"Exploring a critically important topic in today's church, *A Ministry of Discernment* looks at the essential role of the laity in receiving God's revelation. Suggesting bishops are the gateway between the *sensus fidelium* found in the local church and the *consensus fidelium* that guides the church as a whole, Dr. Osheim offers Ignatian discernment as a mode for discovering and cooperating with the action of the Spirit in the apostolic community. There is a freedom in what is offered, with the teaching function of the bishop grounded in mutual learning and listening with the faithful. The process offered here would also serve pastors and parish staff as they discern the movement of the Spirit within their parishes."

> — Marti R. Jewell, DMin
> Associate Professor
> School of Ministry, University of Dallas

"This is a timely book, echoing the concerns of Pope Francis for a listening church, a more dialogic church, a synodal church. Amanda Osheim here enriches the current theology of the *sensus fidelium* by demonstrating the value of Ignatian discernment as a model for local bishops in listening to the Holy Spirit in their churches and bringing local senses of the faith to bear on the teaching of the universal church. This important book will be welcomed by bishops, theologians, and laypeople for its deep spirituality and practical insights."

> — Rev. Dr. Ormond Rush
> Associate Professor
> Australian Catholic University

"Recently, theologians have explored the *sensus fidelium*, an ancient concept more honored in theory than in practice. Utilizing Vatican II and documents promulgated since then, Amanda Osheim outlines how an understanding of the Church as a communion invites bishops to a practice of discernment through dialogue with the people of the local church. Her perspective yields new theological insights. She further argues that this discernment requires new practices and structures. By plumbing the riches of *The Spiritual Exercises* of Ignatius and the structures of the Society of Jesus she offers concrete suggestions for seeking the *sensus fidelium*."

— Zeni Fox
School of Theology and Ministry, Seton Hall University

"*A Ministry of Discernment* views episcopal authority through the lens of Christian spirituality. By doing so, Amanda Osheim offers a fresh approach to both 'teaching' and 'listening' in the church. *A Ministry of Discernment* displays a fine understanding of the ecclesial dimension of faith and an equally impressive grasp of Ignatian discernment, including its implications for those who exercise oversight in a body whose every member is called to discern the movement of the Holy Spirit. This book is rich in insights for the present and future of the Catholic Church."

— Richard Lennan
Professor of Systematic Theology
Boston College
School of Theology and Ministry

A Ministry of Discernment

The Bishop and
the Sense of the Faithful

Amanda C. Osheim

A Michael Glazier Book

LITURGICAL PRESS
Collegeville, Minnesota

www.litpress.org

A Michael Glazier Book published by Liturgical Press

Cover design by Monica Bokinskie. Image: Detail. The Ludwigskirche in Munich, 1908, painting by Wassily Kandinsky, 1866–1944. Courtesy of Wikimedia Commons.

Excerpts from *The Constitutions of the Society of Jesus and Their Complementary Norms: A Complete English Translation from the Official Latin Texts*, by the Society of Jesus, edited by John W. Padberg, Copyright 1996 by Institute of Jesuit Sources, are used with permission of the Institute for Advanced Jesuit Studies, Boston College, Chestnut Hill, Massachusetts.

Excerpts from documents of the Second Vatican Council are from *Vatican Council II: Constitutions, Decrees, Declarations; The Basic Sixteen Documents*, edited by Austin Flannery, OP, © 1996. Used with permission of Liturgical Press, Collegeville, Minnesota.

Excerpts from *Ignatius of Loyola: The Spiritual Exercises and Selected Works*, from The Classes of Western Spirituality, translated by George E. Ganss, copyright 1991 by George E. Ganss, Paulist Press, Inc., New York/ Mahwah, NJ. Used with permission of Paulist Press. www.paulistpress.com.

Scripture texts in this work are taken from the *New Revised Standard Version Bible*, © 1989, Division of Christian Education of the National Council of the Churches of Christ in the United States of America. Used by permission. All rights reserved.

1	2	3	4	5	6	7	8	9

Library of Congress Cataloging-in-Publication Data

Names: Osheim, Amanda C., author.
Title: A ministry of discernment : the bishop and the sense of the faithful / Amanda C. Osheim.
Description: Collegeville, Minnesota : Liturgical Press, 2016. | "A Michael Glazier book." | Includes bibliographical references and index.
Identifiers: LCCN 2016007168 (print) | LCCN 2016015435 (ebook) | ISBN 9780814683194 (pbk.) | ISBN 9780814683446 (ebook)
Subjects: LCSH: Catholic Church—Bishops. | Jesuits. | Sensus fidelium. | Discernment (Christian theology)
Classification: LCC BX1905 .O84 2016 (print) | LCC BX1905 (ebook) | DDC 262/.122—dc23
LC record available at https://lccn.loc.gov/2016007168

To my parents, David and Rosemary Osheim,
who remain my first and best teachers in the ways of faith.

Contents

Abbreviations

AA	*Apostolicam Actuositatem*
AS	*Apostolorum Successores*
CD	*Christus Dominus*
CIC	*Code of Canon Law*
DV	*Dei Verbum*
LG	*Lumen Gentium*
SC	*Sacrosanctum Concilium*
UG	*Unitatis Redintegratio*

Preface

What is the sense of the faithful?

To a degree, Roman Catholic theology has rich resources for answering this question: The sense of the faithful (*sensus fidelium*) is the indwelling of the Holy Spirit within the baptized. Through the Spirit, the faithful are adopted daughters and sons of God. Formed into a family by a common faith, laity, religious, priests, and bishops share an ability to recognize God's revelation which makes them witnesses to Christ whose lives embody the church's apostolic tradition. The *sensus fidelium* is God's faithfulness to the church through the Holy Spirit and allows the church in turn to be faithful to God in its pilgrimage.

Answering this question becomes more difficult, however, if we want more than a theological definition of the *sensus fidelium* as a *concept* but, instead, are seeking to understand the *content* of the *sensus fidelium*. When it comes to the question of what the faithful believe and know—the substance of faith incarnated in history and culture—answers are harder to come by. Yet answers to this question are needed for the *sensus fidelium* to be a source of the church's understanding of God's mystery. Without a means of knowing the *sensus fidelium* substantially, we risk limiting the *sensus fidelium* to a platitude about God's presence in the church rather than fully exploring the *sensus fidelium* as a way of more deeply cooperating with the Holy Spirit for the church's life and mission.

Why is knowing the substance of the *sensus fidelium* difficult? In part because the *sensus fidelium* doesn't come to us neatly summarized in doctrinal propositions about faith and morality. Rather, it arises out of the work of the Holy Spirit who makes the church one, holy, catholic, and apostolic. The Holy Spirit makes us one with others in Christ. As the body of Christ and people of God, we learn to receive and respond to the gift of faith: our faith is both personal and communal. Through the Holy Spirit our union in faith is also apostolic. We receive the Good News of Jesus Christ handed on by the apostles who are sent to the world at Pentecost. As "missionary disciples" ourselves, we continue the apostles' work of handing on, or traditioning, our faith.[1] The Holy Spirit's indwelling, which empowers us to receive the apostles' faith and to live out our faithful response, leads to growth in holiness as we are united more intimately with God, who invites us to join in the divine life.[2] Participating in the divine life as human beings means unity, faith, and holiness are expressed through our histories and cultures, and so the church is catholic. The Holy Spirit, through whom the Son was incarnate in history and culture, incarnates the body of Christ within our histories and cultures as well.

The *sensus fidelium*'s link to the very life and nature of the church means the sense of the faithful is a spiritual reality. As noted above, this is not to say the *sensus fidelium* is abstracted from our earthly lives; rather, the *sensus fidelium* is a spiritual reality because it is rooted in the work of the Holy Spirit. To know the *sensus fidelium* means we must know the Holy Spirit at work within the church. Consequently, if we wish to know the *sensus fidelium*'s substance, we will need to take into account the church as one, holy, catholic, and apostolic—complex spiritual realities that cannot be captured through blunt instruments such as opinion polls.

---

[1] Francis, Apostolic Exhortation *Evangelii Gaudium* (The Joy of the Gospel) (Washington, DC: United States Conference of Catholic Bishops, 2013), 24. All citations from *Evangelii Gaudium* are taken from this translation.

[2] Second Vatican Council, *Dei Verbum* (Dogmatic Constitution on Divine Revelation), in *Vatican Council II: The Basic Sixteen Documents*, ed. Austin Flannery (Collegeville, MN: Liturgical Press, 2014), 2. All quotations from the Vatican II documents are taken from this translation.

These spiritual realities require us to have more than one method of knowing the *sensus fidelium*. The church is rooted in the mystery of God, which we will never fully comprehend but which we may grow to understand in diverse ways. Theologians have been at work to develop both the theory and practice of knowing the *sensus fidelium*, work that should be further prompted by the International Theological Commission's inclusion of the *sensus fidelium* as a criterion of Catholic theology.[3] Without offering an exhaustive list of theologians' efforts, several examples provide a sense of their projects. Orlando Espín considers how coherence among Scripture, tradition, and popular piety manifests the " 'faith-full' intuitions" of the *sensus fidelium* in Latino/a spirituality.[4] Ormond Rush argues that the role of the *sensus fidelium* in determining the canon of Scripture is itself a normative process for discerning the church's faith and emphasizes the need for mutual, dialogical reception among the faithful, theologians, and bishops.[5] Natalia Imperatori-Lee turns to aesthetics and literary narrative as expressions of the *sensus fidelium* at the intersection of the personal, communal, historical, and cultural.[6] Edward Hahnenberg suggests methods from practical and contextual theology, such as ethnography, may help us enter more deeply into the personal lives of the faithful in order to perceive the *sensus fidelium*.[7]

[3] International Theological Commission, "Theology Today: Perspectives, Principles, and Criteria," Vatican website, 35–36, http://www.vatican.va/roman_curia/congregations/cfaith/cti_documents/rc_cti_doc_20111129_teologia-oggi_en.html.

[4] Orlando O. Espín, "Tradition and Popular Religion: An Understanding of the *Sensus Fidelium*," in *The Faith of the People* (Maryknoll, NY: Orbis Books, 1997), 66–67.

[5] Ormond Rush, *The Eyes of Faith: The Sense of the Faithful and the Church's Reception of Revelation* (Washington, DC: The Catholic University of America Press, 2009).

[6] Natalia Imperatori-Lee, "Latina Lives, Latina Literature: A Narrative Camino in Search of the *Sensus Fidelium*" (paper presented at the annual meeting of the Catholic Theological Society of America, Milwaukee, WI, June 2015).

[7] Edward Hahnenberg, "Through the Eyes of Faith: Difficulties in Discerning the *Sensus Fidelium*" (paper presented at the annual meeting of the Catholic Theological Society of America, Milwaukee, WI, June 2015).

Focused   This book offers an additional approach to knowing the *sensus fidelium* that responds to a particular problem. At times the search to know the sense of the faithful seems blocked by the question of who is faithful—in other words, which members of the church we ought to trust as sources of the *sensus fidelium*. The question is a fair one. The church recognizes that some persons, while they appear to be part of the church, do not act with love for God and others (see LG 14). It would be hard to describe these persons as faithful to the God who both redeems us through love and calls us to love. Further, as Avery Dulles and Richard Gaillardetz have noted, participation in the church's communion forms and matures an individual's sense of faith.[8] Thus it seems we must differentiate not only between Catholics who love and Catholics who do not love but also between Catholics along a spectrum of formation throughout the church's communion.

or who?   Answering the question of whom we should trust as witnesses to the *sensus fidelium* presents serious difficulties. It would require that we make determinations about the holiness of others in order to gauge the intimacy of their participation in God's life—not a *yet* simple task, given our own limitations and sinfulness. After all, even when canonizing saints, the church has an extended process for verification, including submission of evidence, and relies as well on the clarity gained through historical distance from the potential saint. Further, the sanctity of particular persons is not normative for the church, though it may be illuminative. Conversely, in the *sensus fidelium* we hope to discover the faith not only of individuals but of persons joined by the communion of the Holy Spirit. Attempting to sort between the sheep and goats in that communion is not only practically daunting but, in all

---

[8] Avery Dulles, "Second General Discussion," in Catholic Common Ground Initiative, *Church Authority in American Culture: The Second Cardinal Bernardin Conference* (New York: Crossroad, 1999), 119; Richard R. Gaillardetz, "Power and Authority in the Church: Emerging Issues," in *A Church with Open Doors: Catholic Ecclesiology for the Third Millennium*, ed. Richard R. Gaillardetz and Edward P. Hahnenberg (Collegeville, MN: Liturgical Press, 2015), 95.

humility, we have to acknowledge that it is God's task and not ours (Matt 25:31-46). If, in order to know the *sensus fidelium*, we must first determine who is faithful, then it seems we may be stumped. On the one hand, not all in the church's communion represent the *sensus fidelium*, and some in the church's communion represent the *sensus fidelium* more fully than others. On the other hand, determining on a case-by-case basis which persons in the church's communion represent the *sensus fidelium* is beyond our ability, and even if it were not, we would need to look into the lives of many individuals in order to arrive at the communal sense of the faithful.

Yet what if we take a more subjective path to knowing the *sensus fidelium* so that the emphasis is not on others' holiness but rather on our own: How do *we* know the *sensus fidelium*? In other words, how might we develop into persons who can discern the Holy Spirit well? This book explores spirituality as a means of forming persons of discernment who may better know the *sensus fidelium*. The *sensus fidelium* is a spiritual reality; through spirituality we may better discern that reality as it is expressed in the church's one, holy, catholic, and apostolic life.

In order to undertake this exploration of spirituality in a way more likely to provide practical outcomes for knowing the *sensus fidelium*, the following chapters build a comparative model of discernment. The first element in this model is the bishop's discernment of the *sensus fidelium* in the local church, or diocese. Bishops aren't the only ones who need to know the *sensus fidelium*; the *sensus fidelium*, however, has a particular claim on the bishop: it is a source for learning the apostolic tradition that the bishop is to teach.[9] Thinking through the spiritual process of how the bishop learns from the *sensus fidelium* helps to root the bishop's teaching ministry in learning from the local church, an essential aspect of the church's catholicity. Focusing on the bishop's ministry provides

---

[9] Richard R. Gaillardetz, "The Office of the Bishop within the *Communio Ecclesiarum*: Insights from the Ecclesiology of Jean-Marie Tillard," *Science et Esprit* 61, fasc. 2, 3 (September 2009): 178–79.

us with a means not only of exploring how the *sensus fidelium* is known but also of developing the theology of episcopal ministry within the local church.

The second element of the comparative model is the spirituality of discernment cultivated through Ignatius of Loyola's *Spiritual Exercises* and the structures that support discernment in the Society of Jesus. Ignatian spirituality has a strong connection with discernment, not only in the discernment of spirits, but also through practices that aid us in becoming persons who habitually receive and respond to God's communication of love within salvation history. The Society's structures embody this spirituality of discernment and ground obedience and authority within communal discernment in order to unite the Society's members in fulfilling Christ's call to mission.

Turning to Ignatian spirituality and Jesuit structures is not intended as a means of imposing this part of the church's heritage on either bishops in particular or the church as a whole. Other spiritualities can offer us insights into the nature and process of discernment, and other structures may facilitate discernment. Rather, paying close attention to Ignatian spirituality and the structures that embody discernment within the Society offer us one way of imagining the bishop's discernment of the *sensus fidelium* in the local church and of reconsidering how the local church's structures may facilitate that discernment.

Ignatian spirituality and Jesuit structures offer us a model for discernment rather than a mold into which all discernment must fit. By viewing the local church and the ministry of the bishop through the lens of Ignatian spirituality and Jesuit structures, a comparative model of discernment can be created. The first four chapters of this book are pairings that help build the model. The first pairing describes the *sensus fidelium* in the larger context of the church as an apostolic communion and the bishop's ministry within the local church. The second pairing considers how discernment is developed through the *Spiritual Exercises* and is embodied in the Society of Jesus' structures. The fifth chapter translates insights from Ignatian discernment and Jesuit structures into the context of the bishop's ministry within the local church. It suggests spiritual practices that form the bishop into a person of discernment who receives the *sensus fidelium*, and structures of the local church that facilitate the bishop's ministry of discernment.

The book moves from ecclesiological theory to imagining spiritual practices and church structures in the hope of contributing not only to the academic conversation about the *sensus fidelium* but also to the ways the church practically lives out our response to the Holy Spirit. Those reading this book who wish to see the more immediate shift from theory to suggestions for practice may read from chapter 1, which lays out some foundational principles of the church and *sensus fidelium*, and then proceed to chapter 5, which points toward practical conclusions for ministry within the local church. Intervening chapters may then be explored to gain a deeper background. Chapters 2 through 4 provide analysis of the bishop's ministry, Ignatian spirituality of discernment, and the structures of the Society of Jesus that are the foundations for the conclusions reached in chapter 5.

Chapter 1, "Receiving God through Each Other: The Church's Apostolic Communion," situates the *sensus fidelium* in a church which comes into being through the authentic, limited, communal, and transformative reception of God's self-gift, or revelation. The Holy Spirit works for this reception in all the baptized and enables us to respond by gifting ourselves in return. This reception and response empowered by the Spirit creates the *sensus fidelium*. Through the Holy Spirit, the church as a whole both learns and teaches. We join the church's communion by learning to receive God's self-gift through others, and our lives are witnesses to a revelation that in turn teaches others.

Through reception and response, the church is an apostolic communion: we are united in a shared faith that sends us on mission. Within an apostolic communion, in which no one group of people knows God's mystery completely, authority and obedience must be more than command and acquiescence. Rather, through authentication we receive others' authoritative insights into God's mystery in ways that allow these insights to become internal, shared truths that prompt our obedience. Authentication occurs when we learn from others through dialogue by asking honest questions and being willing to admit that some of our past answers may have been mistaken. It is within this apostolic communion that the bishop must discern the *sensus fidelium* through a union with the local church in which he continues to learn the apostolic faith.

Chapter 2, "Surveying the Local Church: The Bishop's Role and the Diocese's Structures," looks closely at how ecclesial documents from both Vatican II and following the council conceive the bishop's ministry within the local church with particular regard for how the bishop may receive the local church's faith. These documents, which are normative for the bishop's ministry, reflect Vatican II's shift to envisioning the church as an apostolic communion. Thus they highlight the need for the bishop's dialogue with the local church and describe the bishop's need for personal characteristics and virtues to aid his ministry with the faithful in relational rather than autocratic ways.

Yet the imaginative shift in understanding the church as an apostolic communion is not entirely reflected in these documents. Rather, they retain elements of a church that inclines to institutionalism, which divides the church between the bishops, who teach, and the rest of the faithful, who learn. This means there are some critical absences within the documents that are obstacles for the bishop's discernment of the *sensus fidelium*. First, dialogue is viewed as a means for better implementation of the bishop's pastoral plan rather than as the opportunity for the bishop to learn the apostolic faith. Second, the bishop's symbolization of the universal church's faith is not complemented by an understanding of how the bishop becomes the symbol of the local church's faith. Third, the documents do not adequately describe how the bishop cultivates personal qualities and virtues not only *for* his ministry but also *through* his ministry. By turning to Ignatian spirituality and Jesuit structures, these absences can begin to be addressed.

In chapter 3, "The *Spiritual Exercises*: Developing Persons of Discernment," the *Spiritual Exercises* is explored as more than simply a means of making a singular discernment. Instead, the *Exercises* provides spiritual practices that form persons of discernment: those who discern authentically by consciously engaging in the limited, communal, and transformative ways we receive and respond to God. For Ignatius, to discern is to make distinctions that help us to see ourselves more clearly in relation to God and others, so we may authentically overcome ourselves and join in the communication of love.

Growth into a person of discernment has several aspects: aiding the communication of love by distinguishing between our internal thoughts and those that arise externally to us; the use of imagination to see our personal history in relation to salvation history; the development of humility in order to receive and respond to Christ's mission of salvation; cultivation of indifference to answer Christ's call as fully as possible; and awareness of consolations and desolations as ways of attending to our growth into persons of discernment. Exercises that form us in making these discernments develop a spirituality that makes discernment a habitual part of our conscious response to God, which we undertake both personally and communally.

Chapter 4, "The Society of Jesus: Structures of Discernment and Processes of Authentication," shifts from considering the spirituality of a person of discernment to the structures of discernment that embody and facilitate this spirituality within the Society of Jesus. Particular attention is given to how discernment grounds obedience and authority in the Society. Obedience is intended to be more than external acquiescence to the will of authority. Rather, the companion who obeys his superior is to share the will of the superior, which requires an internal transformation. Conversely, a Jesuit superior's will gains authenticity because it is shaped by his reception of his companions' discernments. Processes of authentication join the superior and his companions in a mutual search for the divine will. By engaging in discernment and processes of authentication with his companions, the superior fosters a union of wills within the community that allows the companions to join together as they participate in Christ's salvific mission.

For the good of the Society, the superior's discernment is further aided by particular persons who are empowered to counsel and raise concerns with the superior about the integration of his personal spirituality with his ministry. These persons become part of the Society's structures that help to ensure its spirituality of discernment will guide its common life and mission. Through these structures, the Society both cares for the superior as a person and also for the well-being of the Society and its mission.

Chapter 5, "Discerning the *Sensus Fidelium*: Episcopal Spirituality and Diocesan Structures," finishes construction on the comparative model of discernment begun in the previous chapters. By following the blueprint of knowing authentically by acknowledging the limited, communal, and transformative ways we receive God's self-gift, it translates insights from Ignatian spirituality into a vision of how the bishop becomes a person of discernment who learns to receive the *sensus fidelium* personally and who responds through his ministry. Through personal practices of discernment, the bishop simultaneously cultivates the habits necessary for growth in holiness and learns to receive the faithful of the local church. By receiving the *sensus fidelium* discerningly, the bishop becomes a symbol of the local church's faith, which in turn shapes his ability to teach within the local church in ways that may be received meaningfully by the faithful and that foster a union of minds. Renovated and newly constructed diocesan structures which embody communal and dialogical processes of authentication are suggested, and persons who are empowered to aid the bishop in integrating his personal spirituality with his ministry of discernment are identified.

Finally, a note about language. As is evident already in this preface, I use the first person frequently in this book. There is a risk of presumption in writing about "we" "us" and "our" with regard to faith and spirituality, but those risks are worth several rewards. First, I write as a Roman Catholic theologian. The ideas and suggestions that unfold in these pages are intended to reflect my position within the church as one member of a family of faith; using the first person reflects my hopes for this family. This is not

intended to exclude "extended family" from other Christian de-
nominations. Rather, it is meant to reflect Vatican II's indication
that Catholics advance in ecumenism in part by attending to the
need for renewal within the Roman Catholic Church (UR 4). Refining discernment of the *sensus fidelium* within Roman Catholicism may increase our ability to discern the Holy Spirit at work
in other Christian traditions as well. Second, writing critically
about spirituality is a step toward abstracting the spiritual life
from the people and communities who live it. To avoid further
removing spirituality from lived experience and to invite readers
to consider more personally the implications of spirituality for
their own lives, I have chosen to use more personal language.
Third, in these pages I write quite a lot about what the bishop in
the local church ought to do; these prescriptions are, however,
grounded in a larger vision of what we as a church ought to do.
The bishop's need for personal conversion and learning to fulfill
his ministry are part of the universal call to holiness; we are all
called to conversion and learning in order to fulfill our baptismal
vocation.

This book is the product of several stages of development, and
I am deeply grateful for the guidance and support I have received
throughout its evolution. Courses with Michael Byron and Patrick
Quinn at the St. Paul Seminary School of Divinity formed my early
thinking about the Holy Spirit, ecclesiology, and the *sensus fidelium*.
Mentors and colleagues in Campus Ministry at the University of
St. Thomas shaped my understanding of ministry. As my initial
ideas coalesced into a dissertation at Boston College, Michael
Himes, my director, offered not only affirmation and support but
also many of the theological foundations upon which this project
is built. My committee members, Michael Fahey and Catherine
Mooney, were generous with both their time and comments and
were instrumental in refining my articulation of theology, spirituality, and history. I am thankful for Richard Gaillardetz's and
Ormond Rush's scholarship as well as for the enthusiasm they
expressed for this project as the manuscript took shape. Kevin
Ahern, Robert Beck, John Edwards, and John Waldmeir were

invaluable for their comments on chapter drafts, as well as for working through ideas with me in conversations. In writing both the dissertation and book, Nicholas Austin, Meghan Clark, Jim Fellows, Christine Kaiser, and Katie O'Neill supported my aspirations and grounded me in friendship. At Loras College I am blessed by colleagues and students who make the daily life of academia a joy, particularly the faculty and staff of the Religious Studies and Theology program. Finally, I am grateful beyond expression to my parents, David and Rosemary Osheim. Their commitment to sharing in all my joys and cares, and confidence in the gifts they fostered in me, accompany me always. It is their steadfast love that gives me the ability to trust in God's enduring faithfulness and the inspiration to seek God's presence within the church and all people.

Chapter 1

Receiving God through Each Other:
The Church's Apostolic Communion

> *Rebbe Shmelke of Nikolsburg, it was told, never really heard his teacher,*
> *the Maggid of Mezritch, finish a thought because as soon as the latter*
> *would say "and the Lord spoke," Shmelke would begin shouting in*
> *wonderment, "The Lord spoke, the Lord spoke," and continue shouting*
> *until he had to be carried from the room.*[1]

Perhaps it is easy to forget the awe Rebbe Shmelke feels. We may be so overwhelmed by the noise of our lives that God's words are lost within the daily cacophony, or in the face of evil and suffering we may grapple more with God's silence than with God's words. Yet in both the Jewish and Christian traditions, God speaks to enter into human history and act for salvation. God speaks, and the world is created from a watery chaos; Abraham and Sarah enter a covenant; a people are liberated from oppression into freedom; prophets call for justice. For Christians, God's speech enters the world as Jesus Christ, the incarnate Word.

Implicit in Rebbe Shmelke's wonder are two important aspects of God's speech, or revelation, which are also causes for contemplative awe. First, it is not only that God speaks but also that we

---

[1] Quoted without further attribution in Annie Dillard, *The Writing Life* (New York: Harper and Row Publishers, 1989), 35.

1

God speaks. We hear.

hear. We are capable of receiving God's revelation. Second, we
hear God's words through others. God's revelation is mediated
via our communication with each other. Our reception of revelation through others is the foundational reason that a Roman
Catholic bishop's ministry ought to include discernment of the
sense of the faithful. Yet, in order to understand the shape of that
discerning ministry and to propose the spiritual practices and
church structures that allow it to flourish, we must first understand more about how receiving revelation through others shapes
the church's common life of faith.

This chapter explores the intersection of revelation, reception,
and the church in four sections. The first, "Receiving God's Self-
Gift," views God's revelation as an invitation to join in the divine
life. God's invitation to us is received in authentic, limited, communal, and transformative ways. In order to receive and respond
well to the invitation, we must engage in discernment that allows
us to be both hearers and doers of God's word (Jas 1:22). The
second section, "Receiving with the Spirit," considers the Holy
Spirit as co-witness with the apostles to revelation. Through the
Holy Spirit's faithful presence, the church is in turn empowered
to remain faithful to God. Both the ministry of bishops and the
sense of the faithful are manifestations of the Spirit's ongoing action within the church and are ways by which God's revelation is
known and communicated. Third, "Models of Faithful Reception"
investigates how reception is conceived differently in two models
of the church: institution and apostolic communion. These models
form how the church imagines reception occurring within the
church's life and inform how bishops and the faithful receive from
each other. The final section, "Receiving with Discernment," follows the contours of the church's reception when it is marked by
discernment. Dialogue that incorporates processes of authentication and learning is necessary for the church's full and faithful
reception of the God who speaks.

These four sections provide the theological context for the
bishop's discernment of the _sensus fidelium_. They point as well to
three implications for discernment. First, discernment needs to be

a virtue, that is, discernment is an ongoing and personally transformative habit of episcopal ministry. Second, the bishop's discernment occurs in a church that is both learning and teaching.
Episcopal discernment empowers the bishop's teaching ministry
because, in his discernment, the bishop learns from others. Third,
just as our reception of faith occurs within contexts of culture and
history, so too does the bishop's discernment of that faith. The
primary context for episcopal discernment of the sense of the
faithful is the local church. • R ʒ h t h c r e.

I. Receiving God's Self-Gift

Revelation is the communication of God's self, or God's self-
gift. Through revelation we do not receive ideas "about God";
rather, we receive God. To be sure, in the process of receiving
revelation, we do come to make claims about who God is; in its
essence, however, revelation is God's gift of self to us. Through
self-gift, God does not remain aloof, waiting apart from humanity
in an infinitely prolonged game of hide-and-seek. Instead, by
sending the Son and Spirit, God dwells among and within us. *Dei
Verbum* describes this mystery:

> It pleased God, in his goodness and wisdom, to reveal himself
> and to make known the mystery of his will, which was that
> people can draw near to the Father, through Christ, the Word
> made flesh, in the holy Spirit, and thus become sharers in the
> divine nature. By this revelation, then, the invisible God, from
> the fullness of his love, addresses men and women as his
> friends, and lives among them, in order to invite and receive
> them into his own company.[2]

---

[2] Vatican Council II, *Dei Verbum* (Dogmatic Constitution on Divine Revelation),
par. 2, in *Vatican Council II: Constitutions, Decrees, Declarations; The Basic Sixteen
Documents,* ed. Austin Flannery (Collegeville, MN: Liturgical Press, 2014). Unless
otherwise indicated, all citations of Vatican II documents come from the Flannery
edition.

God's revelation teaches us not only who God is but also who we are called to be. *Dei Verbum* reminds us that God isn't "just talk": God's self-communication through Christ and the Spirit is an invitation to join in the Trinity's divine life. When we receive God's self-communication, God receives us so that we become "sharers in the divine nature."

Our participation in the divine life is God's saving gift to us, and our salvation begins with that gift's communication. What is the divine life like? Augustine imagined the Trinity itself as loving self-gift. The Father continually gives himself to the Son; the Son continually receives the Father and gives himself in response; and the Spirit is the bond of love between the Father and Son.[3] Through this dynamic bond of love arising from mutual self-gift, the Trinity is three persons in one God. If the divine life is a communion flowing from mutual self-communication, then our participation in the divine life will be like it: a communion rooted in communication, a graced reality both created and expressed by receiving each other and giving ourselves in loving self-gift. The path of revelation is one of communication, of self-gift. We walk that path by receiving God's Word, and our journey of reception transforms our capacity to share God's revelation with others.

Reception and response. Our reception of God's self-communication calls for a response. When God's self-communication falls on deaf ears, God's invitation is left unopened. When the invitation is authentically received, however, we discover that God's offer to join in the divine life means that we cannot remain stationary. We are sent by Christ and empowered by the Spirit to walk a path that wends ever-more deeply into the divine life. On that pilgrimage we carry with us not only God's self-gift but also God's way of communicating that gift: the mutual offering and return of love that marks the Trinity. We receive God through our creation in the divine image, the waters of baptism, and consecrated bread and

---

[3] Augustine, *On the Trinity*, in *A Select Library of the Nicene and Post-Nicene Fathers of the Christian Church*, vol. 3, ed. Philip Schaff (Grand Rapids, MI: Eerdmans, 1988), vi, 5.

wine of the Eucharist. Yet through the incarnation, God also receives us. God did not use our humanity as a ventriloquist uses a puppet. Rather, the permanence of the union between divine and human in Jesus Christ tells us that if the path of God's revelation is self-communication, then the purpose of that path is communion.

Through the faithful reception of God's self-communication within history, the church comes into being and discovers its mission. The church originates in reception of revelation because through it believers are brought into saving union with the triune God and each other. God's loving address to the human person initiates a graced reciprocity of reception. Through the communication of God's very self in Christ and the Holy Spirit within history, humans are invited to share in the divine life. By receiving God's invitation with faith, believers respond in kind by communicating themselves into union with God and others through their self-gift.[4] God reveals not in order to communicate propositions but in order to invite humanity into relationship with God's very self. Through the incarnation that invitation takes the form of self-gift, and with the aid of the Holy Spirit the believer receives this gift and responds through loving self-gift as well. This mutual exchange, always initiated and empowered through divine grace, creates the church through communion and propels the church's mission.

---

[4] J.-M. R. Tillard, *Church of Churches: The Ecclesiology of Communion* (Collegeville, MN: Liturgical Press, 1992), 17. "If we had to sum up in one word the real context of Salvation, as much individual as collective, announced in the Gospel of God, we would use, following many of the Fathers, *communion*, the word which sums up Acts. It is surely not by chance that down to the present time Jewish and Christian thought have conveyed a view of the 'authentic man,' underlining the fact that the human being finds his authenticity and affirms his full singularity only in communion. According to this thinking, the drama of our history is precisely that man has become an isolated being, creating a broken world in which individuals live side by side without establishing authentic bonds of communion. In this way, humanity has condemned itself in reality to a state of non-existence. It has reduced itself to becoming hardly more than a collage of individuals."

Apostles

An apostolic reception. The church's apostolicity is based on this mutual reception and is rooted in a communion brought about by the Holy Spirit. The church is apostolic in faith. Through tradition and Scripture, the apostles communicated to others "what they themselves had received" through their own experience of Christ with the aid of the Holy Spirit (DV 7). The content of the apostolic tradition is God's revelation, more particularly, the revelation of the Word incarnate. Yet the church is also apostolic in action. If our mission is to communicate to others *what* we received, we are also empowered to communicate the *way* we received it: authentically, limitedly, communally, and transformatively.

While the Word of God is eternal, the incarnation of the Word occurred within time: "Grace supposes culture, and God's gift becomes flesh in the culture of those who receive it" (EG 115). Just as Jesus' personal communication of God in action, parable, and symbol was shaped by such contexts as first-century Palestine and Second Temple Judaism, so our reception and response to revelation is shaped by our own, multiple contexts. Our communication with God occurs within history, and that historical context means the church's ability to participate faithfully in the conversation requires acknowledgment of the way we know God. Thomas Aquinas's dictum is important: our way of knowing shapes what we know.[5] More colloquially, this might be translated as "when you're a hammer, everything looks like a nail." The point is that whenever we learn something, we don't come as blank slates but rather with capacities, whether natural, developed, or infused, that give us a certain ability to perceive and understand.

What is our way of knowing as a church? First, we know as human beings, creatures of God who are made in God's image; there exists a correspondence between God and human beings that makes authentic communication with and knowing of God possible. Second, we know as human beings, creatures of God who are historical and finite and therefore limited. God is a mys-

[5] Thomas Aquinas, *Summa Theologica*, vol. 1, trans. Fathers of the English Dominican Province (New York: Benziger Brothers, 1947), I, q. 12, a. 4.

tery who will always go beyond our ability to comprehend completely. Further, we are also impacted by the limitations of sin, both personal and social. In humility, we acknowledge that God communicates with us through—and not simply despite—our limitations. Third, while we can come to know things "for ourselves," we seldom if ever come to know "by ourselves." Rather, we are dependent on those who come before us: our communities, families, and friends who help us learn. Fourth, in speaking about the knower as a Christian, the church also affirms that our capacity for knowing and understanding God is transformed through the power of the Holy Spirit. When we become part of Christ's body in baptism, we begin to share the mind of Christ (Phil 2:1-11). Our love of God and neighbor is the path of self-gift that leads to more intimate communion. This communion itself produces in us a type of knowledge as the Holy Spirit fosters us as daughters and sons of God. The path of knowing that the church walks in order to participate in the divine life is authentic, limited, communal, and transformative. This way of knowing impacts the church's shared apostolic witness, in other words, our common reception and communication of God's revelation.

A historical reception. Without attention to how we know, or receive God's Word of salvation, the church's ability to judge how we in turn communicate that salvation faithfully is put at risk. While the incarnation teaches us that we should not fear the historical and transitory, as human beings we may be tempted to overcome our finitude by trying to make the momentary into the eternal. The Synoptic Gospels share the story of the transfiguration, literally a "mountaintop moment," that Peter, in the midst of fear or excitement, wishes to prolong by making three dwellings. Yet for the disciples, the transfiguration is not an invitation to remain in place but is rather a confirmation of Jesus' prediction that it is necessary to move forward to Jerusalem and the betrayal, suffering, death, and new life that stand on the horizon. For those of us who know the "whole story" the gospels tell, it can be easy to think Peter foolish for not trusting that passion precedes glory for the Son of Man; we know the transfiguration is not the final chapter. In the midst of our personal lives, however, we may be aware of the times we have mistaken an oasis for the end of the journey. Similarly, it may be difficult for us as a church to discern the difference between the message and the media through which that message is communicated; between the moral and the specific practices by which we live out that moral; between the teaching and the words we use to teach.

If the church grows in its understanding of revelation, it is because we learn anew in each generation to express that revelation in our lives of faith. A literary example helps illustrate the continual need for reception and re-expression. In Jane Austen's *Pride and Prejudice*, Mr. Collins is clearly delighted when Lady Catherine de Bourgh lowers herself from the heights of the aristocracy to offer her vicar advice; he lauds her "condescension."[6] In the United States, a country that often imagines itself as radically egalitarian, condescending behavior is not praised but is seen as betraying an inflated sense of self-worth over against another. Not only has the word changed in meaning over time, the differing political and social structures of nineteenth-century Britain and the twenty-first-century United States shape that word's meaning. Something quite similar happens within the church's expression of faith as well. Thomas Aquinas brought to bear both faithfulness and intelligence in describing the church's belief about the Eucharist. His word "transubstantiation" has described this mystery for centuries for Roman Catholics and offered an oasis in the midst of early, quite violent disputes as to the nature of the Eucharist.[7] Yet Pope Paul VI acknowledged that while the mean-

[6] Jane Austen, *Pride and Prejudice*, in *The Complete Novels of Jane Austen*, The Modern Library (New York: Random House, n.d.), 270.

[7] "[I]t cannot be claimed that the Council of Trent defined anything in regard to the philosophy to be used in interpreting the eucharistic celebration. All we can conclude is that the Council of Trent found in Thomas's Aristotelianism a theological system capable of interpreting the eucharistic doctrine that had matured, and been formulated during, the controversies and discussions of the Middle Ages." Enrico Mazza, *The Celebration of the Eucharist: The Origin of the Rite and the Development of Its Interpretation*, trans. Matthew J. O'Connell (Collegeville, MN: Liturgical Press, 1999), 248.

ing of the Thomistic description needs to be retained, the church also needs to find other ways of explaining its belief.[8] In a similar vein with regard to the Gospel, Pope Francis explains:

> While it is true that some cultures have been closely associated with the preaching of the Gospel and the development of Christian thought, the revealed message is not identified with any of them; its content is transcultural. Hence in the evangelization of new cultures, or cultures which have not received the Christian message, it is not essential to impose a specific cultural form, no matter how beautiful or ancient it may be, together with the Gospel. (EG 117)

Today we do not often describe our reality in terms of substance and accidents; the philosophical ideas that allowed the word "transubstantiation" to be meaningful do not translate with equal coherence to all cultures. As the metaphysical categories Thomas developed from Aristotle have receded in the face of new ways of describing reality, the word "transubstantiation" may be more limited today in its authentic ability to express the church's faith in a way that allows for that belief to be received communally and transformatively.

Yet the challenge the church faces is not simply one of trying to distinguish between the essence God's self-gift and the changing

---

[8] Paul VI, Encyclical *Mysterium Fidei*, Vatican website www.vatican.va/holy _father/paul_vi/encyclicals/documents/hf_p-vi_enc_03091965_mysterium _en.html. Paul VI refers to the Council of Trent's articulation of eucharistic theology, indicating: "These formulas—like the others that the Church used to propose the dogmas of faith—express concepts that are not tied to a certain specific form of human culture, or to a certain level of scientific progress, or to one or another theological school. Instead they set forth what the human mind grasps of reality through necessary and universal experience and what it expresses in apt and exact words, whether it be in ordinary or more refined language. For this reason, these formulas are adapted to all men of all times and all places" (24). Yet Paul VI also recognizes a distinction between the concepts and their expression: "[Expression] can, it is true, be made clearer and more obvious; and doing this is of great benefit. But it must always be done in such a way that they retain the meaning in which they have been used, so that with the advance of an understanding of the faith, the truth of faith will remain unchanged" (25).

ways we communicate this revelation in order that it be received and lived in each generation—though that is crucial. There is also a need to distinguish between those historical and cultural ideas and actions that accrue in the Christian tradition but are not necessarily expressions of revelation, or may even be counter to God's revelation. For instance, the church's relationship with chattel slavery has been varied by region and era. At times, both in word and action, Catholics acted to mitigate or prohibit slavery. At other times, however, Catholics both engaged in and fought for slavery. To the extent that Catholics justified slavery through an appeal to the apostolic faith or thought slavery compatible with the Gospel, the church's apostolic witness was rendered both false and dangerous.[9]

[9] For primary sources and insight into the social-political context see Kenneth J. Zanca, ed., *American Catholics and Slavery, 1789–1866: An Anthology of Primary Documents* (Lanham, MD: University Press of America, 1994). While in 1839 Pope Gregory XVI's *In Supreme Apostolatus* addressed slavery with vehement opposition, many American Catholics interpreted this as a prohibition on the "slave trade" rather than on slavery itself. American Catholics regarded slavery in various ways, yet even many who abhorred the idea of slavery and expressed compassion for the enslaved made no effort to change the religious, economic, and political practices that justified slavery. Bishop Spalding of Louisville, Kentucky, feared freeing the slaves would end in their loss of faith: "But where the dominant religion is Protestant it becomes very difficult in practice to decide how the slaves can be emancipated to their spiritual and also temporal profit. Almost all the Catholics who are Negroes are found in the states of the South, and those who are emancipated and go to the states of the North become almost all, at least their children, within a short time Protestants, or else indifferent and infidel. In my dioceses, for example, there are from two to three thousand such Catholic Negroes, who are among the best and most devout of my flock. Now I am convinced that if these were suddenly emancipated in the present circumstances of violence and war, they would all be lost to the Church and to heaven: and so would also be the sad result with the others" (211). In addition, the apostolic tradition was used in attempts to uphold slavery. Bishop Verot of St. Augustine, Florida, stated in a sermon: "I wish to show, on the one side, how unjust, iniquitous, unscriptural, and unreasonable is the assertion of Abolitionists, who brand slavery as a moral evil, and a crime against God, religion, humanity and society; whereas, it is found to have received the sanction of God, of the Church, and of society at all times and in all governments. On the other

A discerned reception. Yves Congar is helpful in pointing out two aspects of the church that must be distinguished in order to grasp the differences between creaturely versus sinful limitations on our historical reception of God's self-gift. The first aspect of the church is its divine institution, reflected in essential elements of the church's life such as revelation, sacraments that unite us to God, and the apostolic ministries.[10] Due to these divine roots, the church is an agent of God's salvation; these are institutions that redeem. As God's gifts, these institutions in themselves are not open to change, though our understanding and human expression of them may reflect aspects of the divine mystery more or less clearly. The attempt to find new language to describe our eucharistic beliefs is an example: the sacramental essence of the Eucharist does not change but, rather, our understanding and expression of it may.

In addition to these divine roots, Congar notes a secondary aspect of the church. As the communion of the redeemed, the church's members are in need of salvation; we are still in the midst of a salvific pilgrimage with God and each other. This means that in addition to the natural limits we have as finite beings attempting to live in relationship with the mysterious God, there is another limit, that of sin. So, not only will our expressions of faith fall short, they will also be hindered by personal and social sin. The church is called to trust that the grace of God continues to work through our brokenness and not simply around it. We proclaim a savior who rose after dying broken on a cross, and it is through the crucifixion and not only after it that God is mysteriously at work. *He works in all things*

Nevertheless, as an apostolic church growing in communion with God, we also have a responsibility to reflect deeply on our traditions and to discern through them how we are being faithful

---

side, I wish to show the conditions under which servitude is legitimate, lawful, approved by all laws, and consistent with practical religion and true holiness of life in masters who fulfill those conditions" (202).

[10] Yves Congar, *True and False Reform in the Church*, trans. Paul Philibert (Collegeville, MN: Liturgical Press, 2011), 85–86.

to God's revelation—or are not. Failure to discern, or poor discernment, may result in a lack of faithfulness to God: the gift is rejected, or our response is stunted. If the church's mission is to be a sacrament of salvation, then a failure to reflect on the essence of that salvation and to translate it thoughtfully into new contexts is a failure in the mission. Such failures in the mission have the potential to damage others' relationships with God and with the community of faith. They can also denigrate and alienate the people with whom the church hopes to share the Good News with the result that the Gospel becomes "bad news" instead. Finally, and ultimately quite related to the church's faithfulness to God and its communication of the Good News to others, lack of discernment between the eternal and historical breeds disagreement and turmoil within the church, threatening relationships of love and justice. Here we may well think of Christian participation in the African slave trade as a scandalous countersign to the Gospel, the effects of which are still all too real today.[11]

II. Receiving with the Spirit

We are called to be a church that redeems while acknowledging that we ourselves are in progress toward redemption. Without acknowledging the limitations that our creatureliness and sin place on our communication of God's revelation, our knowledge of the apostolic faith that lights the path into the divine life is dimmed. In order to authentically receive and respond to God's

---

[11] Laënnec Hurbon, "The Slave Trade and Black Slavery in America," trans. John Bowden, in *1942–1992: The Voice of the Victims*, ed. Leonardo Boff and Virgil Elizondo (London: SCM Press, 1990), 90–100. In addition to the lasting personal and institutional effects of slavery within the United States, Hurbon argues, "[T]he history of the slave trade and the slavery of the Blacks which began with the discovery of the New World is still part of our modern world and of Western civilization, and is even the background without which neither anti-black racism nor the present under-development of the African continent would be unimaginable" (90).

gift of salvation, however, we also need to account for the Holy Spirit's role in the communal and transformative aspects of reception, which help us to discern God's authentic self-gift within the limits of human finitude and sin.

The apostles' message, mission, and authority came from Christ, and the apostles' witness was a proclamation of salvation. Through their witness to Christ, the apostles communicated salvation authentically.[12] If the apostles were co-missioned by Christ to share in a salvific mission, then the Holy Spirit is co-witness to the authenticity of that salvation.[13] The Holy Spirit does not constitute the apostolic tradition but, instead, "His role is to actualize, to interiorize, to personalize what Christ said and did once for all men and all times, and thus to *witness with* the apostles or Christians."[14] The Spirit recalls the teaching of Christ to the apostles so it may be handed on; as the ever-faithful witness to Christ, the Spirit ensures that the church's divine institutional roots remain alive even as the Spirit prompts church members to lives of conversion and holiness in faithfulness to our divine roots.[15]

Through the Holy Spirit, the recollection of Christ through the apostolic tradition does not become stale or ineffective. Instead, the Holy Spirit acts to deepen the church's insight into revelation, which "involves not merely a fidelity of memory, but also a fidelity of living, vital adherence."[16] The deposit of faith itself is immutable, and nothing can be added to what the apostles received and witnessed in Christ. Through the Holy Spirit, however, the church grows in its understanding of the meaning of that revelation, which is shown both in our ability to recognize the Gospel and our ability to express it in words and action.[17] The Holy Spirit mediates in a dynamic and generative manner between the eternal

---

[12] Yves Congar, *Tradition and Traditions* (London: Burns and Oats, 1966), 26.
[13] Ibid., 19.
[14] Ibid., 19. Emphasis in original.
[15] Ibid.
[16] Ibid., 15.
[17] Ibid., 21.

God who is revealed within history and the communication of that historical revelation throughout all time.[18]

Congar explicates the relationship between communion and the apostolic tradition: "The aim of the apostolic witness as it is transmitted, and its effective result if it is received, is to join or assimilate the faithful to the witnesses themselves. The Church spreads by the association of new disciples to the apostles, and exists essentially as a communion of faith with the apostles."[19] This means the church's union and mission are mutually conditioning; the mission's purpose is communion, and communion empowers and shapes the mission. Thomas Rausch writes, "What resulted from the reception of the apostolic preaching by those who became the converts of the apostles and other early Christian missionaries was the Church itself."[20]

Sharing the apostolic faith. By the second century, the ministry of handing down and guarding the apostolic tradition was associated with the episcopate.[21] Through the bishops' teaching ministry, the Spirit makes it possible for the church to confidently confess its ecclesial traditions as authentic expressions of the apostolic tradition.[22] Historical and scriptural sources indicate that some form of normative, pastoral leadership centering on witness to Christ, worship, and adjudication of practical concerns is inherently part of the church's faithful practice. These sources also demonstrate that the existence, structure, and relationship of the episcopacy to the local church developed throughout the apostolic and subapostolic periods. The episcopacy is part of the apostolic

---

[18] Ibid., 22. "The deposit of faith is entrusted to a Church living out historically the history of salvation. It allows for a kind of 'midrashic' activity in actualizing it, and even, in a sense, in bringing it to its full achievement: to preserve it 'with the aid of the Holy Spirit,' is to live by it."

[19] Ibid., 14.

[20] Thomas Rausch, "Reception Past and Present," *Theological Studies* 47 (1986): 499.

[21] J. N. D. Kelly, "'Catholic' and 'Apostolic' in the Early Centuries," *One in Christ* 6, no. 3 (1970): 283.

[22] Yves Congar, *I Believe in the Holy Spirit*, vol. 2 (New York: Crossroad, 1983), 46.

tradition; like all aspects of the apostolic tradition, however, the form a bishop's ministry takes is conditioned and discovered through history and culture.[23]

Episcopal ministry is one way the Holy Spirit manifests God's faithfulness to the church; it is, however, not the only way.[24] The apostolic succession of the episcopate is contextualized within the apostolicity of the whole church: "[T]he 'hierarchical' function exists within the communion of the *ecclesia*."[25] Vatican II's Constitution on the Church, *Lumen Gentium*, illustrates this understanding of the church. The document does not begin immediately by defining the church but with a meditation on the mystery of the triune God. Within the context of God's mystery, the corresponding mystery of the church is discussed through evocative, scriptural images such as "the people of God" and "body of Christ." Only after describing the entirety of the church in its relationship to God are particular vocations within the church—such as the roles of bishops, laypersons, and religious orders—discussed. While the church believes episcopal ministry is graced with the Spirit, in *Lumen Gentium* the activity of the Spirit throughout the church is also stressed. The church as a whole, and not only the episcopacy, is apostolic.

Three senses of faith. The Holy Spirit's work throughout the church invokes the *sensus fidei* (sense of the faithful person), *sensus fidelium* (sense of the faithful people), and *consensus fidelium* (consensus of the faithful peoples). These three terms describe how the Holy Spirit works personally and communally to aid the

[23] For an historical and theological examination of the development of the episcopacy in the apostolic and subapostolic church, see Francis A. Sullivan, *From Apostles to Bishops: The Development of the Episcopacy in the Early Church* (New York: The Newman Press, 2001).

[24] Raymond E. Brown, *An Introduction to the New Testament* (New York: Doubleday, 1997), 295. Sullivan's scriptural analysis in *From Apostles to Bishops* often references Brown's interpretations from this text, as well as Brown's more explicit exploration of the early church in *The Churches the Apostles Left Behind* (Mahwah, NJ: Paulist Press, 1984).

[25] Congar, *I Believe in the Holy Spirit*, 45.

church's faithful witness. In maintaining the church's apostolicity within history, the Holy Spirit does not operate on the church but within and through the communion of the faithful. Received into the church, we in turn receive the indwelling of the Holy Spirit, whose internal witness gives knowledge of God through Christ. The *sensus fidei* points to a particular type of knowledge within believers. This knowledge is rooted in personal union and communication with God and the church; it is knowledge gained through the active reception and return of God's love.[26] Francis Sullivan describes the *sensus fidei* as both an instinct and a disposition and compares it to the virtue of faith; Zoltán Alszeghy indicates it is "an experiential knowledge based on what has been lived," in contrast to an intellectual knowledge.[27] Pope Francis both characterizes the *sensus fidei* as an instinct and links it with the ability to discern "what is truly of God" (EG 119). This instinct for faith is not merely a gauge by which a person of faith determines whether an action or idea coheres with the apostolic tradition. Rather, the *sensus fidei* forms the basis for the believer's life as a daughter or son of God and is also the living expression of faith. Through the *sensus fidei*, the church has not only Scripture but also an authentic and living tradition.[28]

In the local church, or diocese, the love of God is drawn together and mediated through history and the community of faith. Sullivan distinguishes between the *sensus fidelium*, which refers to the common faith expression of the local community, and the

---

[26] "For what we call the *sensus fidelium* is rooted precisely in this lived margin, this space of truth that emerges between the received Word and what it becomes through the power of the Spirit for the believer who tries to conform himself to it. . . . Thus life itself is a commentary which renders explicit the Word that is received, and this unfolding adds to the understanding of the objective data themselves." J.-M. R. Tillard, "*Sensus Fidelium*," *One in Christ* 11, no. 1 (1975): 15.

[27] Francis A. Sullivan, "The Sense of Faith," in *Authority in the Roman Catholic Church*, ed. Bernard Hoose (Burlington, VT: Ashgate, 2002), 86; Zoltán Alszeghy, "The *Sensus Fidei* and the Development of Dogma," in *Vatican II: Assessment and Perspectives*, ed. R. Latourelle, vol. 1 (New York: Paulist Press, 1988), 139.

[28] For the relationship between the *sensus fidei* and Scripture, see part 2 of Ormond Rush, *The Eyes of Faith: The Sense of the Faithful and the Church's Reception of Revelation* (Washington, DC: The Catholic University of America Press, 2009).

consensus fidelium, which indicates agreement in the church's universal communion. The Spirit's abiding presence within the church provides the faithful of the local church with an instinct for both developing and recognizing authentic expressions of faith that accord with the content of revelation transmitted by the apostles.[29] Such expressions are clothed with the cultures, histories, languages, and rituals particular to the local church. In a sense, church traditions bear a dual identity. They reflect not only the apostolic faith but also the contexts in which they are expressed. These identities are not necessarily opposed to each other but invite what Pope Francis describes as a synthesis: God's self-communication is embodied in our histories and cultures as the church receives, lives, and hands on its tradition (EG 123, 143).

As the *sensus fidelium* of a local church is received by other churches, a universal *consensus fidelium* may develop. The aim of the *consensus fidelium* is not to flat pack one local church's faith for global distribution to the universal church; rather, the *consensus fidelium* is a recognition that a local church's faith is shared by the universal church as well, though that faith may be expressed diversely through local histories and cultures. The *consensus fidelium* may come forth when the truth to which a local church's *sensus fidelium* points is recognized as contributing to the common good of the local churches in universal communion.[30] For example, in his 1991 encyclical *Centesimus Annus*, Pope John Paul II referred to the preferential option for the poor.[31] The phrase originated in the local churches of Latin America in the 1960s and 1970s and reflected the cultural synthesis resulting from the Gospel's reception, interpretation, and expression within the political and social

---

[29] The Spirit dwells within the church, though it is well to note that the Holy Spirit is not hypostatically united with the church as the Son's divine nature was united to human nature in the incarnation. The distinction is important: we hold Jesus Christ to be sinless; not so the church, inasmuch as we are the communion of the redeemed and not only the institution that redeems.

[30] Sullivan, "The Sense of Faith," 88, 90.

[31] John Paul II, *Centesimus Annus* (1991), 11, Vatican website, http://w2.vatican.va/content/john-paul-ii/en/encyclicals/documents/hf_jp-ii_enc_01051991_centesimus-annus.html.

context of the poor.[32] Here reception is at work both within the Latin American local churches' reception of Scripture and in the universal church's reception of the preferential option for the poor as a universal *consensus fidelium*. Gustavo Gutierrez writes that the preferential option for the poor is "the most substantial part of the contribution from the life and theological reflection of the Church in Latin America to the universal church."[33] In turn, as the preferential option for the poor is received by local churches as the *consensus fidelium*, it is interpreted and expressed through the cultures and histories of those local churches.

The bishop and the sensus fidelium. *Lumen Gentium* states, "The whole body of the faithful who have received an anointing which comes from the holy one cannot be mistaken in belief. It shows this characteristic through the entire people's supernatural sense of the faith when, 'from the bishops to the last of the faithful,' it manifests a universal consensus in matters of faith and morals" (LG 12).[34] Here the *sensus fidei* is upheld as an essential element of

---

[32] "This commitment—the expression 'preferential option for the poor' is recent but its content is biblical—is an essential component of discipleship." Gustavo Gutierrez, "The Option for the Poor Arises from Faith in Christ," *Theological Studies* 70 (2009): 319.

[33] Ibid., 318.

[34] This statement from *Lumen Gentium* is open to two related criticisms. First, is consensus in the church ever erroneous, that is, consensus about something antithetical to the apostolic faith? The historical record seems to indicate at certain times and places the church reached consensus about praxes it later abandoned or condemned. Second, in critiquing Vicentius's statement that "Christianity is what has been held always, everywhere, and by all," Newman writes, "[W]hat is meant by being 'taught *always*?' does it mean in every century, or every year, or every month? Does '*everywhere*' mean in every country, or in every diocese? . . . [H]ow many Fathers, how many places, how many instances constitute a fulfillment of the test proposed?" John Henry Newman, *An Essay on the Development of Doctrine* (Whitefish, MT: Kessinger Publishing, 2007), 76. As a criterion for determining the church's faith, *Lumen Gentium*'s statement presents the same difficulties as does Vicentius's. *Lumen Gentium* 12 may be nuanced in two ways that are justified by its context within the constitution. First, not every consensus within the church is a manifestation of the apostolic faith; instead, consensus about the apostolic faith must be reached through ecclesial discernment. Second, the statement need not be interpreted as a criterion

the church's faithful response that incarnates the Gospel throughout history. This faithfulness is not first based on the holiness of the church's members but is rooted in God's faithfulness to the church through the abiding presence of the Holy Spirit. Through the Spirit, the apostolic faith of believers is "aroused and sustained" as a living, embodied tradition (LG 12). Further, the *sensus fidei* is a gift shared by all within the church.[35] It provides the context for the bishops' role in the church's apostolicity.[36] J.-M. R. Tillard writes:

> [I]n all this the Magisterium acts "in osmosis" with the *sensus fidelium*. Not that it therefore trails behind popular faith, contenting itself with ratifying what the latter perceives. It exercises a function of its own, a function which the Spirit has not entrusted to others. But this function requires that the Magisterium should draw from the very life of the People of God

---

for adjudicating truth, but rather as an affirmation of belief in the Holy Spirit who witnesses to the apostolic faith throughout the church and not only within the hierarchy.

[35] Tillard interprets 1 John 2:27 as the bestowal of a lasting anointing by the Spirit through which "that teaching of Jesus, present in the believer, gives him the intimate meaning of the truth (vv. 20–21), and instructs him in all things; the Christian is henceforth 'born of the Spirit' (John 3:8). Having arrived at this degree of spiritual maturity he has no more need to be taught (1 John 2:27): the only thing that still matters is that he should remain in Jesus and allow himself to be taught by God (cf. John 6:45)." J.-M. R. Tillard, "*Sensus Fidelium*," *One in Christ* 11, no. 1 (1975): 13–14. This interpretation points to two aspects of the *sensus fidei*. First, it underscores the inalienability of the Holy Spirit's presence through the sacrament of baptism. Second, however, it alludes to the dialectic of grace and sin: one may respond more or less fully to the Spirit, and therefore one's life may be a greater or lesser expression of the *sensus fidei*.

[36] The term "magisterium" has held various meanings in church history and has thus been used to describe diverse groups within the church. I will follow Francis Sullivan, who notes that "in modern Catholic usage, the term 'magisterium' has come to be associated almost exclusively with the teaching role and authority of the hierarchy. An even more recent development is that the term 'magisterium' is often used to refer not to the teaching office as such, but to the body of men who exercise this office in the church: namely, the pope and bishops." Francis Sullivan, "Magisterium," in *The New Dictionary of Theology*, ed. Joseph A. Komonchak et al. (Collegeville, MN: Liturgical Press, 1987), 617–23.

the reality to be discerned, judged, and promulgated or "defined." For it has to exercise all its activity upon the Word *as received and lived* in the Church.[37]

The *sensus fidelium* is not an inferior source of authority but is rather a foundation for the teaching authority of bishops. Through their participation in and reception of the *sensus fidelium*, bishops are formed in their own ability to know God and thus to minister for the good of the church's communion and mission.

III. Models of Faithful Reception

If the church communicates for communion, we must ask what communicative models mark the church, and what practical consequences they hold for a mutual reception of self-gift that is both reflective of and sustained by God's grace. A model is not monolithic and may not capture everything that occurs within the church. Yet models can be helpful for pointing out certain tendencies, strengths, and weaknesses that are influential for how we perceive God, the church, and each other. Models seek to describe what is happening in the church's life but can also serve as corrective prescriptions for our practices that help us better envision and embody the church.

Since Vatican II, the ecclesiology of communion has become a primary model for how the Roman Catholic Church imagines itself. The council's dual retrieval of the scriptural images of the body of Christ and people of God in such documents as *Lumen Gentium* and *Gaudium et Spes* has implications for the church's practice and structures and contrasts with how the church tended to view itself in the centuries immediately preceding Vatican II.

---

[37] Tillard, "*Sensus Fidelium*," 28. Italics in original. "Those having a responsibility in the leadership of the Church have, indeed, to *recognise* with their own charism and *receive* this *sensus fidelium* in which they also participate, as baptized Christians." J.-M. R. Tillard, "Reception-Communion," *One in Christ* 28, no. 4 (1992): 319. Italics in original.

The imaginative shift in the church's self-perception has to do with how we understand reception within the church and what we ought to do to foster it.

Reception in an institution. Partly in response to Reformation ecclesiology, in the centuries preceding the Second Vatican Council, an institutional model of the church developed. Whereas Congar refers to the church's institutions as its rootedness in God's salvific gifts, Avery Dulles employs the phrase "institutional model" to describe a view of the church that prioritizes hierarchical ministries and emphasizes the church's organizational structure.[38] The institutional model gained prominence due to the polemics of the Reformation. Martin Luther emphasized justification as an interior reality and criticized some external trappings of the Roman Catholic Church as offering an illusory path to salvation rooted in human endeavor rather than divine grace. This led some Roman Catholic theologians to conclude that Luther believed the "true" church to be an invisible, internal reality. In other words, these theologians thought Luther eschewed the ways in which the church is made visible through its practices and structures.[39] Robert Bellarmine's description of the church at the beginning of the seventeenth century displays a Catholic response to this reading of Luther's ecclesiology. Bellarmine defined the church as a visible society composed of rational beings united by the profession of the same faith and the reception of sacraments,

[38] See Avery Dulles, *Models of the Church* (Garden City, NY: Image Books, 1978), 39–50.

[39] Michael Himes, "The Development of Ecclesiology: Modernity to the Twentieth Century," in *The Gift of the Church*, ed. Peter Phan (Collegeville, MN: Liturgical Press, 2000), 47. *De servo arbitrio, D. Martin Luthers Werke* (Weimar, 1883–), 18:652. "Luther had cautioned that 'the church is hidden and the saints are unknown' and on occasion expressed his insistence on the word of God as the *sole* authority in the Church by denouncing canon law and hierarchical authority, especially that of the papacy and episcopacy. Read unsympathetically, such statements seemed to lead to the conclusion that there are two quite different meanings of the word 'church': one, the true Church known by God and revealed at the final judgment, and the other, the earthly institution whose membership might or (more likely) might not coincide with the true Church."

under the headship of legitimate pastors, most particularly Christ's earthly vicar, the pope.[40]

As a response to Luther's ecclesiology as interpreted by Roman Catholics, this definition of the church works well: Bellarmine points to the incarnational quality of the church. Our expression of a common faith is embodied within history through sacraments and structures. In our own time, which has suspicion of institutions, often for serious causes, Bellarmine's definition also reminds us that leadership has the potential to be sacramental and not only scandalous. Further, the definition's emphasis on the church as a "rational society" means that just as faith and reason may be brought together beneficially in Catholic theology, the very life of the church also invites our rational affectivity as an essential element of the church's full humanity.[41]

The definition's serious liability is that it makes no mention of two persons of the Trinity and refers to Christ only in terms of his vicar. Abstracted from his own further theological reflections and a historical context that included many attempts at episcopal and ecclesial reform, Bellarmine's definition promotes a view of the church as first and foremost a social body with laws, functions, and authorities rather than as a graced communion of the triune God with humanity.[42] David J. Stagaman writes that in this definition of the church, which was widely disseminated through the

[40] Himes, "The Development of Ecclesiology," 47. Himes quotes Bellarmine's definition from *Disputationes de controversiis Christianae fidei adversus huius temporis haereticos*, 3 vols. (Ingolstadt, 1586–1593), 4.3.2.

[41] Here I presume that in Bellarmine's time we may still be able to describe our emotional lives as part of our rational natures rather than as alien to it.

[42] For example, underscoring the bishop's role was not necessarily (or at least not only) an imposition of episcopal power but may also have been a reminder to absentee bishops of the necessity of residency in order to minister to the souls in their care. Lack of residency was a chronic problem in the Middle Ages. Bishops varied widely in their commitment to their ministry and, if in residence, their way of responding to the needs of the local church, secular power dynamics, and relationship to the papacy. Though from an earlier period, Southern offers enlightening depictions of episcopal variety in the thirteenth century: R. W. Southern, *Western Society and the Church in the Middle Ages* (London: Penguin Books, 1970), 190–210. Further, Bellarmine's definition aside, the Middle Ages also saw the rise of conciliarism in the church, which reflected ongoing negotia-

manuals used to train seminarians, "Ecclesiology becomes hier-archology, the Church a fixed and set structure of offices where issues of authority are paramount."[43] In the nineteenth century, the institutional model's focus on the bishops to the exclusion of the laity led to Giovanni Perrone's division of the church into two factions: the *ecclesia docens* (teaching church), or bishops, of whom the term "church" was most properly predicated, and the *ecclesia discens* (learning church), or the laity, who "were to accept what they had been taught based on the authority of the teaching Church."[44]

One of the dangers of a sharp distinction between the teaching and learning church is that it contributes to institutionalism: focus is given to the church's leadership and law, rather than to the abiding presence and continuing activity of the Holy Spirit throughout the church.[45] By dividing the church into two camps, the mutual reception and response involved in communication for communion

---

tions over the origin and location of authority within the church, as well as the church's relationship with secular power.

[43] David J. Stagaman, *Authority in the Church* (Collegeville, MN: Liturgical Press, 1999), 109, 110.

[44] Bernard P. Prusak, *The Church Unfinished: Ecclesiology through the Centuries* (Mahwah, NJ: Paulist Press, 1989), 249–50. Here the bishops' ability to teach authoritatively is abstracted from their ministry, and "magisterium" is made coterminous with "episcopacy." Perrone's was not the only ecclesiology of the period, and he was influenced by Johann Adam Möhler's presentations of ecclesiology grounded in the activity of the Holy Spirit and Christ. Nevertheless, ultramontanism, which Perrone promoted at Vatican I, "was an attempt to ensure the unity and good order of the Church by creating a highly centralized, omni-competent papacy exercising its authority through a hierarchical chain of command in which the bishops were the principal links." Himes, "The Development of Ecclesiology," 60.

[45] The theoretical models of the church prevalent at any one period of the church's history do not, of course, preclude the Holy Spirit's presence within the church. "God is mediated through historical circumstances, not above, below, or around those circumstances," and that mediation is first and foremost the result of God's faithfulness. Michael J. Himes, "The Ecclesiological Significance of the Reception of Doctrine," *The Heythrop Journal* 33, no. 2 (April 1992): 150. Nevertheless, theory may deeply influence practices and relationships, and the ecclesiological question is what concepts of "church" nurture human cooperation with the Spirit and with each other.

is obscured. Instead, the Holy Spirit provides the hierarchy with the authority to communicate truth and renders the laity docile to magisterial teaching. In this unidirectional form of reception, the bishops are not dependent on the church; rather, through their reception of the Holy Spirit, bishops become the sole architects of communion and the independent arbiters of apostolicity. Exclusive attention to the hierarchy as "giving" and the laity as "receiving" narrows authority to apostolic succession. The result is that the bishops' ministry is no longer contextualized within the apostolicity of the whole church, and the need for bishops to receive the faith through the *sensus fidelium* is unrecognized.

A time of transition. While Vatican II highlighted the church as a communion, in turning to a second communicative model it is well to remember that the institutional model stands close to us in the church's historical journey. Practices and structures— whether societal or ecclesial—do not adapt easily to new paradigms and may require our conversion on several levels. The institutional model may still be the lens through which we view communion, so that the body of Christ is seen primarily as the union that results from assent to magisterial teaching. Further, as Pope Francis has noted, the church as a communion may become guilty of a "spiritual worldliness," craning inward upon itself to such a degree that turning to look outward becomes a pain in the neck, restricting the church's range of mission (EG 93–94). In describing the church as a communion, then, it is also necessary to remember that the Holy Spirit not only makes the church one but also holy, catholic, and apostolic. Through the creedal marks of the church, communion is deeply linked to apostolicity: the church's communion is marked by Christ's co-missioning and the Spirit's co-witnessing, and the church is a body sent forth on a pilgrimage of salvation. This pilgrimage is our lived response to God's gift.

By exercising our responsibility as a communion of pilgrim witnesses, the church cultivates holiness by receiving more deeply the mystery of our own salvation and incarnates catholicity as we learn to offer ourselves as a sacrament of salvation within diverse cultures and contexts.[46] Reflection on the church's interior life ought not be an exercise in parochialism in which the church's communion becomes a sanctuary of complacency or self-sufficiency (something to which any group is susceptible); rather, it is an opportunity for dynamic reengagement with the diverse members of one body who have a common call to apostolic mission, holiness, and catholicity. A communion that is spiritually worldly and overly influenced by institutionalism may be distinguished from a communion that is enlivened by mission by describing the second model of the church as an apostolic communion. This model holds together the church's union and mission by uniting two metaphors: the church as the body of Christ in pilgrimage as the people of God.[47]

Reception in an apostolic communion. In an apostolic communion, the church as a whole is both teaching and learning through mutual communication and reception. Reception, lived out in the church's mission, occurs within the church's communion in several ways: we receive from God, through each other, and as a communion of churches. First, God's initiative in self-communication is the foundation for all ecclesial reception. Communion in God, the source and goal of the human person, occurs through the reception of God's self-gift offered through the divine missions of the Son and

---

[46] EG 116. "In the diversity of peoples who experience the gift of God, each in accordance with its own culture, the Church expresses her genuine catholicity and shows forth the 'beauty of her varied face.' In the Christian customs of an evangelized people, the Holy Spirit adorns the Church, showing her new aspects of revelation and giving her a new face."

[47] The *Final Report* from the 1985 Extraordinary Synod of Bishops stated, "The ecclesiology of communion is a central and fundamental idea in the documents of the [Second Vatican] council." 1985 Extraordinary Synod of Bishops, *The Final Report*, AFER 28, nos. 1–2 (February–April 1986), C1. In *Evangelii Gaudium*, Francis prefers the metaphor of the people of God to that of the Body of Christ: "The Church, as the agent of evangelization, is more than an organic and hierarchical institution; she is first and foremost a people advancing on its pilgrim way towards God. She is certainly a *mystery* rooted in the Trinity, yet she exists concretely in history as a people of pilgrims and evangelizers, transcending any institutional expression, however necessary" (111; emphasis in original).

Spirit. Christianity is based on the claim that through God's gracious and new initiative, the human person's final end is communion with God. Though this final end is beyond humanity's natural powers to attain, God's revelation of the final end is undertaken in such a way as to take account of our humanity, most explicitly in the incarnation.[48] Neither is the church abandoned to the waiting room of history but, rather, we receive the Spirit as companion for our pilgrimage. When we nourish God's gift by giving ourselves in a mission of love, the church's path becomes a history of salvation, stretching out to the fullness of the kingdom. Through this spiritual and historical process we are incorporated into Christ, and Christ is incorporated into us.[49]

The basis for active reception of God's self-communication is the divine word proclaimed and the human "Amen" given to that word. Through this reception, the word is not simply heard but also put into practice.

> In the Church of God . . . nothing exists which is not "communion," beginning evidently with love. That brings in also in a very full way the Word of truth, which is not reduced to a pure intellectual proclamation. It is inseparably Word pronounced and Word accepted, Word declared and Word "received," announcement and *Amen* declared on this announcement to the point that one cannot be in the truth without also "putting it" into action.[50]

Through reception, God's authentic self-gift is transformed into a word of life-giving faith, which in turn transforms the recipients into a communion through their lived response. To receive Christ is to be drawn into the life of communion with God and thus to live out that communion's mission in love.

---

[48] Congar, *Tradition and Traditions*, 238.
[49] Ibid., 255.
[50] Tillard, *Church of Churches*, 125.

Tillard also reminds us that Christians are not born but rather are made through divine adoption.[51] Christian identity comes through entrance into the church, which is transformative: "To become a Christian, one needs to be *received* into the communion of all those who share this divine origin. It concretely means to be *received* into the communion of the Church and to *receive* there, together with faith, the eschatological gifts of God. Christian identity is acquired only through this *reception*, never by human birth."[52] Received into the church, the believer in turn receives the eschatological gifts of God, in which the once-for-all of Christ's death and resurrection are continually made present and which call the church forward on its journey into the fullness of life in God.

Tillard's description of the church's reception of God opens to a second form of reception within an apostolic communion: among the faithful. Our faith is received through the mediation of others, and Congar comments, "[I]t is normal for persons to depend on one another in order to achieve their supernatural destiny."[53] The faith received results not only in a communion with God but also in fellowship with others. Believers share a communal consciousness such that the ground of their relationship with God and encounter with the world is based in the same revelation.[54] Congar indicates: "The unity of persons in the Church is not a 'fusion,' but a 'communion': a large number of persons possess in common the same realities . . . as the content of their inner life, their memory and thus of their consciousness. Thus they are not conscious

---

[51] J.-M. R. Tillard, "Tradition, Reception," in *The Quadrilog: Tradition and the Future of Ecumenism*, ed. Kenneth Hagen (Collegeville, MN: Liturgical Press, 1994), 330. "Since the city of the Christians 'is in heaven' (Phil 3:20) and because Christians are 'fellow-citizens of the saints of the household of God' (Eph 2:19), no one on earth is Christian by birth. The johannine Gospel speaks of the necessity of a rebirth, a birth from above, a birth out of water and Spirit."

[52] Ibid., 331. Italics in original.

[53] Congar, *Tradition and Traditions*, 241.

[54] Ibid., 314–15.

of their *personal* opinions but of the teaching of *the Church* that derives from the apostles."[55]

Congar construes faith not as opinion but as a conviction whose content is given to us by others in unity with the apostles.[56] The church's apostolicity, characteristic of all believers through their baptism, means all believers are "missionary disciples," responsible witnesses of revelation who have a role in incarnating and handing on the apostolic tradition (EG 120). The same Spirit who enables the individual's reception of and response to the Word also joins the individual believer to the communal confession of the church. We know God personally because we receive God communally.

Third, in an apostolic communion we receive God not only through each other personally but also as a "church of churches." Tillard writes that we come to faith as living, independent subjects. The local church is a communion of these believing subjects. The bishop's faith is the faith of his local church, and he represents the faith of that church to the other churches for recognition as apostolic.[57] The grounding of each local church in the apostolic tradition through the Holy Spirit allows local churches to receive one another and thus to have a universal communion. Conversely, through this process of reception, the universal church is present in the local church:

> But the fact that the Churches are, in their communion of faith and life, one single and unique Church of God, marks their reciprocal relationships. It is put into practice and expressed by their "reception": they mutually "receive" each other as Church. . . . This possibility of "reception" of doctrine, of canons, of liturgical forms, decisions of one Church by the

---

[55] Ibid., 320. Italics in original.

[56] Ibid., 315.

[57] Tillard, *Church of Churches*, 134. "The faith of the bishop is, in reality, that of his Church. In old practice, besides, his Church presented him for ordination because it recognized in his faith the deposit transmitted to it and preserved by it."

others has always been perceived as a very basic consequence of *communion* in faith.[58]

Mutual reception within and among local churches is necessarily a continuous process of confirming the churches' faithfulness to the apostolic tradition and thus advancing their unity. The bishop's ministry is essential for the process of reception among local churches which forms the *consensus fidelium* of the universal church: bishops receive the *sensus fidelium* of their local church, communicate that faith to the universal church, and in turn offer the mind of the universal church to the local church.[59] Thus the bishop's growth into a personal symbol of the local church's *sensus fidelium* is vital for the church's faith as a whole.

By attending to multiple forms of reception, imagining the church as an apostolic communion paints a more complex picture of the church's communication for communion than does the institutional model. In the latter model, the process of receiving God's saving revelation is fairly straightforward; however consistently the model may function in practice, we nevertheless have a clear "flow chart" of reception: from God to the bishops to the rest of the church. Reception in an apostolic communion does not flow in straight lines of command. Rather, there are intersecting circles of mutual influence: families, parishes, religious orders, local churches, ecumenical initiatives, ecclesial organizations for

[58] Ibid.

[59] See Richard Gaillardetz, "The Reception of Doctrine: New Perspectives," in *Authority in the Roman Catholic Church*, ed. Bernard Hoose (Burlington, VT: Ashgate, 2002), 108–10. Also: "Reception also involves formal decisions on the part of those authorities who represent and serve the unity of the Church. In the classical model of reception the bishop symbolized the link between the local church and the apostolic Church; the bishops also maintained the communion between the local church and the universal Church by participating in conciliar gatherings. Sometimes it was the role of the bishops in council to initiate a process of reception through formal conciliar decisions. . . . Sometimes the authority of the bishops served to give formal approval to a process of reception already underway, thus bringing the process to a juridical close." Thomas Rausch, "Reception Past and Present," *Theological Studies* 47 (1986): 503.

charity and justice, parochial schools, national bishops' conferences, synods, the curia, and papacy. Reception in this model of
the church is far from easy to systematize, though it does better
reflect the interdependence and messiness of human history. How
in the midst of these intersecting circles are we to distinguish
between God's salvation and changing historical expressions of
it? Between authentic interpretations of the Gospel and sinful
distortions? How can we be transformed together into the body
of Christ and walk faithfully as the people of God?

IV. Receiving with Discernment

The questions raised by reception in an apostolic communion
call for reflection on forms of ecclesial discernment—in other
words, discernment that is undertaken both personally and communally in order to receive and respond to God's self-gift authentically and transformatively. Our ability to discern is grounded in
the *sensus fidei*. Yet if this baptismal gift of the Spirit is to be fruitful,
it must be unwrapped by the graced choices we make to be good
receivers. Even though discernment may be sacramentally innate
through the *sensus fidei*, discerning is a way of knowing—of receiving—that requires thoughtful development. Later chapters will
investigate spiritual practices and church structures that assist
discernment's development. Yet the apostolic communion model
itself points to contours of discernment that bear keeping in mind.

Discernment and dialogue. Since the church comes to know God
through reception of the divine self-gift, an apostolic communion
challenges a strict division of the church into the *ecclesia docens*—
the bishops who teach and transmit—and the *ecclesia discens*—the
laity who learn and receive. The assertion that the apostolic tradition is entrusted to the entire church and that the Holy Spirit works
throughout the church to further the reception and communication
of the apostolic faith emphasizes that the bishops do not have a
privileged source of revelation apart from the church, and that
the entire people of God has a role in the church's salvific mission.

Though division of the church into two factions of "teachers" and "learners" is not tenable in an apostolic communion, it may still be said of the church that it is, as a whole, both teaching and learning.[60]

The church's teaching and learning, shared in diverse ways by the laity and bishops, maintain the church in its apostolic communion. Ormond Rush describes the truth communicated in institutional ecclesiology as *"monologic orthodoxy* in which the truth comes from above from a single authority."[61] In contrast, in order to promote apostolic unity, communion ecclesiology "presupposes a *dialogic orthodoxy* in which the truth is discovered 'from below' through a process of dialogue."[62]

One of the benefits of promoting dialogue is the opportunity to engage more closely with those with whom our faith is shared and to discern the relationship between action, intent, and meaning. In his important essay "On Consulting the Faithful in Matters of Doctrine," John Henry Newman used the word "consult" in a quite narrow manner, which emphasized how faithful practices are observed: "Doubtless [the laity's] advice, their opinion, their judgment on the question of definition is not asked; but the matter of fact, viz. their belief *is* sought for, as a testimony to that apostolical tradition, on which alone any doctrine whatsoever can be

[60] "*Docens* and *discens* are two determinants of the same, sole community; they are two adjectives which qualify two functions of the whole community; they are not two nouns which introduce a dichotomy in the community. To be both teacher and learner emerges as a dual function of one and the same Church and not as two fractions of the Church or within the Church." Leonardo Boff, "*Ecclesia Docens* and *Ecclesia Discens*," in *Who Has a Say in the Church?*, ed. Jürgen Moltmann and Hans Küng (New York: Seabury Press, 1981), 48.

[61] Ormond Rush, "Determining Catholic Orthodoxy: Monologue or Dialogue," *Pacifica* 12, no. 2 (June 1999): 126. Emphasis in original. See Avery Dulles, *Models of the Church*, 47–48. Dulles's list of the benefits of this model includes a foundation for the uncertainties of the present in a past which is considered secure and a strong sense of one's identity in relationship to one's church.

[62] Rush, "Determining Catholic Orthodoxy," 126. Emphasis in original.

defined."[63] For Newman, the *"fidelium sensus* and *consensus"* is a "branch of evidence," and he compares them to a clock which might be "consulted" for the time of day.[64] Newman's argument encountered fierce criticism in his own time, which tended to institutional ecclesiology. Within an apostolic communion, however, consultation may be understood more broadly.[65] Dialogical consultation may better allow for the meaning and purpose behind faithful behaviors to be disclosed and thus diminish the observer's tendency to superimpose her or his own explanations onto the observed behavior. It is one thing, for example, to observe faithful Christians engaged in devotion to Our Lady of Guadalupe; one goes a step further by inquiring of the faithful what their piety means in relation to the church, their families, and their cultural and political contexts.[66] In other words, dialogue allows us to

---

[63] John Henry Newman, "On Consulting the Faithful in Matters of Doctrine," in *Conscience, Consensus, and the Development of Doctrine* (New York: Doubleday, 1992), 393.

[64] Ibid.

[65] Ibid., 392–93. Newman indicates that he uses the word "consult" in its popular meaning as in "consulting our barometer" or to "consult a watch or a sun-dial," as opposed to its more technical meaning of "consult *with*" or "take *counsel*." Thus the quotation above continues: "In like manner, we may 'consult' the liturgies or the rites of the Church; not that [they] can take part whatever in the definition, for they are documents or customs; but they are witnesses" (393). In the context of communion ecclesiology, Newman's view of consultation with the laity is the minimal requirement for reception of the *sensus fidelium*; the more technical terminology, which he does not intend to employ in this essay, is both appropriate and necessary.

[66] The necessity of dialogue in the consultation process reflects "a philosophic change since Newman's day, from an epistemological question, how the church knows the truth of the faith tradition, to a hermeneutical question, how the church, in different times and places, comes to understand the faith tradition. Communication of the faith from the church in one time and place to another requires delicate instruments of interpretation if the catholicity of the faith is not to be lost." Paul G. Crowley, "Catholicism, Inculturation and Newman's *Sensus Fidelium*," *The Heythrop Journal* 33, no. 2 (April 1992): 168. Francis highlights the importance of popular piety for the inculturation of the Gospel: "Nor is it devoid of content; rather it discovers and expresses that content more by way of symbols than by discursive reasoning, and in the act of faith greater accent is placed on *credere in Deum* than on *credere Deum*" (124). Dialogical consultation aims at

discern—or see—further into others' witness and opens up the possibility for a deeper reception of one another's *sensus fidei*, a necessary step in knowing the *sensus fidelium*.

The purpose of discerning via dialogue is the church's diverse unity in mission. In monological orthodoxy, the requirement for unity may be mere uniformity. Conversely, dialogically based unity better allows for diversity because through it the church learns to recognize an underlying consensus of faith woven through diverse cultures and practices. After discussing the limitations of orthodoxy upheld by a monolithic unity based in hierarchical authority, on the one hand, and orthodoxy that devolves into "totally incommunicable liberal pluralism," on the other, Walter Kasper indicates "the only alternative is orthodoxy regarded as a process based on dialogue. This approach is based on the conviction that truth in the Church has to emerge from a process of dialogue between all the charisms and tendencies."[67] Dialogue aims at forming consensus in the church through the process of listening. Thus dialogue toward consensus involves, and implicates, all members of the church in a spiritual process.[68] Dialogue serves as discernment's context and catalyst.

Discernment and authorities. The role of the people of God in the reception and transmission of the apostolic faith poses the challenge of recognizing diverse sources of authority. While the institutional model associated authority with the hierarchy alone, in

---

developing the faithful's reflective interpretation of their piety as well as gaining through that reflection a greater insight into the *sensus fidelium*.

[67] Walter Kasper, *An Introduction to Christian Faith* (New York: Paulist Press, 1980), 150.

[68] Kasper describes an epistemology "which differs from both authoritarian and from democratic processes of decision. Consensus in faith and the determination of a consensus is a spiritual process. It can only be detected by the *sensus fidei* produced by the Spirit, an interior feel, a sort of sixth sense for faith. . . . Often a purely intellectual process will not produce agreement or clarity about where truth ends and error begins. Nevertheless the Church must make unequivocal statements at least on fundamentals. This is only possible by spiritual judgment. The only way to be sure of the shared truth in the faith is by doing the truth together." Ibid., 145.

an apostolic communion authority arises from the co-witness of the Spirit shared by all Christians through their baptism. Kasper indicates that dialogue is the mark of genuine authority within the church, and it is therefore particularly incumbent on the bishops:

> Institutionalized authority is—or is meant to be—something like institutionalized freedom. It ought to be a centre of communication, responsible for seeing that everyone has a say. In this general dialogue it ought to articulate and emphasize shared basic convictions, but too often it is prevented from doing so by its own isolation and inability to communicate. Today in the Church we suffer, not from an excess of authority, but from a lack of genuine authority which is in a position to articulate the faith that is binding on all in such a way that all people of good will can see themselves represented in it and a consensus is created.[69]

Here Kasper construes authority in terms of how bishops do—or do not—foster dialogue and guide the church in orthodoxy. A discussion of authority also introduces questions of obedience in a church whose members are each graced by the Holy Spirit to be responsible communicators of the apostolic faith. Kasper writes, "An attitude of obedience to ecclesiastical authority is not the principal expression of the ecclesiality of faith. Membership of the Church is not demonstrated by blind obedience, but by listening to others and being willing to accommodate them."[70] Empowered by the Spirit, all the baptized may communicate authentic knowledge of God; all the baptized are sources of authority within the

[69] Ibid., 148. See also Sullivan: "As we have seen above, the basic notion of *koinonia* is sharing or participation. Hence, the exercise of hierarchical authority will meet the requirements of an ecclesiology of communion to the extent that it promotes the participation in the life of the Church of all its members, according to the gifts and capacities of each. On the contrary, authority will fail to meet the requirements of an ecclesiology of communion when it so restricts active participation to the few, that the many are prevented from having that share in the life of the Church of which they are capable." Francis Sullivan, "Authority in an Ecclesiology of Communion," *New Theology Review* 10, no. 3 (August 1997): 24.

[70] Kasper, *An Introduction to Christian Faith*, 143.

church. Yet if this is the case, how can we understand obedience in the church?

Nicholas Lash helps to address this question by contextualizing the relationship of authority and obedience within the greater question of how truth is known. Religious belief is not a different kind of knowing from other knowledge; in our knowing we "believe" many things that have not been proven demonstrably to us.[71] We can, however, ask for authentication for our belief.[72] Central to Lash's question is whether truth is something that human beings create, or whether it is received and therefore something that calls for discernment, appropriation, and creativity.

Part of discerning authoritative sources within the church is acknowledging that each human authority is limited. Since no single human authority can stand in place of the absolute authority of God, both authority and obedience are the result of recognition, or discernment, of the truth through multiple, particular authorities.[73] Lash writes, "Ultimately, the only authority is the authority of truth: the truth that is God, the source and ground of all truth. The 'problem' of authority, therefore, is the problem of establishing criteria for the discernment and prosecution of truth: for 'hearing' the truth and 'doing' it."[74] A variety of authorities, however, presents the need to foster a common mission, which through the Spirit is both the church's gracious reality and essential responsibility.[75]

Having set up the problem of authority within a church that is in its entirety the communicator of the apostolic tradition, Lash asks: "Where the christian discernment and appropriation of truth is concerned, in what sense can there be experts who 'know,' who stand in relationship to Christ such that, as mediators of his knowledge of God, they are entitled to be the recipients of unqualified

---

[71] Nicholas Lash, *Voices of Authority* (Shepherdstown, WV: Patmos Press, 1976), 79. Here, as elsewhere in this book, Lash is deeply influenced by John Henry Newman.

[72] Ibid., 83.

[73] Ibid., 33.

[74] Ibid., 24.

[75] Ibid., 39.

trust on the part of the rest of the believing community?"[76] To answer this question, he follows Newman's thought in *Lectures on the Prophetical Office* by inquiring whether church leaders, scholars, or saints can be the ones who "know." Church leaders manifest God's fidelity to the church when in particular circumstances and through divine assistance they define a teaching as somehow normative for the life of the church. Bishops do not have access to a source of revelation apart from the church, however, and thus it seems they cannot be the only ones who know.[77] Scholars have technical expertise in some sources of Christian knowing; this expertise, however, can yield quite varied interpretations, and scholarly sources are not the only sources of Christian knowledge.[78] Finally, while saints do exemplify the relationship between holiness and knowledge of God, Lash notes that having one's heart in the right place is perfectly compatible with being wrongheaded.[79] Thus each of these groups has something to offer to Christian knowing, but no one group is at all times the only authoritative source for all Christian knowing. Lash concludes that these three groups, "symbolically" representative of the three-fold office of Christ, must remain in creative tension with one another:[80]

> This tension, which is constitutive and not destructive of the believing community, will be, at one level, a tension between groups of functionaries—between church leaders and scholars, for example. At another level it will often be a tension which the individual christian experiences within himself: a tension between pastoral prudence and scholarly integrity, for example; or between the trustful generosity of living faith and the caution characteristic of scholarly enquiry.[81]

[76] Ibid., 91.
[77] Ibid., 91–92.
[78] Ibid., 92–94.
[79] Ibid., 95–96.
[80] Ibid., 97.
[81] Ibid., 98.

If Lash is correct about the necessity of this tension in the church, then no one authority may claim to stand alone; we must discern the truth these authorities know personally because the church participates in knowledge of God communally. For Lash, obedience is found in the recognition of truth, and not merely in acquiescence to the authority who communicates that truth. The problem of authority is the "criteria on the basis of which truth, both practical and theoretical, is discerned, responded to, appropriated, and embodied."[82] Within Lash's conception, we may give obedience to each of these three general groups within the church, but that obedience need not be blind. Asking for truth to be authenticated does not remove the possibility of an obedient response to the truth expressed through these authorities; rather, it renders obedience a more complete expression of the believer's acquiescence to God.[83] Lash writes:

> We are saved by Christ's obedience not because it was blind but because it was obedience, because it was unswerving and total response to perceived truth. This is not to deny that at its focal point—in the garden and on the cross—it was an obedience to truth that was only "darkly" perceived. And obedience to darkly perceived truth always carries within it, as part of its constitutive agony, the risk of being profoundly and disastrously mistaken.[84]

Identifying authorities within the church and seeking authentication from them begin the process of transition from an external communication of truth to a mutual communication of truth; it is the movement by which God's truth, initially external to us, comes to dwell within and thus to transform us into persons of faith capable of responding to God through our lives.[85] Conversely, authorities should see in others' requests for authentication an opportunity to follow the "God whose self-expression as a man has

---

[82] Ibid., 99.
[83] Ibid., 110.
[84] Ibid., 112.
[85] Ibid., 10–11.

Responding to God.

convinced us, wooed us, compelled us to answering recognition, love, and trust."[86] Discernment is a process of authentication reflecting this dynamic of mutual authority and mutual obedience.

Discernment and learning. The discernment that is authentic, limited, and communal becomes transformative as well when we acknowledge our need to learn of God from one another. While "magisterium" is associated with "teaching function," Frederick Crowe argues for an explicit acknowledgment of the necessity of learning within the church, and for an intelligent, reasoned, and methodologically coherent understanding of the process by which the church learns.[87] By recognizing the process of learning, Crowe proposes that the church is ultimately living out its call to discipleship.

> Jesus, we know, advanced in wisdom and age. He learned obedience from the things he suffered. He strove to the very end to learn the divine will, ready always to do it, but asking whether there was not another way than the one the Father seemed to have chosen. Indeed, he asked questions of others, too, not all of them rhetorical surely, some of them presumably in order to learn the answers. . . . To affirm then that we are a learning Church is simply to affirm our Christian discipleship, a pattern of life that in this as in other matters is modeled on Jesus of Nazareth. We do indeed belong to a learning Church, and our learning Church had a learning founder. There should be no more than a momentary hesitation in making so simple an affirmation.[88]

Crowe notes that the process of learning itself raises problems that we may find difficult to accept. The first is the recognition

---

[86] Ibid., 11.

[87] Frederick Crowe, "The Magisterium as Pupil: The Learning Teacher," in *Developing the Lonergan Legacy: Historical, Theoretical, and Existential Themes*, ed. Michael Vertin (Toronto: University of Toronto Press, 2004), 288.

[88] Frederick Crowe," "The Church as Learner: Two Crises, One *Kairos*," in *Appropriating the Lonergan Idea*, ed. Michael Vertin (Washington, DC: The Catholic University of America Press, 1989), 373.

that when we learn we must ask questions about things of which we are ignorant. The church needs to admit that there are questions to which we do not yet have answers. The second is the realization that when questions are asked, ideas about possible answers are produced—and some of these ideas will be wrong. Therefore, beyond admitting that there are questions that we cannot yet answer, the church also needs to concede that some ideas of how to answer these questions have been mistaken.[89] Refusing to acknowledge these aspects of the church's learning does not change the fact that the church learns but instead hinders our ability to engage the learning process—to be transformed disciples.

In order to reclaim the church's learning function, Crowe suggests that it is necessary to think through the Christian message in relation to the church's pilgrimage through history:

> Let us be clear on what we are doing and what we are not doing. We are not proclaiming a new God, a new Christ, a new Holy Spirit. All these are divinely given in revelation; and just as we had nothing to do with the giving of revelation, so we can do nothing to change it, nor should we wish to change it. We are asking, however, what God's revelation, given through Hebrew images and in Hebrew language in scriptural times and scriptural places, means for us today.[90]

The participation of the laity in the process of learning is crucial for determining how the church's communication is coherent today, not only for the church's sake but also for the sake of its mission.[91] Crowe finds inspiration for this learning process in

---

[89] Crowe, "The Magisterium as Pupil," 289.

[90] Ibid., 290. Crowe's essay was originally an address to the Paulinian Conference held at St. Paul's College, Winnipeg, on February 12, 1990.

[91] "The *instinctus*, the spiritual discernment, the religious needs, the true sense of direction of the body of the faithful carry the dynamism of the faith where the Spirit wills: into the turbulent stream of human problems and searchings, on to the floor of the workshops where mankind is building its future. For faith is for man as he is, and is 'catholic.'" Tillard, "Sensus Fidelium," 28.

Bishop Bernard Hubert who suggested at an extraordinary synod that the bishops "go back and discuss the themes considered with the members of the people of God responsible for the mission of the church."[92] Crowe interprets the bishop as inviting "feedback from the people of God, based on their experience of the world we live in," discussion that should include every member of the church.[93] In the learning process of consultation, the laity become teachers. More recently, the desire to learn from the faithful was reflected in the preparatory survey sent out to all the churches for the Extraordinary Synod on the Family.[94] The church deepens its redemption by embracing its divine roots: we learn to discern and discern in order to learn.

Lash and Crowe help to bring out the questions of reception in an apostolic communion in relation to the *ecclesia discens* and *docens*: How does the church come to a realization of truth, or learn, given multiple sources of authority? The conclusions of both scholars return us to the necessity of dialogical discernment and help to describe the contours of that dialogue. For Lash, this dialogue acts as part of the process of authentication that provides for mutual trust and mutual obedience within the church; for Crowe, it is only through the genuine asking of questions—including asking questions of the laity and the formulation of answers that

[92] Crowe, "The Magisterium as Pupil," 292. Crowe quotes the report of Bishop Hubert's statement in *L'Osservatore Romano*, Weekly Edition, English (December 16, 1985), 12. See also Tillard: "Indeed, even at the level of the understanding of the content of Revelation and of the rendering explicit of its elements, those faithful who have no hierarchical responsibility cannot be seen as simply receiving what is determined by the heads of the Church enlightened by the researches of theologians or other specialists in 'educated faith'; the faithful have a specific part to play in this knowledge of the whole Church of the truth given to Jesus Christ." Tillard, "Sensus Fidelium," 12.

[93] Crowe, "The Magisterium as Pupil," 292.

[94] Lorenzo Baldisseri, Letter to Cardinal Timothy Dolan, October 18, 2013. scribd.com/doc/180575701/Vatican-questionnaire-for-the-synod-on-the-family. In his capacity as secretary general of the Synod of Bishops, Cardinal Baldisseri asked that dioceses distribute the synod's preparatory document "as widely as possible to deaneries and parishes so that input from local sources can be received regarding the themes and responses to the questionnaire, as well as any helpful statistics, for the preparation of the *Instrumentum laboris*."

may be at times wrong—that the church develops as a learner and is thereby enabled to teach.

V. Conclusion

If dialogue as a spiritual reception and mutual exchange is a means of discerning the apostolic faith, then practices and structures that incarnate that dialogue by incorporating processes of authentication and learning are necessary. What are these practices and structures? In order to address that question, later chapters investigate one aspect of the dialogical process, the discerning reception of the *sensus fidelium* by the bishop within the local church.

Reception of the *sensus fidelium* represents for bishops, as it does for all believers, participation in an apostolic communion embodied within history through a living tradition. While each of the faithful has a baptismal vocation for transmitting the faith, an apostolic communion recognizes a particular role for the bishops in authoritatively defining and teaching the faith they receive. Three implications arise from this claim.

First, while not all that the bishop receives requires further doctrinal definition, a continual attitude of discerning reception is important. The bishop's discernment of the *sensus fidelium* ought to be a virtue in two senses of the word. To be a virtue, this discernment must be habitual. While dialogically based discernment is vitally important at times of crisis within the church, it is always necessary and may help to prevent the church's unity from devolving into polemics. In addition, this discernment will also be virtuous if it develops the bishop's own capacity to know and respond to the activity of the Holy Spirit at work throughout the church, as well as within his own spiritual life. The virtue of discernment should lead to both conversion and communion and authenticate the bishop's authority through his spirituality.

Second, magisterial authority is not the only authority in the church. As Lash reminds us, God is the ultimate authority, and others within the church participate in this authority through the ways in which they know God. It is necessary for bishops to take into account in a positive, rather than in a competitive, manner other ecclesial authorities. This recognition is enacted when the need of learning from these authorities through honest questioning toward authentication is embraced and when the possibility of mistakes in developing answers is acknowledged as a quite human part of the process of coming to know. The *Spiritual Exercises* and the structures of obedience and authority within the Society of Jesus will help us construct a comparative model for incorporating these first two implications into the bishop's ministry of discernment within the local church.

Third, the *sensus fidelium* is always contextualized within history. Sullivan's description indicates that the *sensus fidelium* may be valid for the church of a particular time and location without necessarily becoming normative for the universal church. Nevertheless, the bishop's representation of the *sensus fidelium* is an essential part of learning the *consensus fidelium* of the universal church. This necessarily means that the bishop must draw distinctions between all that goes on within and around the church and the work of the Holy Spirit which is always mediated through diverse people, cultures, times, and locations. This is not to say that the bishop "distills" the activity of the Holy Spirit from the events of history in such a way as to make the expression of the apostolic tradition ahistorical. Rather, it points to the importance of understanding the local church as the context for the bishop's discernment, a subject taken up in the next chapter.

Chapter 2

Surveying the Local Church: The Bishop's Role and the Diocese's Structures

> *When I am frightened by what I am to you, then I am consoled by what I am with you. To you I am the bishop, and with you I am a Christian. The first is an office, the second a grace; the first a danger, the second salvation.*[1]
>
> —Augustine, Bishop of Hippo

Augustine provides us with a way to understand the bishop's relationship to the *sensus fidelium*: who the bishop is "with" the faithful is the foundation for who the bishop is "to" the faithful. In other words, the bishop's person and ministry are connected. Through the sacrament of episcopal ordination, the bishop's office—or ministry—is one of teaching, governing, and sanctifying. The Catholic tradition of sacramental theology, formed in part by Augustine's own response to disputes in the early church, holds that grace works through the sacrament itself; lack of personal holiness on the part of the bishop does not negate God's ability

---

[1] Augustine, "On the Anniversary of His Ordination. P. L. 340," in *Selected Sermons of St. Augustine*, trans. and ed. Quincy Howe, Jr. (New York: Holt, Rinehart and Winston), 215.

to work through him.[2] Yet belief in grace's effectiveness does not absolve the bishop from the need to grow in personal holiness through his ministry. *Lumen Gentium*, Vatican II's Dogmatic Constitution on the Church, helps make this connection clear by following its description of the hierarchical and lay vocations with a chapter on the universal call to holiness. All the baptized are called to enter more deeply into the divine life of mutual self-giving and receiving, offer and response, that leads to participation in the life of God, who is the holy one. Through his ministry, the bishop is answering this call by living out his personal response to God's gift. This response, which is his ministry, itself shapes the person the bishop becomes. As Augustine notes, the process of being formed personally through ministry is no light matter, and we can hear in his words an echo of Paul's insistence that we work out our salvation in fear and trembling (Phil 2:12).

While the bishop's development in holiness takes a variety of forms, the questions of this chapter are twofold. First, how is the bishop's discernment of the *sensus fidelium* not only a requirement of his office but also formative of his personal holiness? Second, how does the bishop's personal holiness allow him to receive and represent the *sensus fidelium* of the local church? Developing answers to these questions is to some degree the goal of later chapters as they explore insights from Ignatian spirituality and Jesuit organizational structures that may have fruitful implications for an episcopal spirituality of discernment and for diocesan structures that support the bishop's discernment. Yet before turning to those resources, it is necessary first to survey the landscape of the local church and the bishop's ministry in relation to it. Such a survey helps us to perceive what is already, at least ideally, present within the local church that may serve as a foundation for the bishop's

---

[2] "If a bishop breaks communion with the college of bishops, he loses his ability to teach and rule in the name of the Church. However, since the Donatist controversy in the time of Augustine, an ordained minister out of communion with the Church does retain the ability to confer the sacraments validly even though these are considered to be illicit, that is, unlawful." Susan K. Wood, *Sacramental Orders* (Collegeville, MN: Liturgical Press, 2000), 33.

discernment of the *sensus fidelium* and his formation through its reception. A survey also assists us in noticing what may either be lacking or in need of further development in the guidelines for episcopal ministry in the local church and in the diocesan structures that facilitate this ministry with regard to the *sensus fidelium*.

In order to develop and reflect critically on the ideals already in place within the local church, this chapter proceeds in four sections. The first, "A Local and Universal Ministry" describes the bishop's ministry in relation to the local and universal church in order to gain a broad context for the bishop's ministry of unity in an apostolic communion. Next, "The Bishop as Personal Symbol of Unity" describes the personal qualities bishops are encouraged to develop for their ministry in the local church. "Structures of Unity," the third section, shifts to a consideration of the persons and organizational structures of the local church that either support the bishop's personal qualities or provide the bishop opportunities for dialogical discernment. Finally, "Critical Developments" points to areas in which further development of the ideals stated in these documents is needed in order for bishops to be formed by the *sensus fidelium* into personal symbols of their local churches' faith.

Four texts, with varying degrees of authoritative claims on the bishop's ministry, help in constructing this landscape. The first two are documents of the Second Vatican Council. *Lumen Gentium* establishes the ecclesiological framework for the bishop's ministry. *Christus Dominus* (Decree Concerning the Pastoral Office of Bishops in the Church) has its roots in *Lumen Gentium* and communicates the council's extended reflection on episcopal ministry.

A general directive at *Christus Dominus*'s conclusion is the genesis of the second two documents that deal with episcopal ministry. *Apostolorum Successores* (Directory for the Pastoral Ministry of Bishops) was published in 2004 by the Congregation for Bishops and is a revision of an earlier directory from 1973. The updated directory incorporates ideas from Vatican II documents, the 1983 *Code of Canon Law*, and John Paul II's *Pastores Gregis* (the 1992 postsynodal apostolic exhortation on the episcopal vocation).

Apostolorum Successores aims at providing bishops with an extensive guide to facilitate their pastoral ministry.[3] As a curial document, it does not have the same authority as the council documents themselves; it draws, however, on church sources which are normative, and its directives have a certain collegial authority among bishops.[4]

Finally, *Christus Dominus* also directed that canon law be revised in order to better reflect the principles of episcopal ministry articulated by Vatican II. This contributed to the creation of the fourth document under consideration in this chapter, the 1983 *Code of Canon Law*. While not a theological source *per se*, canon law often attempts to safeguard and to promote the church's theological principles and has a role in preserving the church's unity in the practice of its corporate life of faith.[5] The code is juridical and thus tends toward uniformity; however, it often leaves open the opportunity for legitimate diversity. This corresponds to the will of the 1967 Synod of Bishops, which indicated that revisions to the 1917 Code should produce canons that were, among other things, pastoral and reflective of both the needs of bishops and of the principles of subsidiarity and individual rights.[6]

In examining these four texts, the goal is to discover within them what personal attributes of the bishop are identified as en-

[3] Sacred Congregation for Bishops, introduction to *Apostolorum Successores* (2004), Vatican website, http://www.vatican.va/roman_curia/congregations/cbishops/documents/rc_con_cbishops_doc_20040222_apostolorum-successores_en.html. All citations from *Apostolorum Successores* are taken from this translation.

[4] By "collegial authority," I intend to indicate a relationship among the bishops and pope that results from hierarchical communion, and thus not "some vague sort of *goodwill*, but . . . *something organic* which calls for a juridical structure as well as being enkindled by charity." See "Explanatory Note" (LG 2).

[5] See Michael J. Himes, "A Theology for Law," in *The New Canon Law: Perspectives on the Law, Religious Life, and the Laity* (St. Louis, MO: The Catholic Health Association of the United States, 1983), 9.

[6] Adam J. Maida, "The Spirit of the New Code of Canon Law," in *The New Canon Law: Perspectives on the Law, Religious Life, and the Laity* (St. Louis, MO: The Catholic Health Association of the United States, 1983), 70–71.

hancing explicitly or implicitly his ability to symbolize the local church's union in faith, and what structures exist to call forth and cultivate these personal attributes. Before examining these sources, two clarifications are in order. First, these documents express principles for episcopal ministry, and so they tend to articulate the ideals of episcopal ministry. Reviewing these ideals helps us to understand the bishop's vocation within the church and what the church ought to consider "standard" for bishops. Of course, these ideals should also be brought into conversation with bishops' lived experience of their ministry in order to incorporate insights from their practical wisdom. Second, while several of the ecclesial documents under consideration in this chapter employ the term "particular church," designating the diocese as the "local church" provides theological nuances the former term lacks.[7] First, "local church" complements "universal church," whereas "particular" connotes the diocese as a part—or a piece—of the universal church.[8] The notion of "particular" contrasts with *Lumen Gentium*'s insistence that the church of Christ is fully present in the local church, and that the universal church is neither a composite nor a confederation but rather is the communion of local churches throughout the world.[9] Second, the parallel construction between the diocese as the "local church" and the bishop as the "local ordinary" emphasizes the relationship between the bishop and the diocese. Thus this chapter will prefer the use of local church, though it will be used interchangeably with particular church and diocese as quoted in the ecclesial sources.

[7] Patrick Granfield, "The Church Local and Universal: Realization of Communion," *The Jurist* 49 (1989).

[8] Christopher Ruddy indicates that J.-M. R. Tillard preferred the term "local church" as it "better conveys the thoroughly catholic nature of the church of God, through its emphasis on that church's engagement with all of creation and humanity." Christopher Ruddy, *The Local Church: Tillard and the Future of Catholic Ecclesiology* (New York: Crossroad, 2006), 6.

[9] Granfield, "The Church Local and Universal," 456.

I. A Local and Universal Ministry

Augustine roots his ministry as a bishop within the common baptism that makes him one of the faithful, and this points us toward the importance of the bishop's relationship to the local church, or diocese. Such an emphasis does not deny that bishops exercise essential aspects of their ministry when they gather together in synods, conferences, and councils to discern together the *consensus fidelium* (sense of all the faithful peoples) in the universal church.[10] It is in part through that discernment that we understand the church's faith as "catholic": a shared faith in Christ that through the Spirit's mediation is received and responded to by diverse peoples, cultures, and histories, both universally and within the local church. Yet, in order to discern the common faith of the *consensus fidelium* in the universal church, bishops must individually know well the *sensus fidelium* of their local churches.[11]

Rather than thinking of the local church as a piece of the universal church, the Second Vatican Council understood the local church to be fully church. *Lumen Gentium* describes the local church as follows:

> This church of Christ is really present in all legitimately organized local groups of the faithful which, united with their pastors, are also called churches in the New Testament. For these are in fact, in their own localities, the new people called

[10] See John R. Quinn, *Ever Ancient, Ever New: Structures of Communion in the Church* (New York: Paulist Press, 2013).

[11] Hubert Müller indicates, "[T]he reference in Vatican II to the *communio* tradition of the ancient churches has provided a point of departure for the development of a three-leveled ecclesial structure: local church, groups of local churches, universal Church. Such groupings of the local churches facilitate communion among them and a proper inculturation of the gospel, bring those churches into the universal communion, and constitute a frame of reference for realizing the values of diversity in unity and unity in diversity." Hubert Müller, "The Relationship between the Episcopal Conference and the Diocesan Bishop," in *The Nature and Future of Episcopal Conferences*, ed. Hervé Legrand, Julio Manzanares, and Antonio García y García (Washington, DC: The Catholic University of America Press, 1988), 114–15.

by God, in the holy Spirit and with full conviction. In them
the faithful are gathered together by the preaching of the
Gospel of Christ, and the mystery of the Lord's Supper is
celebrated "so that by means of the flesh and blood of the
Lord the whole brotherhood and sisterhood of the body may
be welded together." . . . In these communities, though they
may often be small and poor, or dispersed, Christ is present
through whose power and influence the one, holy, catholic
and apostolic church is constituted. (LG 26)

The council affirms that God calls and gathers together the faithful
through the Holy Spirit, and so the local church is fully the church
of Christ. While the local church does not exist in isolation from
the universal church, through Christ and the Holy Spirit the diocese is nevertheless still truly the one, holy, catholic, and apostolic
church in which we profess our faith. Through union with God,
the local church's faith is expressive of the apostolic faith, and its
people are called to apostolic mission. *Christus Dominus* para-
phrases *Lumen Gentium*'s claim in its definition of the local church:
"A diocese is a section of God's people entrusted to a bishop to be
guided by him with the assistance of his clergy so that, loyal to
its pastor and formed by him into one community in the holy
Spirit through the Gospel and the Eucharist, it constitutes one
particular church in which the one, holy, catholic and apostolic
church of Christ is truly present and active" (CD 11).[12]

The bishop both represents the local church in its unity and
also, through his communion with the other bishops and with the
pope, the union of the local church with the universal. In the
theology of reception, the unity of the local church cannot be sepa-
rated from its communion with the church universal; the local
and universal church are mutually dependent realities based on

---

[12] For the canonical definition of the local church, see *Code of Canon Law* in *New
Commentary on the Code of Canon Law*, ed. John P. Beal, James Coriden, and Thomas
J. Green (New York: Paulist Press, 2000), c. 368. Additional canon citations in this
chapter come from the commentary edited by Beal et al. and are cited paren-
thetically.

koinonia, "a common participation in the gifts of salvation won by
Jesus Christ and bestowed by the Holy Spirit" that "also desig-
nates the bond of fellowship or the community of Christians that
results from our union with God."[13] This unity originates in baptism and is further sought and expressed through the eucharistic
celebration by the bishop with the full and active participation
of the faithful (SC 41). The grace of the Eucharist leads to the
apostolic work of unity, which is both part of the ministry of the
bishop and is also the vocation and responsibility of all the faithful
(AA 2).[14] The church described as an apostolic communion has a
shared faith and a common mission that arises from this faith.

   Lumen Gentium underscores the close relationship between the
local church and its bishop with regard to unity in faith: "Individual bishops are the visible source and foundation of unity in
their own particular churches, which are modeled on the universal
church; it is in and from the [local churches] that the one and
unique catholic church exists. And for that reason each bishop
represents his own church, whereas all of them together with the
pope represent the whole church in a bond of peace, love, and
unity" (LG 23). Here we see that the bishop symbolizes the church
in two interdependent ways. First, the bishop represents the unity
in faith of the local church, and, second, he represents with the
other bishops the unity in faith of the universal church. It is in part
through this dual symbolism that the universal church's com-

---

[13] For a discussion of these terms, see Granfield, "The Church Local and Universal," 451.

[14] "The church was founded so that by spreading Christ's kingdom throughout
the world to the glory of God the Father, every man and woman may share in
the saving work of redemption, and so that through them the entire world may
be truly directed towards Christ. Every activity of the mystical body with this
in view goes by the name of apostolate, which the church exercises through all
its members, though in various ways. In fact, the christian vocation is, of its
nature, a vocation to the apostolate as well." See also Robert J. Kaslyn, Commentary on "Book II: The People of God [cc. 204–746]," in Beal et al., *New Commentary on the Code of Canon Law*, 264–65: " 'Sacred pastors' must also maintain
communion with their fellow believers and this obligation determines the appropriate exercises of authority: to build up the Church as *communio*."

munion can be described as a "church of churches."[15] Since the
local church is truly the church of Christ, when its *sensus fidelium*
is represented by the bishop to the universal church, the bishops
together discern and represent the *consensus fidelium*; in turn, the
consensus fidelium returns to the local church for reception within
the diocese via the bishop's ministry.[16]

   Apostolorum Successores frames its vision of the local church
through the bishop's hierarchical communion with the episcopal
college and its head, the pope: the local church images the universal church and, through hierarchical communion, both contributes to and receives the abundant gifts of the universal church
(AS 5). The document underscores reciprocal communion as a
reality that results from more than the bishop's representation of
the local church to the universal church and vice versa. Rather,
hierarchical communion is to be embodied in both the governance
and life of the local church. Further, according to *Apostolorum
Successores'* description of the principle of communion, the local
church's good is subordinate to the good of the universal church
(58). While giving a great deal of attention to the bishop's ministry
in the local church, the document consistently stresses the bishop's
union with the universal church as the source of his ministerial

---

[15] "The nature of the Church, as early Tradition understands it, is, therefore,
summed up in *communion, koinonia*. It is the Church of Churches. Understood
in full context, it is the *communion of communions*, appearing as a *communion* of
local Churches, spread throughout the world, each one being itself a *communion*
of the baptized, gathered together into communities by the Holy Spirit, on the
basis of their baptism, for the Eucharistic celebration. This existence constitutes
its essence. And the relationship to *communion* with the Father, Son and Sprit
shows its deep-rootedness even in the eternal reality of the mystery of God."
J.-M. R. Tillard, *Church of Churches*, trans. R. C. De Peaux (Collegeville, MN: Liturgical Press, 1992), 29.

[16] In the model of the church as apostolic communion, it must be recalled that
there are diverse forms of "reception and response" within the church. While
the bishops' role in communicating the *consensus fidelium* of the universal church
to their local churches is essential, the *consensus fidelium* may also be communicated partially through other means such as international lay movements, meetings of religious orders from throughout the world, etc.

authority without a complementary emphasis on the bishop's formation through the local church.

In keeping with its title, *Apostolorum Successores* grounds the local church's communion within apostolicity and hierarchy. The bishop is the principle of unity within the local church because he has inherited the apostles' mission, been ordained to the episcopacy, and is in hierarchical communion with the college of bishops (AS Introduction). The idea of the bishop as the principle, guarantee, or foundation who makes unity visible is taken from *Lumen Gentium* 23 and is repeated several times in *Apostolorum Successores*. Emphasis is given to the bishop's symbolization of unity for the local church through his hierarchical communion with the universal church. While the bishop represents the local church within the church's universal communion, relatively little attention is given to how the bishop comes to represent the local church's faith (AS 13). Here the document seems to fall short of its own description of the reciprocal communion between the local and universal church.

As a successor to the apostles, the bishop's mission and identity is tied to the preservation and transmission of God's revelation through Scripture and tradition (AS Introduction). Through the bishops, the witness of the apostles is both preserved and handed on in order to ensure fidelity to the Gospel, which is fundamental to unity. Though *Apostolorum Successores* indicates the church as a whole is characterized by mission and communion, the faithful as a whole are not underscored as witnesses to, or sources for knowing, the apostolic tradition which the bishop is to safeguard and hand on. Instead, the sources for the apostolic tradition tend to be understood as Scripture and magisterial teaching. Of course, both Scripture and magisterial teaching transmit the apostolic tradition, yet so do other aspects of the church's life, such as the *sensus fidelium* and liturgy.

Rather than envisioning an apostolic role for all the faithful within, as well as outside, the church, *Apostolorum Successores* parallels *Lumen Gentium*'s universal call to holiness with a correspondingly universal call to mission (AS 109). The document's affirmation of the link between holiness and mission shows the interplay between these two marks of the church. Yet we might wonder as well how the *sensus fidelium* contributes to the church "internally" as one, holy, catholic, and apostolic. In other words, how the apostolic faith is received and expressed communally within the histories and cultures of the local church, and how the bishop's knowledge of the apostolic tradition is shaped by the local church's holiness in the *sensus fidelium* are not featured topics in this document.

While *Apostolorum Successores* does not provide extensive answers to how the bishop might learn, as well as teach, the apostolic tradition through the *sensus fidelium*, in two instances it provides a strong image for the unity developed through this mutual exchange: perichoresis. In trinitarian theology, perichoresis describes the mutual indwelling of the three divine persons; it characterizes the intimacy of their communion and mission. Scripturally, this indwelling is in part reflected by Jesus' statement, "The Father and I are one" (John 10:30). Later in John's gospel this intimacy of union is extended to others through Jesus' prayer: "As you, Father, are in me and I am in you, may they also be in us, so that the world may believe that you have sent me" (17:21). Here there is a strong sense that communion is necessary for mission. Returning to *Apostolorum Successores'* use of perichoresis, we find a similar connection: mission comes from mutual union, or communion; the apostolic mission flows from the apostolic faith.

In the first instance that perichoresis is used, the document describes a dynamic reciprocity of responsibility for the local church between the faithful and their bishop (AS 66). As the faithful contribute to the life of the church and its mission, the bishop receives their insights and in turn ministers in order to aid the faithful in fulfilling their baptismal vocation. Perichoresis is used a second time to describe the bishop's learning and teaching of the apostolic faith. The bishop receives the apostolic faith as one of the baptized and in turn teaches this faith authoritatively as bishop (AS 118). This affirmation appears in the section on the bishop's teaching ministry, making it more evident that his teaching is dependent on his continual reception of the apostolic faith from the local church. This means that, by assenting to the faith their local bishop teaches, the faithful are asked to recognize their own faith as it is articulated by the bishop.

Thus far, the landscape of the bishop's ministry constructed through these documents from Vatican II has several features. First, the documents describe, though with different degrees of emphasis, an essential and interdependent relationship between the local and universal church: the universal church is a communion of local churches, and the local church exists through this communion. Second, the bishop is central to the realization of this communion, both sacramentally and personally. Finally, the local church's communion with its bishop is primarily spiritual rather than juridical, as it is rooted in the sacramental life that fosters a mutual indwelling between the local church and their bishop. Further, this indwelling is dynamic rather than static, because it propels the local church's communion for apostolic mission. The next section looks more deeply into the bishop's ministry in order to survey more particularly how the bishop becomes a personal symbol unity.

II. The Bishop as Personal Symbol of Unity

According to his ordination, by grace the bishop symbolizes officially the faith of the universal and local churches. Yet in an apostolic communion, we must speak not only of the grace received but also of the reciprocal response of self-gift. In order for a "church of churches" to flourish, bishops must do more than "officially" represent the local church. Rather, to richly represent the *sensus fidelium* of the local church through his ministerial self-gift, the bishop must be formed personally by receiving the gift of the local church's faith as well. Without personal formation by the local church, the bishop's symbolism of the faith that unites the local church is diminished.

How does episcopal ministry in the local church not only make but also shape a bishop into a symbol of unity as *Lumen Gentium* suggests it should? One way of answering this question is to consider how the bishop's ministry forms him into a person of discernment. Chapter 1 described our way of receiving (and thus knowing) God as authentic, limited, communal, and transformative. How we discern is related to how we receive. To discern in light of how we receive means authentic discernment develops through conscious engagement with the limited, communal, and transformative aspects of reception. Persons of discernment are those for whom such engagement is virtuously habitual, who are continually aware of revelation's living reception through the Holy Spirit, and who therefore are able to believe, feel, think, and act in ways that are responsive to God's revelation in Christ. Habitual practices of discernment in turn cultivate one's capacity to know God more authentically by acknowledging limitations, learning communally, and being transformed personally. With regard to the bishop's ministry, we must ask which practices allow him to engage in the authentic, limited, communal, and transformative process of becoming a person of discernment via his reception of the local church's *sensus fidelium*. Through these practices, the bishop grows not only in personal holiness but also in his ability to personally (and not just officially) symbolize the local church's faith.

In order to become a person of discernment, attention must be given to the personal qualities of the bishop that allow his ministry to flourish. When undertaken habitually, these qualities may contribute to practices of discernment that shape the bishop, even as he ministers through them. Turning again to *Lumen Gentium, Christus Dominus, Apostolorum Successores,* and the *Code of Canon Law,* the goal is to recognize what personal attributes and actions of the bishop either explicitly or potentially enhance his ability to grow into a person of discernment in relation to his ministry. These attributes and actions promote authentic discernment when they lead the bishop to personally acknowledge limitations, learn from others, and seek transformation. As these aspects of the bishop's discernment are often intertwined, each document will be reviewed separately for its potential contributions to practices of discernment. Areas for development will be considered in the final section, "Critical Developments."

Lumen Gentium

The ordering of chapters in *Lumen Gentium* provides initial insight for considering the bishop's ministry in relation to his person. As is often noted, the decision of the council to situate its discussion of the church within the mystery of God and, in turn, to place the description of church hierarchy following the section on the people of God refocused the church's understanding of our relationship to God and each other. By placing the mystery of God at the beginning of its reflections on the inner life of the church, *Lumen Gentium* roots the church in the divine communion and mission of the Trinity. Rather than shifting directly to a consideration of hierarchy in its second chapter, the document first discusses the church as the people of God. Thus, when the role of bishops is discussed in chapter 3, the bishop is seen first as a member of the people of God. Called from this people, a bishop ministers within the church when through ordination "a sacred character is impressed" that he may "take the place of Christ himself, teacher, shepherd, and priest, and act in his person" (LG 21). *Lumen Gentium* further describes the bishop's office as a service (*diakonia*), thus clearly emphasizing the nature of his ministry within the local and the universal church (LG 24). As noted above, the bishop's ministry is linked to the universal call to holiness in *Lumen Gentium*'s fifth chapter, since it is through his vocation that the bishop responds to God's self-gift with his own. In addition, the bishop is to uphold the rights and responsibilities of the laity to offer counsel and undertake initiatives in keeping with their expertise and baptismal vocation; he ministers in communion with all the baptized (LG 37).

Christus Dominus

With regard to the bishop's teaching office, *Christus Dominus* indicates the necessity of communicating doctrine in a way both "relevant to the needs of the times" and also meaningful to the persons who will receive it and themselves be teachers of the apostolic faith (CD 13). The same section notes that dialogue, initi-

ated and promoted by the bishop, "should be marked by clarity
of expression as well as by humility and courtesy, so that truth
may be combined with charity, and understanding with love";
dialogue is also to be "characterized by due prudence allied . . .
with confidence. This, by encouraging friendship, is conducive to
a union of minds" (CD 13). Therefore, while according to their
bishop's office the faithful of the local church should recognize
the authority of his ministry, authentic unity does not arise simply
through "official" obedience to episcopal teaching. Rather, reception of the bishop's teaching that results in genuine unity is af-
fected by the bishop's personal qualities, which may help his
teaching to take root meaningfully in the lives of the faithful.

The bishop's ministry of sanctifying also serves the purpose
of unity. Bishops "should aim to make of one mind in prayer all
who are entrusted to their care, and to ensure their advancement
in grace through the reception of the sacraments . . . that they
become faithful witnesses to the Lord" (CD 15). This unity and
growth comes to fruition in part through the bishop's own example of holiness in charity, humility, and simplicity of life.
Through this sanctification, the "ethos of the universal Church of
Christ . . . [is] fully reflected" in the local church (CD 15). This
speaks to the normative relationship of the universal church to
the local; it does not, however, reflect how the local church forms
the holiness of either the universal church or the bishop.

Finally, in their governing role as "fathers and pastors, bishops
should be with their people as those who serve, as good shepherds
who know their sheep and whose sheep know them, as true fathers
who excel in their love and solicitude for all, to whose divinely
conferred authority all readily submit. They should so unite and
mold their flock into one family that all, conscious of their duties,
may live and act as one in charity" (CD 15). This suggests that the
bishop's loving knowledge and care of the faithful facilitates their
obedience to his authoritative role within the church's communion. Further, the faithful's knowledge of their bishop, rooted
in personal relationship, allows communion to flourish.

Code of Canon Law

Canon law describes a number of requirements for appoint-ment to the episcopacy. A bishop must be "outstanding in solid faith, good morals, piety, zeal for souls, wisdom, prudence, and human virtues, and endowed with other qualities which make him suitable to fulfill the office in question" (CIC c. 378, §1). Bish-ops must also have a doctorate or licentiate in Scripture, theology, or canon law or have expertise in these disciplines. In his ministry, the bishop is to have concern for all the faithful in his care and to act with "humanity and charity" toward those not in communion with the Catholic Church (CIC c. 383 §1; §3). Finally, in a manner similar to the documents discussed above, canon law connects the bishop's ministry with his personal virtues:

> Since the diocesan bishop is mindful of his obligation to show an example of holiness in charity, humility, and simplicity of life, he is to strive to promote in every way the holiness of the Christian faithful according to the proper vocation of each. Since he is the principal dispenser of the mysteries of God, he is to endeavor constantly that the Christian faithful en-trusted to his care grow in grace through the celebration of the sacraments and that they understand and live the paschal mystery. (CIC c. 387)

It should be noted that this passage describes the holiness of the local church as proceeding from the bishop; thus the bishop is the dispenser of the mysteries of faith. Here the troublesome connec-tion between the bishop as "dispenser" of mysteries and the remnants of institutionalism leaves unclear how the local church serves as the context for forming the bishop in holiness, or how his ministry might itself contribute to his personal, spiritual in-tegrity (LG 15).

Apostolorum Successores

Of all the documents considered in this chapter, *Apostolorum Successores* provides by far the most extensive description of the bishop's ministry. In order to investigate this document's under-standing of how the bishop is a personal symbol of unity, four areas of focus will be considered: first, the bishop's authority in relation to his holiness; next, the virtues needed for the bishop's ministry; third, ongoing formation for episcopal ministry; and finally, the principles of the bishop's ministry.

Authority and holiness for ministry. Apostolorum Successores in-dicates the bishop's teaching authority is drawn from both Christ's authority and his hierarchical communion with the episcopal college. Through the grace of his ordination and this communion, the faithful are to be obedient to his teaching. Yet the bishop's personal witness lends "authoritativeness" to his teaching, en-abling the faithful to trust his teaching more entirely (AS 119). This witness is cultivated through spirituality and ongoing formation. *Apostolorum Successores* holds together the bishop's authority through the sacrament of ordination with the bishop's need for a spirituality and formation that allows his authority to be practiced effectively. This means the document underscores both the grace of ordination and the bishop's need to grow in his personal capac-ity to know Christ in order to minister well. Communion with Christ is the source of the bishop's authority, and through his spirituality and formation, the bishop is coming to greater union with Christ through holiness. *Apostolorum Successores* also de-scribes Christ as the source of the bishop's spirituality. The bishop responds to the grace received in his ordination by shaping himself to Christ through his ministry (AS 33). Here the document makes a link between the bishop's person and his ministry, as it is in and through his ministry that he grows in personal holiness, which is his intimacy with Christ.

The connection between the bishop's personal holiness and ministry is strengthened by the document's next lines:

> This configuration to Christ allows the Bishop to submit his whole being to the Holy Spirit in order to integrate within himself his different roles as member of the Church and simultaneously head and shepherd of the Christian people,

as brother and as father, as disciple of Christ and teacher of
faith, as son of the Church and, in some sense, father of the
Church, as minister of the supernatural rebirth of Christians.
(AS 33)

Through spirituality, the bishop fosters an integrated personal
identity as one of the faithful who is fulfilling his baptismal vocation through his ministry. Further, the bishop's integration of his
person and ministry through intimacy with Christ is not for his
own sake alone but rather his growth in holiness serves the local
church as well. Conversely, his ministry itself is then a pilgrimage
to personal holiness (AS 46). Through love, the bishop offers
himself to the church in order to foster unity and also attends to
the faithful's growth in holiness, while through his example of
intimacy with Christ, the faithful may grow in holiness as well
(AS 34).

Apostolorum Successores describes Mary as both a spiritual
model and intercessor for the bishop's growth in holiness. In particular, through Mary's example, the bishop learns to contemplate
Christ as well as the worth of pondering God's revelation in his
heart (AS 35). Mary's holiness is to provide hope for the bishop's
own growth in union with God while her motherly love is to
pervade the bishop's ministry for both the church's unity and its
mission.

Through prayer the bishop finds hope to continue despite dis-
couragements and grows in love of Christ manifested in love of
others. The bishop's crozier is symbolic of prayer's importance,
as *Apostolorum Successores* imagines prayer as the shepherd's staff
which supports him at all times as he journeys with God's people
(AS 36). The document commends particular spiritual practices
to the bishop, including the eucharistic liturgy, adoration, Liturgy
of the Hours, Scripture meditation, the rosary, and *lectio divina*.
He is also to set aside time each month for recollection and to go
on retreat each year (AS 46).

Virtues for ministry. The bishop grows in personal holiness
through virtues that aid his ministry, and *Apostolorum Successores*
details the significance of a number of these virtues. Faith, hope,

and love help the bishop become a sacrament of grace for others (AS 37). Love, or pastoral charity, integrates the bishop's personal and ministerial life in the face of the many demands made on him. While the document does not detail how pastoral charity promotes the bishop's integrity of life, it draws on Augustine's definition of the bishop's office as a ministry of love, as well as John Paul II's indication that through love, the bishop does not exist for himself but rather for others (AS 38). Thus the document suggests that Christ's model of service will be particularly important in order for the bishop's ministry to both foster and reflect pastoral charity.

The virtue of faith calls the bishop to attentiveness so that he may "discover what the Holy Spirit is saying to the Churches with regard to eternal salvation" (AS 39). It is notable that the Spirit is described as speaking "to" rather than "through" the local churches, particularly since the next line in the document emphasizes that the bishop's way of hearing the Spirit is through reflection on Scripture and doctrine, as well as growth in theological knowledge. Certainly these three sources are essential for recognizing the Spirit's voice; the witness of the faithful to the Spirit's work through their lives is, however, conspicuous by its absence.

Faithful attending leads to action, and the virtue of hope fosters the bishop's strength for his ministry through trust in God's promises and confidence in his vocation. Hope directs the bishop to minister for the church's mission with both creativity and fortitude (AS 40). Thus hope is characterized by the bishop's perseverance in trusting God and in fulfilling his ministry.

In addition to the theological virtues, *Apostolorum Successores* highlights a number of other virtues for the bishop's ministry: prudence, fortitude, humility, obedience, celibacy, and poverty. Prudence helps the bishop apply wisdom to practical needs in order to govern well; divine wisdom and evangelical prudence combine to help the bishop meet the needs of the church while making judgments through divine, rather than only human, reasoning (AS 41). Prudence does not lead the bishop to avoid risks but rather to choose the right risks in order both to preserve the church's traditions and to develop new initiatives. Prudence also requires that he dialogue with the faithful, respecting their rights and responsibilities while fulfilling his own duties responsibly. Fortitude is related to prudence, as it grows through patient perseverance in the face of practical challenges. As a virtue it should help the bishop teach the apostolic faith with conviction and be combined with meekness in imitation of Christ (AS 42).

Humility is described as a primary virtue, which argues that it ought to have a higher place on *Apostolorum Successores'* list of virtues than it in fact occupies. In humility, the bishop acknowledges his weaknesses. Knowing his limitations means the bishop is aware of his need for compassion from the faithful, and that his salvation is still in progress. Further, through humility, the bishop recognizes that his authority for making decisions is accompanied by the risks of error. Therefore, through humility, the bishop should "remain open to dialogue with others, always ready to learn, to seek and accept the advice of others" (AS 42). Learning from others personally translates to the bishop's ability to make good choices ministerially.

Obedience helps the bishop draw closer to Christ. By following Christ more entirely, the bishop becomes a personal witness of obedience whose ministry gains authenticity (AS 43). Celibacy and continence allow the bishop to offer himself to others completely, and an ascetic lifestyle enables his embrace of Christ's death in his daily life (AS 44). Through material and spiritual poverty, the bishop imitates Christ more closely in his way of life and manifests Christ's mission to preach the Gospel to the poor (AS 45). The bishop's poverty should be reflected in his manner, way of dress, and home so that wealth does not become an intimidating barrier between him and the materially poor. Poverty also ought to prevent the bishop from giving preference to the wealthy and powerful and help him in directing material resources appropriately in order to fulfill the church's mission, including care for the impoverished. Finally, *Apostolorum Successores* lists a number of human virtues that need the bishop's consistent attention in order to become part of his life and ministry: "a rich humanity, a good and loyal spirit, a constant and sincere character, an open, forward-looking mind, a sensitivity to the joys and sufferings of others, a thorough self-mastery, kindness, forbearance and discretion, a healthy readiness to engage in dialogue and to listen, an habitual attitude of service" (AS 47).

Formation for ministry. To cultivate this daunting spectrum of virtues and thus grow in his personal capacity for ministry, the bishop needs continual formation in four areas: human, spiritual, intellectual and doctrinal, and pastoral (AS 49). Formation is not elective but is rather described as the bishop's duty. As with holiness, growth in these four areas is linked with the bishop's personal ability to witness effectively to Christ through his ministry.

Human formation recognizes that the bishop's ministry is shaped through grace and manifested in his ability to be in relationship with others. The human virtues listed above characterize the bishop's personal openness to encountering others in ways that transform his ability to minister. Human formation speaks to the ways the bishop can enter more deeply into the life of the faithful within the local church and accompany them in pastoral solidarity: "In this way, his humanity will become richer, simpler, more authentic and more transparent, so as to reveal the mind and heart of the Good Shepherd. The Bishop, like Christ himself, should manifest the most genuine and perfect human qualities if he is to share the daily life of his people and to be one with them in times of joy and sorrow" (AS 50). *Apostolorum Successores'* intuition is that the closer the bishop's human qualities are to those of Christ, the more his ministry will take incarnate form in the life of the people and mediate Christ's presence. This rich description of human formation speaks to the importance of dialogue and encounter, though again the primary emphasis is on the bishop's self-gift without reference to ways the bishop's human formation allows him to receive the *sensus fidelium.*

Spiritual formation calls the bishop to constant conversion to Christ as he embraces the gift of his baptism through his pastoral ministry. Continual conversion through spiritual formation invests his ministry with holiness and in turn encourages the bishop to aid the faithful in fulfilling their own call to holiness (AS 51). Intellectual and doctrinal formation advance the bishop's ability to grow personally in order to fulfill his teaching ministry within the context of the local church. Reading theology is both a means of continuing to explore revelation and of preparing for dialogue with theologians. Theology contributes to the bishop's ability to teach in relation to current events and may strengthen his discernment of how particular theologies cohere with the apostolic tradition so as to make sound judgments (AS 52).

Through pastoral formation, the bishop's awareness of the needs of the local church in relation to its particular times and circumstances increases. Spiritual, human, and intellectual formation are ultimately aimed toward the bishop's pastoral formation as well. This formation involves dialogue so the bishop may learn the needs of the local church, explore pastoral practices, and determine the resources needed for ministry. Bishops are to consult experts in ministry and the social sciences and to engage in study of the liturgy and canon law (AS 53). Here again, dialogue is an essential part of formation, though while the laity may be involved in his dialogue as experts, their experience of living faithfully is not explicitly mentioned.

Apostolorum Successores notes several ways the bishop may make his formation in these four areas habitual, though it also emphasizes that, like other members of the faithful, the bishop is primarily responsible for his own formation. In addition to the forms of prayer and reflection noted above, the bishop is also encouraged to find times for rest each day, take a regular day off, and vacation once a year. These are described as times of Sabbath that are both necessary and a way of following Jesus' own call to rest. Further, the study of doctrinal and pastoral documents is encouraged to build his communion with the pope and his brother bishops and in order to learn ways of furthering his own pastoral work. The bishop should also study theology, culture, and society in order to be aware of developments within these areas and how to evaluate them. In addition to these individual means of formation, the bishop is to take advantage of formation opportunities with other bishops. Within the local church, the presbyteral council and cultural events are occasions for formation, as is consultation with pastoral and spiritual experts (AS 54).

Finally, the document notes that formation occurs within the bishop's daily ministry:

> [H]is lived communion with other members of the People of God, through daily contact with priests and lay faithful, provides the setting in which the Spirit speaks to him, reminding him of his vocation and mission, and forming his heart through the vibrant life of the Church. Hence the Bishop should always adopt an attitude of careful listening to what the Spirit is saying to the Church and in the Church. (AS 54)

This statement is one of *Apostolorum Successores'* strongest indications that the bishop receives personal formation through his ministry in the local church. While it does not reference the *sensus fidelium* explicitly, the life of the church is the living tradition of faith empowered by the Spirit—the *sensus fidelium*. The passage links the bishop's personal formation ("his heart") with his ability to minister well ("his vocation and mission"). Cultivating an "attitude of careful listening" that is consistently a part of the bishop's personal way of fulfilling his ministry may require the aid of particular virtues such as humility. To be formed through listening means the bishop must attend to the Holy Spirit at work within the church, including the *sensus fidelium*, which the bishop receives through his "lived communion" with the people of God in the local church.

Principles for ministry. Apostolorum Successores begins its most extensive discussion of the bishop's ministry in the local church by stating seven principles for the bishop's ministry: trinitarian, truth, communion, cooperation, respecting others' competence, placing the right person in the right post, and justice and legality. The document views these principles as contributing to reciprocal communion—or at least continuity—between the bishop's ministry in the universal and local church (AS 55).

Through the trinitarian principle of his ministry, the bishop ministers in God's name. Thus he is the image of the Father who fulfills Christ's offices of governing, teaching, and sanctifying and gives the church life through the Spirit (AS 56). *Apostolorum Successores* does not explicitly connect the trinitarian principle of the bishop's ministry with the church's foundation in the mystery of the Trinity as described in *Lumen Gentium*'s opening chapter. Developing this connection might further relate the bishop's ministry to the church's shared trinitarian identity and also better contextualize the bishop's ministry within the people of God and the *sensus fidelium*.

The principle of truth touches explicitly on the bishop's ministry of teaching: God's revelation is both the source and guide for pastoral decision making (AS 57). The bishop's grounding in truth allows him to illuminate the church's pilgrimage. Truth is known through Scripture as well as through "the Magisterium of the Church's living tradition" (AS 57). This phrase is an interesting one, as we can interpret it in at least three ways. In an apostolic communion, magisterial teaching is part of the church's living tradition. The church's living tradition, however, does not only consist of magisterial teaching but also the faithful expression of God's self-gift in diverse ways, such as the faith of the baptized, liturgy, and art and architecture.[17] Therefore, this phrase may refer to the magisterial teaching that *in part* makes up the church's living tradition. A second way of interpreting this phrase is by putting the emphasis on who is teaching—the magisterium, or bishops. In that case, this phrase would emphasize how the church's tradition as a whole has been received and expressed through the bishops' teaching. A third interpretation, and one

---

[17] "For there are as many ways of consulting the faith of the Church as there are ways that the deposit of revelation has been handed on in her teaching, life, and worship. These include Sacred Scripture, the writings of the Fathers and Doctors of the Church, the sacred liturgy, the decrees of councils, the works of theologians, traditional beliefs and practices, etc." Francis A. Sullivan, *Magisterium: Teaching Authority in the Roman Catholic Church* (Eugene, OR: Wipf and Stock Publishers, 1983), 104.

inconsistent with the church envisioned as an apostolic communion, is that this phrase narrowly equates the church's living
tradition with magisterial teaching. In any of these interpretations,
however, leaving out the *sensus fidelium* as a source for knowing
God's revelation and emphasizing solely how the bishop offers
truth to the faithful short-circuits the document's articulation of
truth as a principle of episcopal ministry by ignoring the *sensus
fidelium* as one way in which the church expresses truth and the
bishop learns truth.

The principle of communion is rooted in *Lumen Gentium*'s description of the bishop as the principle and foundation of unity.
This unity is not stagnant but rather reflects the diversity of the
body of Christ, which the bishop is to both promote and protect
(AS 58). It is important to note here as well that dialogue is tied
to the bishop's ability to know the common good of the local
church by being present to the faithful, engaging them in constant
dialogue, studying research relevant to the intersection of religion
and the social sciences, and taking the advice of trustworthy counselors (AS 58).

As noted earlier in the chapter, *Apostolorum Successores'* description of the principle of communion also indicates the local church's
good is subordinate to the good of the universal church, just as
smaller communities within the diocese are subordinate to the
diocese's needs. The document's language of subordination seems
to arise from a particular interpretation of the church's hierarchal
communion.[18] In an apostolic communion, due to the bishops'
mutual reception of one another, the church has a communion
through its hierarchy. Through the Holy Spirit, the church's unity
is a communion of mutual gift and reception; this mutuality means
the good of the local and universal church is interrelated and mutually dependent rather than subordinate. *Apostolorum Successores'*

---

[18] For insight into the differing views of Walter Kasper and Joseph Ratzinger
regarding the relationship of the local and universal church, see Kilian McDonnell,
"The Ratzinger/Kasper Debate: The Universal Church and Local Churches,"
Theological Studies 63 (2002): 227–50, and "Walter Kasper on the Theology and
Praxis of the Bishop's Office," *Theological Studies* 63 (2002): 711–29.

use of hierarchical communion to subordinate the good of one of the members of the communion to others is not in keeping with the reciprocal communion described earlier in the document, though it does reflect the document's relatively strong emphasis on the universal church's faith and norms and how they may be applied to the local church without a complementary consideration of how the apostolic tradition may be expressed through the local church and received by the universal church.

Three principles of the bishop's ministry are closely related: cooperation, respecting others' competence, and selecting the right person for the right post. Cooperation recognizes that the bishop ought to welcome all the faithful to join in the church's mission and that their participation is not only a right but also a duty of the Christian life. Further, through cooperation, the bishop fosters the faithful's sense of responsibility as well as their freedom of initiative in relation to their vocations, so long as that freedom does not infringe on the local church's common good (AS 59). By respecting the competency of others, the bishop promotes subsidiarity within the local church; instead of taking on roles that may be fulfilled well by others, the bishop encourages others in their own good work while coordinating their efforts for efficient and harmonious collaboration (AS 60). By acknowledging the gifts of the faithful that help them to build up the church and fulfill its mission, the bishop is able to guide particular persons to positions within the local church that serve the diocese's common good (AS 61).

Lastly, the principle of justice and legality holds the bishop accountable for knowing and respecting the rights of others within the church. It reminds him as well that he is also bound by canon law, whose purpose is described as promoting justice within the church so that all may contribute their gifts in charity (AS 62; 65). Canon law, as a juridical system, fosters a certain uniformity within the church, which is manifested in *Apostolorum Successores'* indication that the bishop should not govern the church according to his personal preference (AS 62). Focused as it is on the bishop's governance, we need not interpret this statement in opposition to the bishop's personal formation that allows him to fulfill his ministry. Rather, the diocese is not akin to a suit that is custom tailored to the bishop's personal preferences. While the bishop's ministry must always be personal in order to be effective, he must not simply adapt the church to fit his own interpretations, as that risks violating not only legality but also, more broadly, the justice that canon law seeks to bring about. Even with this admonition in mind, we must also ask how the bishops can promote changes within canon law so that it may better reflect both the pastoral needs and the faith of the local churches.

Potential Practices for Discernment

While these documents do not explicitly envision the virtues and principles of the bishop's ministry as ways of discerning the *sensus fidelium*, they do offer potential to build on. More specifically, the documents help us consider several ways in which the bishop could become a person of discernment through his ministry by acknowledging the authentic, limited, communal, and transformative ways he receives and responds to God's self-gift. Through such discernment practices, the bishop may both be formed in holiness and also become a symbol of the local church's faith.

First, *Lumen Gentium*'s structure suggests that we must first see the bishop as part of the people of God, and *Apostolorum Successores* emphasizes the relationship between the bishop's personal holiness and ministry. Growth in personal holiness is important not only for the bishop's own union with Christ but also for his ability to minister well as a witness to Christ. This form of holiness is not simply intellectual but also shapes the bishop's ability to be in relationship with others in a Christlike way and thus mediate Christ's presence to the local church. Growth in holiness is personally transformative for the bishop because through holiness he receives and responds to God's self-gift more authentically. In turn, the bishop's personal witness helps the faithful to move beyond a relatively shallow obedience to official authority, to having trust in the personal authoritativeness of the bishop as well. The need for growth and ongoing formation is an acknowledgment of the bishop's personal limitations as well as a mandate for continual conversion to Christ. Further, the bishop's ministry is to be communal: it arises through his reception of the grace of baptism that joins him to the body of Christ, and he lives out his response to grace with and for others (AS 34).

Second, the bishop's personal holiness grows through virtues related to his vocation. This is significant, as virtues are not meant to be theoretical but rather are the habitual attitudes and actions that shape—and transform—us. For example, through the virtue of pastoral charity, the bishop moves from being a person who acts lovingly to a person of love. Such a transformation cannot occur within a vacuum but rather takes shape within the bishop's ministry. Further, the need to cultivate virtue indicates that the bishop has limitations and must continually grow into his ministry. This need is not eliminated but rather is reinforced by virtues such as humility that confirm the bishop's need to receive compassion from others in his weakness, a form of love that strengthens the bishop in his conversion. Virtues help the bishop become an example to others, and when he lives out these virtues in his ministry, the faithful have the opportunity to see holiness as a "work in progress" in their midst. The virtues that help the bishop to become holy are not for himself alone but enable the bishop's loving self-gift that is essential for communion.

Third, the need for ongoing formation suggests the bishop must be continually learning, and that this learning takes place in numerous ways. While the documents tend to presume the bishop's ability to answer questions, the need for learning requires the bishop to admit what he does not know and to ask questions. This acknowledgment necessarily turns the bishop to God and others as sources for answering his questions. A wide range of sources is recommended for the bishop's learning, ranging from theology and liturgy to culture and the social sciences. While the bishop's learning of the apostolic faith is often confined to Scripture and magisterial teaching in these documents, his need to learn from the faithful is also included as an important element in his formation.

Fourth, these documents underscore the necessity for dialogue within the local church, particularly for pastoral decision making, though such dialogue is also essential for the bishop's learning and so for his ministry. Both canon law and *Apostolorum Successores* indicate a broad spectrum of persons with whom the bishop ought to consult. Dialogue with the faithful as well as experts in particular fields promotes the bishop's learning about the local church's context, needs, and resources. Further, *Christus Dominus* describes dialogue as building friendship and the union of minds. Episcopal virtues such as courtesy, sincerity, and kindness outline a ministry rooted in dialogue instead of dominion, which builds up a union of friendship with others. A union marked by friendship speaks to a certain mutuality of reception and self-gift that should characterize dialogue within the local church, and friendship itself is a type of ongoing human formation for the bishop.

Fifth, the principles of the bishop's ministry are frameworks that call forth practices of virtue and make the need for particular sorts of formation more evident. For instance, if the bishop's ministry is to be guided by the principle of truth, then discovery of truth is necessary. *Apostolorum Successores* focuses on learning truth through Scripture and magisterial teaching, which are both certainly necessary. Yet the discovery of truth can be limited neither to intellectual formation nor to these two sources. Through spiritual formation, the bishop learns through his intimacy with God, a knowledge that is more fully developed if the bishop's spirituality unites with human formation to help him receive the *sensus fidelium*. Further, the search for truth—good for its own sake—is often catalyzed by the questions that arise within daily life. For example, the particular questions the bishop faces as he ministers within the local church mean that virtues such as prudence are necessary as he makes decisions that are both rooted in truth and that address concrete needs. Similarly, fortitude will be needed in order to aid the bishop's own process of discovering truth in the midst of complex pastoral situations.

From these documents it is evident that the bishop's person and ministry are deeply interconnected through his spirituality.

Growth in holiness through virtue, ongoing formation, and principles of ministry lead to personal transformation by recognizing limitations to the bishop's knowledge and abilities and requiring a communal approach to ministry, including learning from and collaborating with others. Thus the initial result of our survey is a ministerial landscape that has the potential to help the bishop become a person of discernment with regard to the *sensus fidelium*. After considering the structures of the local church, we will return to this landscape to review these personal qualities in relation to the bishop's ability to become a personal symbol of the local church's faith.

III. Structures of Unity

In the previous section, we saw that a great deal is asked of the bishop personally in order for his ministry to flourish officially. Archbishop John R. Quinn writes, "Authentic discernment calls for evangelical patience, for openness to do the will of God, and for humble listening for the voice of God."[19] He also notes that "communion, if it is not to remain an abstraction, has to have concrete shape" that is embodied in the universal church through structures such as episcopal synods, patriarchates, and councils.[20] In the local church's communion, diocesan structures have potential to be venues for dialogue and accountability.

Christus Dominus notes the bishop's ministry necessitates both personnel and resources that reflect the needs of the local church (CD 22). *Apostolorum Successores* further indicates that through their baptism, the faithful are called to contribute to the life of the church and the fulfillment of its mission. To that end, the document suggests diocesan structures should be viewed by the bishop as opportunities for mutual collaboration between the bishop and

[19] John R. Quinn, *Ever Ancient, Ever New: Structures of Communion in the Church* (Mahwah, NJ: Paulist Press, 2013), 3.
[20] Ibid., 8.

faithful for the good of the local church (AS 165). Therefore, structures of participation are not an addendum to the church's communion and mission but are rather integral to it. Further, the spirituality of communion that should characterize the bishop's ministry is both manifested and reinforced through these structures. The dialogue these structures promote should unite the bishop and faithful in the essentials of the apostolic tradition while creating the opportunity for developing accord around open questions about the church's life (AS 165). *Apostolorum Successores* tends to view these structures of participation in light of their practical effects. Hence, they are tied to the bishop's governance of the local church, as dialogue is necessary for determining how to apply the church's resources to pastoral needs and opportunities. In keeping with this practical purpose, the intent of these dialogues should be clear and their outcomes concrete (AS 165). While the benefits of a well-organized and efficient gathering are appreciable, longer processes and openness to results that are not always tangible are necessary in order for dialogical discernment to take place.

Seven local church structures are particularly relevant to consider as opportunities for dialogue: diocesan synods, pastoral visitations, presbyteral councils, the college of consultors, finance councils, pastoral councils, and diocesan curia. These structures are the people and institutions that inform the bishop in his care for the diocese. They are vital to consider because they potentially provide a range of means for the bishop to encounter, know, and learn from the *sensus fidelium*, as well as for the faithful to participate in and shape pastoral planning.

Diocesan synod. Apostolorum Successores roots the diocesan synod in hierarchical communion: synods draw together the bishop's governance of the church with his ministry for the church's unity (AS 166). By linking the diocesan synod to hierarchical communion, the document describes the synod's task as the application and adaptation of the universal church's laws and standard practices to the local church (AS 168). This means the synod is not envisioned by this document as an occasion for further discerning the apostolic faith of the local church.

The synod is an occasional celebration within the local church, convened by the bishop, with the consultation of the presbyteral council (CIC, c. 461, §1). The bishop determines when to convoke a synod in order to fulfill his ministry of governance in light of the pastoral needs of the local church (AS 171). While the bishop ultimately decides on the synod's topic, the faithful should be asked to submit their ideas for the synod, and priests are to be encouraged especially to propose topics about the local church's governance (AS 173). Synods require a great deal of work, as they involve not only the practical aspects of bringing together large portions of the diocese to discuss diverse matters but also the spiritual and intellectual preparation of the faithful. These preparations facilitate dialogue with those faithful who directly participate in the synodal discussions, as well as the understanding of the local church as a whole about the matters of faith and pastoral action the synod explores.

Canon law dictates numerous people who, as a result of their office in the church, are to attend the synod, including coadjutor and auxiliary bishops, vicars general and episcopal vicars, representatives from the presbyteral council, and laity. Laity are chosen either by the pastoral council in a manner approved by the bishop, or, if the diocese lacks a pastoral council, are chosen in another manner determined by the bishop (CIC, c. 463, §1). Further, the bishop may also invite observers from other churches or ecclesial communities with whom the Catholic Church is not in full communion (CIC, c. 463 §3). Neither those with advanced degrees in theology nor lay ecclesial ministers are explicitly mentioned in the list of attendees, though it would seem that in dioceses where such experts are available, their assistance in planning and participating in the synod could be fruitful. *Apostolorum Successores* indicates the synod ought to include faithful from a wide range of vocations who also reflect the local church's social diversity and geographic locations. Further, members of the synod should be chosen for their exemplary lives of faith, commitment to the church's mission, and practical wisdom (AS 169). Balance between the numbers of lay faithful and clerics represented will need to be carefully considered if the composition of the synod is to reflect the local church, even though the synod participants are to be cautioned that the synod is not a representative body of the people of God in opposition to the bishop (AS 171).

Liturgical celebrations are at the heart of the synod and are open to the whole diocese; those gathered for worship may receive presentations on church teaching and pastoral action as well. The synod discussions themselves are reserved for those officially invited to participate. The bishop is to have a direct and active presence during synod sessions, though he may delegate others to attend particular sessions in his place. *Apostolorum Successores* affirms canon law's indication that questions proposed may be freely discussed, but it counterbalances this statement by drawing on a second Vatican document, which places off limits those topics contradictory to church doctrine or that cannot be decided by the synod (AS 174).[21] Votes taken on the synod's discussions are not binding on the bishop but rather are consultative. Even so, apart from serious reasons, the bishop should not distance himself from the conclusions of the synod's majority (AS 171). The outcomes of the synod are drawn up by commissions chosen by the bishop, and once the texts are prepared, he signs by virtue of his office (AS 174). Hierarchical communion is reaffirmed, since after signing the decrees, they are to be sent to the metropolitan bishop and episcopal conference as well as to the Congregation for Bishops and Congregation for the Evangelization of Peoples (AS 174).

Pastoral visitations. Pastoral visitations are mandatory. At the end of a five-year cycle, the bishop ought to have personally visited all the diocese; however, others may represent the bishop if necessary (CIC, c. 396, §1). Through the visitation, the bishop fosters personal relationships within the local church, both with clergy and the lay faithful, in ways that renew and support their

---

[21] Cf. CIC c. 465. See Congregation for Bishops and Congregation for the Evangelization of Peoples, *Instruction on Diocesan Synods*, IV, 4, Vatican website, http://www.vatican.va/roman_curia/congregations/cbishops/documents/rc_con_cbishops_doc_20041118_diocesan-synods-1997_en.html.

lives of faith and inspire their missionary efforts (AS 220). The pastoral visitation is described as the bishop's means of exercising his ministry more directly in the lives of the clergy and lay faithful so that the pastoral visitation is "an extension of his spiritual presence among his people" (AS 223). Virtues cultivated by the bishop should be in evidence in the visitation, both as an example to the faithful and as a means of communicating his pastoral charity.

Apostolorum Successores emphasizes what the bishop offers to the faithful through the visitation. For example, drawing on John Paul II's *Pastores Gregis*, it states: "For the communities or institutions visited by the Bishop, it is an event of grace, reflecting in some measure that great visit with which the 'chief Shepherd' and Guardian of our souls, Jesus Christ, has visited and redeemed his people" (AS 220). While the pastoral visitation may not rise to the level of the incarnation itself, this elevated language does reinforce the significance of the visitation. It is notable that pastoral charity is not characterized here as the bishop's self-commitment in love to learning about or from the faithful but rather as a communication of grace to the faithful. Through pastoral charity, the bishop comes to the faithful as the source of unity within the church. It does not seem, however, that the visit is intended to help the bishop receive or be shaped by the faithful personally (AS 220).

If possible, the bishop is to engage in particular forms of pastoral ministry during his visitation, including celebration of Mass and the sacrament of confirmation; preaching the Word of God; visiting the sick; and meeting with clergy, the pastoral council or other lay leaders, the parish finance council, and children, youth, and young adults who are being formed in faith (AS 221). Learning about the social and religious context of the parish is part of the bishop's preparation for the visit. While we may assume such learning also takes place during the visitation, the document does not explicitly describe the bishop as learning about the parish's social and religious context through his experiences during the visitation (AS 222). Nevertheless, the bishop is to demonstrate his ability to listen, articulate himself, and show interest in the persons he encounters (AS 223). Conversely, those visited are to prepare to receive the bishop in various ways, such as through parish missions or presentations and homilies about the church's communion and the bishop's ministry (AS 222). The perichoresis described elsewhere in *Apostolorum Successores* may be presumed to be in effect for the pastoral visitation; the document's lack of sustained description of the visitation's purpose as moving beyond government and administration to an authentically mutual exchange, however, seems to leave the potential for perichoresis underdeveloped.

Presbyteral council. The council of priests is a mandated, representative body that aids the bishop in caring for the pastoral needs of the local church, with a particular focus on diocesan governance (CIC, c. 495, §1). It is composed of *ex officio* members; priests elected by the diocesan priests to the council, who generally make up about half of the membership; and other priests whom the bishop may appoint at his discretion (CIC, c. 497). The council provides for union among the diocesan presbyterate and serves as a forum for discussion about the local church's governance. Particular attention is given to understanding the local church's context and to the Holy Spirit's work among the people, which help guide pastoral decision making (AS 182). Thus while the presbyteral council's purpose has much to do with the practical governance of the diocese, discernment of the Holy Spirit is also part of its purpose.

The bishop convokes, presides, and determines the subject matter for the council, which has a consultative but not a deliberative role, except in those cases mandated by canon law (CIC, c. 500, §1, §2).[22] The bishop has freedom to make his own decisions apart from the opinions of the council members. Yet, given the importance of the matters the council discusses, when his counselors are united in their opinion, the bishop ought not to act against their

---

[22] Opinions about whether or not any cases require the consent of the presbyteral council differ. Barbara Anne Cusack, Commentary on "Title III: The Internal Ordering of Particular Churches [cc. 460–572]," in Beal et al., *New Commentary on the Code of Canon Law*, 658–59.

advice except for serious and carefully weighed reasons (AS 182). The need to give great weight to the council's unanimous opinion calls forth the bishop's virtue of prudence, which combines the ability to govern practically with divine wisdom.

The presbyteral council may develop its own statutes, subject to the approval of the bishop, but it is dependent on the bishop for its agenda. Potentially, the council offers a more frequent opportunity for consultation than diocesan synods or pastoral visitations. While canon law requires the establishment of the presbyteral council, however, the number of times it meets is not legislated apart from the statutes approved by the bishop (CIC, c. 500).[23]

College of consultors. This college of six to twelve priests takes its membership from the presbyteral council, and its purpose is to ensure the bishop is well assisted in his ministry (AS 183; CIC, c. 502 §1). As with the presbyteral council, the bishop presides over the college, which must be consulted in certain matters of diocesan administration as determined by the episcopal conference (CIC c. 502 §2).[24] Otherwise, the main functions of the college of consultors have to do with administration of the diocese when the episcopal see is vacant or impeded, and with such formal aspects as receiving the letters of appointment for coadjutor and auxiliary bishops.[25]

Finance council. The finance council is also canonically required and is composed of those faithful appointed by the bishop whose expertise in the areas of finance and law is combined with impeccable personal integrity (CIC, c. 492 §1). In addition to consulting on matters of diocesan finance and the preparation of a yearly report, the council is to be consulted by the bishop before he appoints the diocesan finance officer and must also be consulted

---

[23] Ibid., 658.

[24] These consultations generally have to do with administration of personnel, property, and finances. See Robert T. Kennedy, Commentary on "Book V: The Temporal Goods of the Church [cc.1254–1310]" in Beal et al., *New Commentary on the Code of Canon Law*, 1479.

[25] Cusack, *New Commentary on the Code of Canon Law*, 662.

before that officer's removal (CIC 493; 494 §1).[26] While the finance council serves an administrative role, it also exists to ensure transparency in the business operations of the diocese and to help maintain the bishop's integrity.

Pastoral council. In contrast to the councils above, the diocesan pastoral council is not canonically required. Rather, "In every diocese and to the extent that pastoral circumstances suggest it, a pastoral council is to be constituted which under the authority of the bishop investigates, considers, and imposes practical conclusions about those things which pertain to pastoral works in the diocese" (CIC c. 511).[27] Where it exists, the pastoral council is to be convened at least annually (CIC, c. 514 §2). Through the council, the bishop structurally invites all the faithful to join in the church's apostolic mission (AS 184).

The bishop appoints the council's members from among the Christian faithful "who are in full communion with the Catholic Church—clerics, members of institutes of consecrated life, and especially laity" (CIC c. 512 §1). The membership is not representative of the diocese in a republican sense; rather, members are to be chosen "with consideration for different areas of the diocese, social conditions and professions, and roles which they have in the apostolate whether individually or joined with others" (CIC c. 512 §2). The vote of the pastoral council is consultative, not deliberative, and *Apostolorum Successores* cautions that it must not step outside the boundaries of its competency (AS 184). Even so, the document also indicates the bishop should weigh carefully the

[26] The college of consultors must also be consulted in the appointment and removal the financial officer. Cusack, *New Commentary on the Code of Canon Law*, 652.

[27] "While such councils are not mandatory, conciliar and postconciliar endorsement of such councils would suggest that, unless pastoral circumstances warrant otherwise, the bishop should establish such a council. In the drafting stages there were efforts to strengthen the encouragement of councils, more in line with the conciliar texts. However, it was ultimately determined that circumstances among dioceses were quite diverse so the canon should not mandate councils." Cusack, *New Commentary on the Code of Canon Law*, 668.

members' opinions, as the council reflects the faithful's collaboration with the bishop's apostolic ministry (AS 184). While the bishop presides over the council and decides its agenda in relation to pastoral planning for the diocese, he may delegate attendance at its meetings to others (AS 184; CIC, c. 514; 1).[28] The possibility of delegation necessarily reduces the pastoral council's potential efficacy as a means of communicating the *sensus fidelium* directly to the bishop.

Coadjutor and auxiliary bishops and the curia. In addition to the persons and structures listed above, the coadjutor and auxiliary bishops, as well as the diocesan curia, work with the bishop in order to ensure the good order of the diocese and the effectiveness of pastoral work. These persons ought to be consulted by the bishop in virtue of their offices and in light of their responsibility for the good of the diocese. For example, *Apostolorum Successores* speaks of a fraternal relationship between the bishop and auxiliary bishop, in which the bishop invites collaboration and mutual exchange as they attend together to the needs of the local church. Conversely, the auxiliary ought to respect the bishop's authority through obedience (AS 70). Similarly, *Christus Dominus* affirms, "Whenever the bishop is given a coadjutor, the two should not fail to consult one another in matters of greater importance, in order to provide as far as possible for the present and future welfare of the diocese" (CD 26). In addition to their competency in particular fields, curial officials are to be characterized by passion for ministry as well as by lives of faithfulness. They are also to have pastoral responsibilities in addition to their administrative roles in order to maintain personal relationships with the faithful (AS 176).

Potential Structures for Discernment

Philip Selznick indicates that "dialogue is inherent in the idea of community, and dialogue is a requisite for effective authority.

[28] Ibid., 671.

But dialogue presumes a framework of commitment so that people really listen to one another."[29] The diocesan structures described above, whether mandated or recommended, provide institutional frameworks for that commitment and offer a spectrum of opportunities for the bishop to receive and learn from the *sensus fidelium* in a dialogical manner. In particular, the diocesan synod provides the opportunity for widespread formation and discussion both before and during the synod, and through pastoral visitations the bishop may gain experience of diverse members of the faithful within their own contexts. Further, presbyteral councils contribute to unity in apostolic ministry within the local church, and through the diocesan pastoral council, the bishop may receive deeper insights into both the needs and charisms of the faithful. Finally, through the curia, auxiliary bishops, and coadjutor bishop, the diocesan bishop receives both assistance in his ministry and the possibility of spiritual fellowship.

These seven structures of the local church offer organizational frameworks within which the bishop exercises his ministry. Clearly the bishop's ministry is not circumscribed to these structures alone. They present, however, regular opportunities for the bishop to engage in learning through dialogue and to develop those personal virtues that allow limitations to be acknowledged, even as the bishop seeks to know the *sensus fidelium* authentically, communally, and transformatively. The structures reinforce the need for consultation and collaboration if the bishop's ministry is to flourish and offer the possibility for making such consultation and collaboration authentic, particularly when allied with the bishop's personal virtues described in the preceding section. It is less clear that the documents envision these structures as transformational for the bishop, though when allied with personal virtues, the bishop's regular interactions with the faithful of the local church may be a catalyst for his personal transformation.

---

[29] Philip Selznick, "Second General Discussion," in Catholic Common Ground Initiative, *Church and Authority in American Culture: The Second Cardinal Bernardin Conference* (New York: Crossroad, 1999), 142.

IV. Critical Developments

These four ecclesial documents born within and from the Second Vatican Council do a great deal to articulate the bishop's ministry in ways that reflect the church as an apostolic communion. In various ways, they describe and support the bishop's ministry as inherently related to the apostolic tradition that is expressed and received through mutual gift and reception within a church that is the body of Christ on pilgrimage. As noted in the first chapter, however, a vision of the church that tends to institutionalism stands close to us in history. Institutionalism focuses on the bishop as giving and on the faithful as receiving and confines the apostolic tradition to the teaching of the magisterium. Remnants of institutionalism are also found in these documents, limiting their ability to address the two significant questions highlighted at the chapter's beginning: How is the bishop's discernment of the *sensus fidelium* not only a requirement of his office but also formative of his personal holiness? How does the bishop's personal holiness allow him to receive and represent the *sensus fidelium* of the local church? Addressing these questions encourages us to notice what is lacking in the landscape these documents create and to understand more clearly what needs to be developed in order to more fully aid the bishop's discerning reception of the *sensus fidelium*.

The vestiges of institutionalism may be seen in three absences within these texts, which will be explored in this section as critical areas for development. First, episcopal learning is often narrowed to pastoral application rather than pastoral reception, and the *sensus fidelium* is described more as a gauge of pastoral effectiveness rather than as a source of the church's tradition. Second, due to a focus on the reception of the universal church by the local church, the documents give insufficient attention to how the local church is received by the universal church through the bishop's personal symbolization of the *sensus fidelium*. Finally, while the documents emphasize the importance of the bishop's personal growth in holiness through virtues that are applied to his ministry, they do not adequately envision the bishop's formation in holiness through his reception of the *sensus fidelium*, or how virtues may be cultivated through his ministry of discernment.

Narrowing learning via the sensus fidelium. These documents primarily advocate dialogical learning in order that the bishop be better able to undertake the pastoral application of his threefold office. Such learning is certainly important in order for the bishop to respond to the needs of the faithful and not simply impose a pastoral plan on the diocese. Further, it is wise to avoid an overly firm distinction between the bishop's pastoral experience of the diocese as it expresses the Christian faith and how that faith is articulated by the church in doctrinal principles; the pastoral and the doctrinal are not unrelated. These documents, however, generally limit episcopal learning to the realm of pastoral application. The church's apostolic tradition seems to exist at the level of the universal church alone, thus leaving the bishop with the task of finding the best way of implementing this teaching within the local church rather than seeking out the apostolic tradition within the *sensus fidelium* as well. The result may be that learning and consultation lose the character of "theological and moral imperatives" and instead become mere "teaching strategies or teaching methodologies."[30]

The tendency to limit the bishop's learning to the determination of best pastoral practices results in the documents' lack of consideration of the *sensus fidelium* as a source of the church's tradition. Instead, the *sensus fidelium* becomes a gauge of pastoral success rather than an authoritative source of the apostolic tradition that contributes to the bishop's own formation. There is an analogy here to the classroom. Teachers evaluate the effectiveness of their pedagogical strategies and personal gifts for teaching. Reviewing pedagogies is valuable for determining the goals and effectiveness of one's teaching, and personal abilities such as

[30] James Coriden, "Panel Discussion: James Coriden, Avery Dulles, Joseph Komonchak, and Philip Selznick," in Catholic Common Ground Initiative, *Church Authority in American Culture: The Second Cardinal Bernardin Conference* (New York: Crossroads, 1999), 85–86.

establishing rapport, displaying respect, and engaging in dialogue are important for being able to meet students "where they are." Yet these pedagogies and personal gifts are limited if they flow only from the teacher to the student—if, in other words, it is presumed that there is nothing substantial to be learned from the students themselves about the subject being taught and not only the way to teach it. Translated to the bishop's task, this means that the lives of the faithful, in which the church's apostolic faith is received, refined, and developed, are not viewed as having an authoritative claim on the bishop with regard to the content of the church's teaching as well as the form of that teaching.

Focusing on the qualities that are required for the "application" of episcopal ministry within the local church results in the *sensus fidelium*'s role being insufficiently developed in two key areas. First, while the bishop forms the faith of the local church, the *sensus fidelium* is not described adequately as forming the bishop's intellectual and affective understanding of the church's tradition itself. Second, lack of consideration for the *sensus fidelium*'s authority means that, despite the numerous personal qualities cited, there is relatively little description in these documents of how the bishop comes to personally symbolize the local church's faith via those ministerial virtues. In other words, while there is *potential* for such symbolism to arise through the ministerial virtues described in these documents, one of the purposes of these virtues is not explicitly named as the *realization* of that symbolization. Therefore, while the virtues described may well pertain to good practices in episcopal ministry, they lack the more explicit purpose of being practices of discernment that advance a particularly important aspect of the bishop's ministry: learning from the local church's apostolic communion in order to symbolize its faith.

Reception of the local church by the universal church. In these documents, reception of the apostolic faith seems to flow primarily from the universal church to the local, with little development of how the local church's faith is received by the bishop for personal representation to the universal church. The bishop's service is conceived as maintaining the local church in its union with the universal church; the service he might give to the universal church through his ability to symbolize the local church's *sensus fidelium* is largely unconsidered.[31] The bishop's unity in faith with the episcopacy of the universal church is an essential way the local diocese is understood to have received the fullness of the church of Christ and thus be called properly "church." The bishop, however, is also the personal symbol of unity *of* the local church—and not only *for* the local church—through his reception of the *sensus fidelium*.[32]

The relationship between the reception of the *sensus fidelium* and the unity of the local church is important for two reasons. First, the bishop's reception of the *sensus fidelium* is part of how he, as symbol of unity, is meaningfully representative of the local church, its people, and context. If the bishop does not symbolize the expressions of faith that characterize the local church, two risks arise. On the one hand, he may symbolize only an abstract, idealized version of the universal church that does not engage the

[31] Richard Gaillardetz, *Teaching with Authority: A Theology of the Magisterium in the Church* (Collegeville, MN: Liturgical Press, 1997), 45. "The deliberations of bishops in synod or council were not for the early Church, and should not be today, understood as the exercise of a kind of governing board placed over the Church. Rather, synodal and conciliar deliberations are concentrated expressions of the mind of the Churches." Gaillardetz draws on Michael J. Himes, "The Ecclesiological Significance of the Reception of Doctrine," *Heythrop Journal* 33, no. 2 (April 1992): 154: "The capacity of the bishops to reflect the mind of the Church universal conditions and is conditioned by their capacity to reflect the mind of the local churches. The conciliar structure of the church is short-circuited when the bishops cannot or do not act as the corporate voices of their churches."

[32] I take the emphasis of the bishop's ministry of unity in relation to his person from Frank B. Norris, "The Bishop: First Liturgist of the Local Church," in *Shepherds and Teachers: The Bishop and Liturgical Renewal* (Chicago: n.p., 1980), 40–41. "In the last analysis the only cogent theological reason, in my opinion, that strongly argues for episcopal leadership is one that is based on the importance of local church unity-in-love and the need to have that unity (and the continuing struggle to achieve it) symbolized *personally*" (emphasis in the original). A similar idea is expressed by *Lumen Gentium* 23: "The individual bishops are the visible source and foundation of unity in their own particular Churches."

apostolic needs and gifts of the people of God.[33] On the other hand, the bishop may transpose the *sensus fidelium* of another place and time into the local church, thus promoting a pastorally ineffective uniformity rather than true unity.[34]

Second, as noted earlier, through the bishop's ministry, the local church receives the universal church and the universal church also receives the local church. If the bishop does not receive and symbolize the *sensus fidelium* of the local church, he is prevented from being a real symbol, or witness, of the local church within the universal church. This poses a difficulty for the process of reception and thus for the development and articulation of doctrine aimed at recognizing an underlying *consensus fidelium* of the universal church. In order for there to be a "church of churches," the faith of the local church must be part of the universal church's discernment of a shared and catholic faith that is expressed diversely by the local churches.

Developing personally through ministry. In keeping with the tendency of these documents to focus on pastoral application rather than pastoral reception, as well as to emphasize the local church's reception of the universal church, a third area for critical development is how the bishop is formed in holiness not only *for* his ministry but also *in and through* his ministry. As described extensively

---

[33] "Since the bishop presides over the apostolate exercised in the whole diocese it is most necessary that he be acquainted with all its aspects, but especially the moral and spiritual factors that affect people's lives. Otherwise his zeal would be fruitless and ineffective, for it would not be directed to men as they really are; nor can he supply fitting remedies if he does not know the evils and obstacles as they really are." Sacred Congregation for Bishops, *Directory on the Pastoral Ministry of Bishops* (Ottawa, Ontario: Publication Service of the Canadian Catholic Conference, 1974), 101.

[34] "The bishop ought also to have that sense of evolution in human affairs and history which enables him to foresee the changes affecting or threatening his diocese and to provide for them; such, for example, are: large gatherings of people in suburbs of cities, desertion of rural areas, changed hours and employment, workers who are migrant for shorter or longer periods, advances in culture and information, etc. For these and similar reasons it is necessary that pastoral activity be carried on in a way that has in good time been adjusted to changed conditions (cf. GS 5–10)." Ibid.

in *Apostolorum Successores*, the bishop's personal spirituality and ministry should be linked. The relationship between spiritual growth and the bishop's ministerial practices, however, is not fully articulated, particularly with regard to his discerning reception of the *sensus fidelium*.

A return to the analogy of the classroom helps illustrate this point. A teacher may be formed in pedagogical theories and techniques outside the classroom and may also seek areas for professional development as a result of experiences in the classroom. Yet the classroom itself is a crucible of experiential learning: a teacher learns to teach personally in and through the practice of teaching. Similarly, the bishop may engage in spiritual formation outside of his direct ministry with the faithful or seek formation in response to his experiences of the faithful. Yet he also learns to minister personally in and through the practice of ministering. If the bishop is to minister as a person of discernment, then spiritual practices associated with discernment must be developed as he ministers. These spiritual practices are tied to knowing God more authentically by acknowledging limitations, learning communally, and being transformed personally. While these spiritual practices need not be confined to the bishop's ministry, they must also be present in the way the bishop ministers with the faithful if he is to be formed personally by the local church's faith. While many bishops themselves recognize the link between their spirituality and ministry, spiritualities rooted in practices of discernment and integrated with pastoral ministry are needed.[35] Without such integration, the bishop is inhibited in becoming a person of discernment who exercises a ministry of discernment within the church.

Attention to spirituality in relation to practices of discernment is necessary for three reasons. First, while the documents make

---

[35] For example, see George Basil Hume, "Spiritual Foundations of a Bishop's Ministry," in *The Ministry of Bishops: Papers from the Collegeville Assembly* (Washington, DC: United States Catholic Conference, 1982); James S. Sullivan, "Called to Holiness. The Bishop as Sanctifier," in *Servants of the Gospel: Essays by American Bishops on Their Role as Shepherds of the Church*, ed. Leon J. Suprenant, Jr. (Steubenville, OH: Emmaus Road Publishing, 2000).

clear that a relationship between the bishop's personal virtue and the fulfillment of his ministry exists, they do not indicate in great depth how the bishop grows in these virtues. This omission is understandable, as diverse spiritualities are part of the richness of the church, and there need not be one, episcopal spirituality. Further reflection on the development of ministerial virtues in relation to spirituality, however, is needed. Second, the documents do not describe how the bishop moves from dialogue to decision, a step requiring the integration of spirituality with processes of authentication. Receiving God's gift mediated through history and culture is a spiritual process, and discernment is a habit essential to making this process a means of coming to know the apostolic faith personally in order to teach the faith most authentically. Thus the bishop's reception and discernment of the *sensus fidelium*, and his decision about how to act in light of it, is a spiritual process as well.

Third, while these documents emphasize the need for collaboration in his ministry, the bishop at times appears spiritually solipsistic. As Bradford Hinze asks, "Are there any mechanisms for discussing the bishop's accountability in this web of relationship and shared responsibility?"[36] If, through his practices of discernment, the bishop grows in personal holiness, which in turn affects his ability to fulfill his office well, then structures and persons within the local church should aid the bishop's advancement in virtue and assist the bishop in maintaining his spiritual integrity. Though the structures outlined earlier in this chapter may have the potential to ensure such spiritual integrity, it is not evident that their design and implementation aims at realizing such integrity. More positively stated, the mutuality of an apostolic communion forces us to consider that just as the bishop is to have pastoral care for his diocese, so, too, through its structures, the diocese should exercise pastoral care for its bishop.

---

[36] Bradford E. Hinze, *Practices of Dialogue in the Roman Catholic Church* (New York: Continuum, 2006), 41. Hinze is referring to how much influence the consultations of diocesan pastoral councils have on the bishop's deliberations.

V. Conclusion

How is the bishop's discernment of the *sensus fidelium* not only a requirement of his office but also formative of his personal holiness? How does the bishop's personal holiness allow him to receive and represent the *sensus fidelium* of the local church? The documents investigated in this chapter point us to partial answers to these questions but demonstrate the need to develop a more thorough response as well. On the one hand, the church already ideally envisions the bishop's holiness as integrally related to his ability to minister well. The documents describe his holiness in relation to virtues that may contribute to practices of discernment that promote the bishop's authentic reception and response to God's self-gift by acknowledging his limitations, leading him to learn from others, and promoting personal transformation. Further, these documents describe and prescribe organizational frameworks for dialogue marked by authentication and learning.

On the other hand, the church has yet to integrate a stronger understanding of the *sensus fidelium* into our vision of the bishop's ministry. The *sensus fidelium* is not yet understood by these documents as an authoritative source for episcopal teaching that requires practices of discernment in order to be received. Yet it is through receiving the *sensus fidelium* that the bishop may be transformed by the local church's faith into a personal symbol of that faith. This transformation is central to the bishop's ability to minister not only within the local church but also within the universal church as a *consensus fidelium* is discerned. Such reception requires that we be able to describe spiritualities that integrate the bishop's ministry of discernment with his personal holiness, and that we create or reform diocesan structures in order to support the bishop's spiritual integrity.

The next chapters begin to address these areas for critical development. Chapter 3 explores the relationship between discernment, reception, and response in the *Spiritual Exercises*. It aims to provide a more complete description of spirituality and discernment and to discover the practices through which the *Spiritual*

Exercises forms persons of discernment. Through these practices, persons of discernment grow in their ability to receive and respond to God authentically and cultivate virtues such as love, humility, and indifference. Chapter 4 builds on this foundation by describing how discernment functions within the Society of Jesus in terms of the superior's ministry of fostering a union of wills among his companions through processes of authentication. It also examines structures of the Society that aid the superior's spiritual integrity. Together, these chapters form a comparative model that offers insights for an episcopal spirituality of discernment that aids the bishop's development into a personal symbol of the local church's faithful union and strengthens his ability to both learn from and teach the faithful.

Chapter 3

The *Spiritual Exercises*:
Developing Persons of Discernment

> *Discernment is always done in the presence of the Lord, looking at the signs, listening to the things that happen, the feeling of the people, especially the poor. My choices, including those related to the day-to-day aspects of life, like the use of a modest car, are related to a spiritual discernment that responds to a need that arises from looking at things, at people and from reading the signs of the times. Discernment in the Lord guides me in my way of governing.*[1]
>
> —Francis, Bishop of Rome

Chapter 1 argued we ought to envision the church as an apostolic communion in which unity is enlivened by mission. It also indicated that our ecclesial imagination within and following Vatican II is still quite influenced by institutionalism, which sets the church's hierarchy and teaching apart from the larger context of the church's communion and mission. The church documents in chapter 2 illustrated that this imaginative shift is still in process with regard to the role of the bishop in the local church. On the one hand, the need for personal formation and qualities such as humility and dialogue are linked to the bishop's ministry and are

---

[1] Antonio Spadaro, "A Big Heart Open to God," *America* 209, no. 8 (September 13, 2013), http://americamagazine.org/pope-interview.

also those associated with a view of authority that is more relational than autocratic. These documents emphasize the bishop's
holiness as integral for ministry within the local church. Nevertheless, the imaginative shift is not complete as long as these characteristics are perceived as being unidirectional, as having to do
with the bishop as a teacher without regard for the qualities necessary for the bishop to be a learner as well. In other words, these
documents do not take sufficient account of the authentic, limited,
communal, and transformative ways the bishop learns to receive
the local church's sense of faith as part of the living apostolic
tradition. Discerning God's self-gift of revelation received and
expressed through history and culture, which both creates the
church's unity in faith and calls the church to a mission of love,
is essential for the bishop both personally and ministerially. The
bishop's ability to discern the *sensus fidelium* is important because
through discernment, the bishop both grows in personal holiness
and comes to symbolize the faith of the local church. This symbolization is necessary for an authentically mutual reception between the local and universal church, which ought to characterize
the church's catholic unity in the apostolic faith.

   The task in this chapter is to move from examining *why* discerning the *sensus fidelium* is necessary for the bishop's ministry to
exploring *how* such discernment may take place. In the quote
above, Pope Francis describes discernment in terms enlivened by
the language of learning: to discern in Christ's presence is to look,
listen, feel, and read. For Francis, to discern is to respond, but this
response is rooted in reception of the Holy Spirit at work in the
church and world. In Ignatius of Loyola's *Spiritual Exercises*, we
can find the foundation of Francis's personal and ministerial spirituality, a spirituality of discernment. By examining the spiritual
practices embedded within the *Spiritual Exercises*, we can begin to
build a comparative model of discernment which, combined with
chapter 4's discussion of Jesuit structures, helps us envision the
bishop's ministry of discernment within the local church. A spirituality of discernment develops through practices in which we
train ourselves to habitually embrace the limited, communal, and

transformative ways we receive God's self-gift. Through these practices we know and respond to God's self-gift more authentically. Spiritual practices help us to enter more deeply into communion with God and others—thus, intimacy with the holy shapes our holiness so we become persons of discernment and not simply persons who make discernments.

The *Spiritual Exercises* develops discernment as a habit that transforms us through union with God. The virtue of discernment forms us in holiness as we make distinctions that help us to follow our calling by receiving and sharing God's communication of love. Through discernment we receive and respond to God more authentically because we learn from others through our limitations. This learning transforms our self-knowledge as well as how we know God and others. This chapter's goal is to delve deeply into the ways discernment is cultivated through the *Spiritual Exercises*. By turning to this spiritual tradition, which is one part of the church's inheritance, we may enrich our ecclesial imagination regarding the bishop's discernment within the local church. Characteristics of the *Exercises* may affirm Ignatian spirituality itself as helpful for bishops, an affirmation complemented by the long tradition of adapting the *Spiritual Exercises* for use by many different persons within the church. Of course, not everyone resonates with Ignatian spirituality. Thus while the *Spiritual Exercises* is fruitful for identifying spiritual characteristics of discernment, turning to the *Exercises* may also encourage us to seek characteristics of discernment in our other spiritual traditions or assist us in constructing new spiritualities of discernment. Ultimately, the *Spiritual Exercises* offers a model for discernment rather than a mold into which all spiritualties of discernment must fit.

This chapter's exploration of a spirituality of discernment begins with "Spirituality and Learning" by defining the term spirituality and noting how spirituality develops our capacity to learn. "Development and Purpose of the *Spiritual Exercises*" considers both the origins and intentions of the *Exercises* in relation to Ignatius's own growing understanding of how to discern union with Christ's mission. Next, "Discernment in the *Spiritual Exercises*" investigates what Ignatius means by discernment and how the spirituality promoted by the *Exercises* forms persons of discernment. Discernment develops in the *Exercises* through making distinctions, the use of imagination, growth in humility, the cultivation of indifference, and experiences of consolation and desolation. The fourth section, "A Spirituality of Discernment," weaves the previous sections together in order to understand what it means to become a person of discernment and to learn through the *Spiritual Exercises*. The chapter concludes by noting how this spirituality of discernment engages the authentic, limited, communal, and transformative ways we receive God's self-gift.

I. Spirituality and Learning

In the culture of the United States today, being spiritual is sometimes seen as an alternative to being religious. Identifying oneself as "spiritual, but not religious" may suggest a desire for relationship to the divine or the transcendent in ways which are unmediated by a religious tradition or which seek greater freedom from the uniformity that religious traditions are perceived as imposing.[2] Yet the many spiritualities flourishing within Catholicism, as well as in Christianity more broadly, are testament that our relationship to the divine need not preclude a religious tradition's framework; rather, in the Catholic tradition, spirituality and tradition are mutually necessary. Defining spirituality is not a simple task, though it is necessary. On the one hand, in order to study spirituality in a meaningful manner, the term must be understood in some fashion; on the other hand, spiritualities arise within history, and thus the term resists one hard and fast definition.

---

[2] For the correlations between spirituality and religious affiliations, see Pew Research Center, *"Nones" on the Rise: One in Five Adults Have No Religious Affiliation*, Pew Forum, http://www.pewforum.org/files/2012/10/NonesOnTheRise -full.pdf.

Philip Sheldrake notes these problems of defining spirituality and indicates that in contemporary studies "the realization has emerged that specific spiritual traditions are initially embodied in people rather than doctrine and grow out of life rather than from abstract ideas."[3] Sheldrake views the everyday world as the ground of spiritual experience. For Catholics, while spirituality always involves the apostolic tradition, this tradition is rooted in cultures and histories. This means spirituality is not merely an incarnation of an abstract tradition. Rather, as a learned response to the continued activity of God within history, spirituality prevents tradition from becoming either dry historical reenactment or pious nostalgia. Through spirituality, tradition lives because it is received meaningfully within the landscape of our lives. Spirituality's responsiveness to both our current context and the apostolic tradition means that through our spiritualities we learn to both receive and to respond to God's self-gift.

Sheldrake offers a working definition of spirituality as "the conscious human response to God that is both personal and ecclesial."[4] Interpreting the elements of his definition demonstrates its helpfulness for the tasks of this chapter. First, one engages spirituality knowingly and in a purposive manner. Spirituality is therefore not only a commonly held human openness to receiving God's self-gift but also the manifestation of that openness through our response. Its conscious character means that to have a spirituality is to engage in making choices about how we receive God and the ways we respond to God. Through our spirituality, we learn to become aware of God's self-gift and to reflect on the replies we make with our lives. Further, this definition precludes

---

[3] Philip Sheldrake, *Spirituality and History* (Maryknoll, NY: Orbis Books, 1998), 41. "In short, part of the contemporary problem with defining 'spirituality' is associated with the fact that it is not a single, transcultural, phenomenon but is rooted within the lived experience of God's presence in history—and a history which is always specific. Indeed, our basic understanding of what is 'spiritual' and what is 'the Christian life' depends, in part at least, on particular experiences rather than merely on a theological language given for all time."

[4] Ibid., 45.

the idea that spirituality merely mirrors the forms of prayer, devotion, and ethics practiced in the church, whether within the past or one's own historical period. Certainly such an imitation can exist, but in this view, imitation uncoupled from intent is not fully spirituality. Spirituality is a form of active learning in which we are not simply "along for the ride" within our ecclesial and cultural milieus but are rather engaging deliberately in a means of receiving and responding to God. While as individuals we may not consciously label the practices by which we receive and respond to God as "spirituality," our conscious desire to enter into relationship with the divine through these practices is necessary for spirituality to flourish.

Second, Sheldrake's definition emphasizes spirituality as a human response to God's initiative. Rather than a blind groping for God in the void, spirituality is an answer to the God who is revealed within a human history that is both personal and communal. If Christian spirituality aids our reception and response to God's self-gift, then learning to interact deeply with revelation must be a constitutive part of spirituality. Explicit and personal interaction with revelation received through the witness of Scripture and tradition is essential for developing Christian spiritual practices.

You need both.

Third, according to Sheldrake's definition, spirituality cannot be described apart from the individuals who engage in it—thus it is always personal. Yet the claim that spirituality is a response to God's self-communication means that spiritualities are also ecclesial. God's revelation is known through the church, and the conscious response to that revelation is characterized by being communal rather than narrowly individualistic. By insisting on the role of both the person and the church, Sheldrake's definition of spirituality avoids an idealization of the church as somehow existing apart from its historical context: we learn who God is and who we are within history, and our histories are both personal and communal. Spirituality lives within the persons and communities whose graced reception of and response to the apostolic tradition incarnate the church within time and space.

Autonomous + independent.

II. Development and Purpose of the *Spiritual Exercises*

The *Spiritual Exercises* is the result of Ignatius's reflection on his own experiences of, and maturing responses to, God. His notes for the *Exercises* began in the latter part of an eleven-month stay at Manresa, Spain, between March 1522 and February 1523. Ignatius's experience at Manresa was one of deepening conversion and insight. He arrived in the excited flush of his recent conversion and commitment to God, which occurred during his long recovery at Loyola from battle injuries. While he records an almost constant joy in the early months of his conversion, he also notes his lack of maturity in understanding the Holy Spirit's work within him.[5] Obstacles of doubt and scrupulosity arose at Manresa and led Ignatius to develop his capacity to discern what is, and what is not, of God through a greater understanding of the interior workings of the Holy Spirit.[6]

Ignatius writes he learned from God at Manresa as a child learns from a teacher.[7] His experiences there, coupled with his own continuing reflections, led to the development of the *Spiritual Exercises* as a means of growing in personal and apostolic relationship to God. In *The Autobiography*, Ignatius describes ways in which God was beginning to teach him through mystical visions as well as intellectual insights.[8] Though mystical encounters with God continued throughout his life, at Manresa Ignatius had a singularly intense and impactful experience of graceful insight which transformed his knowledge so greatly that he saw everything in a new light.[9] Following this extraordinary experience of insight, and with greater personal knowledge of how to discern the interior workings

---

[5] Ignatius of Loyola, *The Autobiography*, trans. Parmananda R. Divarkar, in *Ignatius of Loyola: The Spiritual Exercises and Selected Works*, ed. George E. Ganss, Classics of Western Spirituality (New York: Paulist Press, 1991), 20. References for *The Autobiography* are given by numbered sections.

[6] For a description of the temptations and scruples that beset Ignatius, see ibid., 20–25.

[7] Ibid., 27.

[8] Ibid., 27.

[9] Ibid., 30.

of the Spirit, Ignatius began to compose the initial notes of the
Spiritual Exercises.[10]

In *The Autobiography*, Ignatius recalls his exercises were written
gradually, through self-reflection. He took note of spiritual principles and practices as he became aware of them in his own experience, and so the *Spiritual Exercises* is a product of Ignatius
learning to be attentive to the Spirit's work within.[11] While the
major portions of the *Exercises* were either written or sketched at
Manresa, the text continued to develop based on Ignatius's experiences and conversations with others until 1541.[12] The exercises
that formed so experientially are also intended to be used practically. George Ganss compares the text to an instruction manual
for playing tennis: reading brings some knowledge, but the exercises are meant to be practiced.[13]

The *Exercises* is not primarily intended as a spiritual self-help
guide for the person engaging in the various exercises, who is
known as the exercitant. Rather, it is more frequently used by
another who "gives" the *Exercises* and guides the exercitant in
discerning the divine gift and human response at work in the
exercitant's prayer and interior dispositions.[14] Originally designed

[10] See John W. Padberg, "General Introduction," in Ganss, *Ignatius of Loyola: The Spiritual Exercises and Selected Works*, 15–26. Padberg offers a discussion of the influence of other spiritual works on Ignatius prior to Manresa, which is particularly helpful in connecting the *Spiritual Exercises* with Ignatius's reading of Ludolph of Saxony's *Life of Christ*.

[11] Ignatius of Loyola, *The Autobiography*, 99.

[12] George E. Ganss, introduction to *The Spiritual Exercises of Saint Ignatius: A Translation and Commentary*, trans. George Ganss (Chicago: Loyola University Press, 1992), pp. 3–4.

[13] Ibid., 3.

[14] "Ignatius, whether by good instinct or by careful reflection, does not speak of the 'director of the retreat.' Instead he uses the term 'the one who gives the Exercises' (*el que da los exercicios*). Involved here is something far more important than words; for me it is the basic truth that the director is God, and with God lies the main responsibility for the success of the enterprise of the retreat. It is God who has invited the retreatant to 'come apart' (Mark 6.31), and it is God too who gives the grace whereby the retreatant responds generously to that invitation." Brian Grogan, "The One Who Gives the Exercises," in *The Way of St. Ignatius of*

for a thirty-day retreat, though often adapted to other formats, the exercises are divided into four weeks with meditations or contemplations assigned for each day. These meditations and contemplations are themselves the spiritual exercises that promote interaction with salvation history: the ways God is at work for salvation within the past and present as well as the full realization of God's salvation in the future. Ignatius also provided additional prayer forms, rules, and notes as important aids for the exercitant's spiritual growth.

daily!

As we undertake different types of physical exercise for various outcomes—running for cardio, stretches for flexibility, weight lifting for muscle building—spiritual exercises have particular outcomes. The purpose of Ignatius's *Exercises* is related to its origins in his mystical encounter at Manresa, which informed key aspects of his reflections and shaped the structure of the *Spiritual Exercises* as a whole. Prior to this encounter, Ignatius was both steeped in the contemplation of Christ's life and aware of the need to discern between different spirits, or external forces, that draw us closer to or farther away from God. Part of what he came to understand in his experience at Manresa was that contemplation of Christ and discernment of spirits were intimately related aspects of his developing spirituality. Connecting discernment of spirits with contemplation involved a shift in Ignatius's perception of why Christ's life was to be contemplated. While he initially contemplated in order to imitate Christ, at Manresa he came to see contemplation of Christ's life as a calling to share in Christ's ongoing, salvific mission to the world.[15] Discernment of spirits was necessary in order to hear and respond fully to Christ's call.[16]

This enlarged spiritual vision, from meditating on Christ's person to cooperating with Christ's mission, had two significant

_____

Loyola: Contemporary Approaches to the Spiritual Exercises, ed. Philip Sheldrake (Bristol: SPCK, 1991), 180.

[15] Hugo Rahner, *Ignatius the Theologian,* trans. Michael Barry (New York: Herder and Herder, 1968), 57–58.

[16] See Padberg, "General Introduction," 33.

impacts on the *Exercises*. First, Ignatius did not interpret Christ's call to mission as meaningful for himself alone. While his self-reflections had personal relevance, Ignatius's observations of his interior dispositions were used to help others share in his spiritual experience and were also informed by his experience in the spiritual counsel of others.[17] The *Spiritual Exercises* was composed for the purpose of offering personal, spiritual guidance and was shaped by the practical experience of this guidance.[18]

Second, and of more direct relevance for this study, the *Spiritual Exercises* offers spiritual guidance with a particular purpose in mind: assisting the exercitant to take part in Christ's salvific mission in the world. Luigi M. Rulla notes Ignatian scholarship has at times divided the *Spiritual Exercises* either into a means to make a particular election (a personal commitment to a discerned way of responding to God) or a means to greater spiritual perfection (growth in holiness). Rulla contends the "originality of Ignatius lies in the intuition that there is a connection between discernment, on the one hand, and election or spiritual growth on the other."[19] As Rulla indicates, the steps laid down in the *Exercises* leading toward an election also serve as a means of fostering deep union with God. Indeed, it is only in the process of coming to a deeper union with God, and thus growing in holiness, that the exercitant can come to know the divine will and be said to make a sound discernment of how to join in Christ's mission. Therefore, the *Spiritual Exercises* centers on discernment of union for mission and so corresponds well to the church imagined as an apostolic communion as described in chapter 1.

After his initial explanatory notes, Ignatius indicates the purpose of these exercises: "[T]o overcome oneself, and to order one's life, without reaching a decision through some disordered affec-

---

[17] Ibid.

[18] Ibid., 61.

[19] Luigi M. Rulla, "The Discernment of Spirits and Christian Anthropology," *Gregorianum* 59, no. 3 (1978): 538. For Ignatius's use of the exercises with persons who had already made an election, see Ganss, *The Spiritual Exercises of Saint Ignatius*, p. 147, no. 14.

tion."[20] The exercises are tools to attain one's purpose, which is expressed in the Principle and Foundation:

> Human beings are created to praise, reverence, and serve God our Lord, and by means of this to save their souls.
>
> The other things on the face of the earth are created for the human beings, to help them in working toward the end for which they are created.
>
> From this it follows that I should use these things to the extent that they help me toward my end, and rid myself of them to the extent that they hinder me.
>
> To do this, I must make myself indifferent to all created things, in regard to everything which is left to my freedom of will and is not forbidden. Consequently, on my own part I ought not to seek health rather than sickness, wealth rather than poverty, honor rather than dishonor, a long life rather than a short one, and so on in all other matters.
>
> I ought to desire and elect only the thing which is more conducive to the end for which I am created.[21]

The themes of the Principle and Foundation deeply shape the intent of the *Spiritual Exercises*, which is to foster the ability to take part in Christ's salvific mission to the world by knowing, desiring, and choosing whatever is for God's greater glory. The exercitant's personal vocation is the means by which he or she participates in salvation history. This history is personal because the exercitant grows in holiness by fulfilling her or his calling to union with Christ. Salvation is also communal, however, as one's personal holiness is discovered and formed by sharing in Christ's salvific mission for all.

Discernment and decision making are essential for coming to greater unity with God for the purpose of salvation, both one's

[handwritten margin note: Conducive to the end for which we are / I am created.]

---

[20] Ignatius of Loyola, *Spiritual Exercises*, in Ganss, *Ignatius of Loyola: The Spiritual Exercises and Selected Works*, 21. References for the *Spiritual Exercises* are given by numbered sections.

[21] Ignatius, *Spiritual Exercises*, 23. See also the description of the Principle and Foundation in Ganss, *The Spiritual Exercises of Saint Ignatius*, pp. 148–51, no. 17.

own and the world's. Therefore, Ignatian spirituality is both personal and apostolic. The exercitant's conversion toward union with God promotes the individual's salvation by promoting the world's salvation; as the exercitant learns how to recognize and enact the will of God, God's salvation is communicated not only to the exercitant but also to others through the exercitant's actions. The exercitant reflects on salvation history in order to better understand his or her own role in advancing this history. Therefore, Ignatius's ultimate purpose in the *Spiritual Exercises* is to promote union with God through a discernment of God's will that both facilitates the exercitant's salvation and allows the exercitant to more fully join in Christ's saving mission.

III. Discernment in the *Spiritual Exercises*

Discernment takes on added weight if learning to receive and respond to God's will is central not only to the exercitant's salvation but also to the world's. Much commentary on the *Spiritual Exercises* focuses on discernment in relationship to the Rules for Discernment of Spirits, which is oriented toward the first and second weeks of a thirty-day retreat and the making of an election.[22] Ignatius uses the word "discern" in a particular manner, however, that illuminates a much broader role for discernment in the *Spiritual Exercises* as a whole. While discernment of spirits and making an election are two parts of the *Exercises* that call for discernment, Ignatius's understanding of discernment informs the entirety of the *Exercises* and is essential for the spiritual process by which one comes to union with God and acts as a collaborator in Christ's salvific work.[23]

---

[22] The "Rules for Discernment of Spirits" are found in sections 313–36 of the *Spiritual Exercises*. Ignatius's thought on elections appears at the end of the second week in section 169.

[23] John Carroll Futrell, *Making an Apostolic Community of Love: The Role of the Superior in the Society of Jesus According to St. Ignatius of Loyola* (St. Louis, MO: Institute of Jesuit Sources, 1970), p. 6, no. 8. Futrell writes that "this discernment 'of spirits' is only a part of a larger, much more complex dynamic process of

Ganss carefully explores the meaning of the word "discern" as Ignatius uses it in the *Spiritual Exercises*:

> [T]o discern is to see deeply in order to recognize and separate; in other words, to identify and distinguish the good spirits from the bad. The Spanish *discernir* (from Latin *discernere, discrevi, discretum,* to separate, distinguish, discern, discriminate) means to know, judge, comprehend, distinguish, or discriminate. . . . "Keenness of insight" and "skill in discerning or discriminating" . . . are the meanings of the English word "discernment" which are most relevant for accurate understanding of Ignatius' thought here.[24]

The *Spiritual Exercises* moves the exercitant toward a particular way of viewing reality in relation to the glory of God and Christ's salvation. This perspective is based on the exercitant's ability to make discernments—separations and distinctions—about external and internal realities, which will be described further below. To discriminate between the good and bad spirits and make an election, the exercitant must first discern by seeing deeply into salvation history, the life of Christ, and present circumstances. This ability to penetrate reality, and thus to learn the will of God and be unified with it, is itself dependent on a series of distinctions the exercitant makes throughout the *Exercises*.

In order to develop the virtue of discernment, exercitants must learn to habitually differentiate between God, themselves, and other parts of creation. Learning to make these distinctions occurs throughout the *Exercises*, which taken as a whole are themselves practices in discernment that form exercitants into persons of discernment. To better understand how the *Exercises* develops the habit of discernment, it is necessary to make a few distinctions of our own by separating the many interrelated aspects of discernment in Ignatian spirituality.

---

discernment or deliberation leading to action . . . in an actual, concrete situation here and now."

[24] Ganss, *The Spiritual Exercises of Saint Ignatius,* p. 190, no. 141.

In order to perceive these aspects of Ignatian discernment, five elements of discernment will be discussed in greater detail in the following sections. First, discernments are made between external and internal realities in order to aid the communication of love. The communication of love is made possible through distinctions that allow for a proper relationship between God, creation, and the exercitant. Next, through imagination the exercitant sees the intersection of her or his personal history with salvation history. Third, through humility the exercitant both receives God's salvation and joins in Christ's call to mission. Fourth, in order to join more fully in Christ's mission, the exercitant develops indifference as a willingness to answer Christ's call as completely as possible. Finally, discerning consolations and desolations further assists the exercitant in evaluating growth in union with Christ.

External and Internal Discernments

Two general arenas of discernment are suggested by the Principle and Foundation of the *Exercises*.[25] The first is external, since exercitants learn to distinguish themselves from God and the created world; the second is internal and involves distinguishing movements of the will, or how the good is perceived and pursued. These two arenas are profoundly related since they mutually inform the exercitant's ability to make further discernments that facilitate union with God.

For example, in one exercise, the exercitant is to consider three forms of thought. The first type is the exercitant's own thought, which is rooted in free will and desire. Ignatius describes the other two types of thought as external and coming from spirits, who may either be good or bad.[26] In the *Exercises*, the need to discern both internal and external thoughts connects the exercitant's "in-

[25] Ignatius, *Spiritual Exercises*, 23. While the "Principle and Foundation" particularly highlights external areas for discernment, i.e., God and creation, its language of desire and elections refers to internal dispositions as well as external relationships.

[26] Ignatius, *Spiritual Exercises*, 32. Ganss indicates God or angelic beings may be good spirits, while devils are the bad spirits. The divine will is known through

ternal" personal conversion toward greater union with God to the exercitant's "external," salvific role in Christ's mission. Distinctions made in one area influence the other. A personal story with an Ignatian interpretation illustrates the relation between these three thoughts and the larger dynamic of conversion for mission.

In kindergarten, one of my classmates was a bit of a bully, and I generally did my best to stay out of her path. One day our teacher sent us home with an important letter for our parents and impressed upon us the responsibility we bore for making sure it got into their hands. I happened to be sitting on the bus behind the bully when my friend and I noticed her letter had fallen out of her backpack and onto the floor. My friend's counsel was to rip it up. At first, I wasn't inclined to follow her suggestion, but then the idea came to me, "Yes! I will strike a blow for all who walk in fear!" I proceeded to rip up the letter and added littering to my crimes by throwing it back on the floor. When the bully noticed her missing letter and saw it in pieces, my dear friend obligingly pointed the finger at me, and I prepared for my life to end. Then, to my surprise and horror, the bully asked in a trembling voice, "Why? Why did you do that?" and began to cry. Suddenly I knew the person who could make a bully cry was not a hero but a monster, a realization that made this sin the headliner for my first confession one year later.

While my friend had certainly not encouraged me to virtue, the other thought—that by doing something mean I could act for justice—seemed to come from "outside" me (I wasn't a perfect kid, but I didn't routinely contemplate vengeance). This external thought impacted my will, or what I chose to do with my freedom, as well as my perception of the false good I chose to pursue. If I had been a five-year-old of greater discernment, I might have realized the distinction between the external thought and my own and made a choice that conformed more to love, such as making sure the letter was returned. Though I lacked such discernment,

---

discerning these spirits. Ganss, *The Spiritual Exercises of Saint Ignatius*, p. 143, no. 4.

the knowledge that I had behaved monstrously was also a thought that came from beyond me, helping me to perceive how I had chosen wrongly, and so to desire forgiveness and to choose conversion toward loving actions.

The goal of both external and internal distinctions is unity. Without separation, no true communication of love, and the gifts of love, between the exercitant, God, and the wider creation may exist: gift and response cannot occur where distinction is not present. Ignatius describes the Contemplation to Attain Love in words reminiscent of Augustine's description of the Trinity discussed in chapter 1:

> Love consists in mutual communication between the two persons. That is, the one who loves gives and communicates to the beloved what he or she has, or a part of what one has or can have; and the beloved in return does the same to the lover. Thus, if the one has knowledge, one gives it to the other who does not; and similarly in regard to honors or riches. Each shares with the other.[27]

The communication of love rests on God's self-gift, which is mediated by Christ and others through the Spirit. By reflecting on God's self-gift in the *Exercises*, exercitants begin to properly understand themselves in relation to God and creation. This proper self-understanding—I am neither God nor someone or something other than myself—both allows the exercitant to receive God's self-gift and to respond through self-gift.

The discernment that acknowledges distinctions between God, others, and oneself allows for the communication of love and thus for apostolic communion. The communication of love is a mutual gift and reception that creates communion; participation in God's saving mission within history is the context in which gift and response are expressed. It is helpful to recall Ignatius's indication

---

[27] Ignatius, *Spiritual Exercises*, 231; see also the description of this exercise as the summit of the *Exercises* in Ganss, *The Spiritual Exercises of Saint Ignatius*, p. 183, no. 117.

that through the *Spiritual Exercises* we learn to overcome ourselves.[28] Communication is a form of self-transcendence. When
we communicate, whether in word or action, we move beyond
ourselves and can be received by others. Distinctions made between themselves, God, and others are integral to the exercitant's
ability to receive the fullness of God's salvific love and also to
communicate this love to others and thus further Christ's salvific
work through self-transcendence.

Imagination and Discernment

Proper distinctions that allow for the communication of love,
and therefore for communion between oneself and others for God's
mission, are promoted throughout the *Exercises* by Ignatius's use
of imagination. Imagination develops the exercitant's capacity to
know God by integrating the exercitant's emotional and physical
life with receiving and responding to God's communication of
love. The imagination is engaged within individual exercises, both
those that promote awareness of the exercitant's sin and those that
invite the exercitant to join in Christ's mission.[29]

In the second week of exercises, Ignatius adds another component to his use of the imagination, the application of the five
senses.[30] In the setting of a thirty-day retreat, this application of
senses occurs at the end of the day, prior to dinner, and involves
a return to the day's earlier contemplations through an imaginative
exploration of the earthly persons and places in the contemplations,
as well as the divine elements. Ganss indicates that the application
of the senses moves the exercitant from meditative to contemplative prayer, that is, the exercitant moves from reflection on salvation history to being entirely present with God within salvation
history.[31] The imaginative exploration of the day's exercises serves

[28] Ignatius, *Spiritual Exercises*, 21.
[29] For example, see Ignatius, *Spiritual Exercises*, section 65, the meditation on
hell, and section 110, the contemplation of the nativity.
[30] Ibid., 121.
[31] Ganss, *The Spiritual Exercises of Saint Ignatius*, pp. 163–65, no. 66.

to integrate more thoroughly the exercitant's intellectual and emotional responses to God, and thus allows the exercitant to rest, entirely and richly, in God.[32]

Hugo Rahner notes the prevalence of two complementary interpretations of the application of senses in the *Spiritual Exercises*. The first interpretation primarily views the application as making the person of Christ and the events of his life, as well as other aspects of salvation history, more accessible to the exercitant's understanding: "This aspect is what I should like to call the 'making present' of mysteries which are otherwise so beyond the grasp of the mind—it is the use of prayer for putting the history of salvation into, as it were, the 'present tense.' "[33] This interpretation views imagination as particularly helpful for those who are new to the exercises and who require greater aid in contemplating the divine mysteries.[34] For instance, consider the impact of entering imaginatively into the fifth chapter of Luke's gospel by putting ourselves into Peter's role as he encounters Jesus: We feel Peter's frustration and fatigue after a night's work with no fish to show for it, experience his anxiety about making ends meet for his family, listen with him to the man who commandeers his boat to speak to the crowd, and join in his disbelief as we follow that man's instruction to cast the nets again (what does *this* guy know about fishing and why am I following *his* instructions?). We also share Peter's astonishment as we see the nets swelling with fish, call with him to our friends for help, strain our legs, backs, and arms to pull the catch onto the boat as the sweat trickles down into our eyes and the lake water splashes over us. Chaos converts to confession as in the midst of all this—the shouting of people at work, boats sinking under their load, fish flapping about on deck—we turn to the one Peter now calls "Lord" and kneel.

---

[32] Ibid. Ganss connects the application of the senses to a growing openness to contemplative prayer.

[33] Rahner, *Ignatius the Theologian*, 192.

[34] Ibid., 191.

Through imagination we "get" Peter because we know how it feels to think our work has been for nothing, and we've likely had the experience of being told how to do our job by someone we think knows nothing about it. We may also learn from Peter that our encounter with Christ happens in the midst of daily life and so be encouraged to imitate his immediate confession of faith rather than putting it off for a "more appropriate" time. The mystery of salvation becomes more present to us because, through our imaginations, we've encountered salvation history personally.

Rahner notes a second interpretation of application of the senses, which perceives imagination as the capacity to know God, developed through the experience of mystical union with God.[35] Imaginative engagement with the created world through the spiritual senses has the potential to become a graced movement into union with the mystery of God. The experience of union with God transcends the temporal and physical world and so transforms the exercitant's vision of the world: all of creation is seen in proper relationship to God, and all creation communicates the divine mystery.[36] This second interpretation moves beyond past aspects of salvation history, such as the earthly life of Christ, to God's salvation at work in the world around us in ways that discernment helps to reveal. If through an imaginative reading of Luke 5 we see that Peter's encounter with and conversion to Jesus happened in the midst of his working life, then we may take a step back from our own lives to look for and wonder about how we respond to God in our own work, and how we are collaborating with God to write the next chapter of salvation history with our lives. Through our imaginations we train ourselves to look for God's presence in all things, including daily experience.

[35] Ibid., 190.

[36] "Everything which is perceived in [sic] seen as coming from God or leading to God. . . . This almost cosmic feeling that all created things perceptible to the senses are bound up together with their 'creator and Lord' (as Ignatius so typically called God) belong to the very essence of Ignatian mysticism." Ibid., 210.

Ultimately, these two interpretations of the application of the senses—making salvation history present and seeing the present as part of salvation history—are, in Rahner's view, complementary:

> This uniting of understanding and heart, reason and imagination, thought and feeling, was what Ignatius wished to teach the exercitant to achieve in the highest form of the Application of the Senses. For him, this form of the Application of the Senses was the very essence of *sentir*—the feeling for the things of God. . . . The soul opens itself to the divine through sense perceptions which are almost as immediate as the impressions of the bodily senses. This more elevated form of the Application of the Senses is in no way opposed to the simpler way which Ignatius alluded to with equal clarity. On the contrary—if the soul nourishes itself by putting salvation history into the present tense . . . it will *ipso facto* be preparing itself, gently and unceasingly, to be taken up into God's love and praise, and by reaching out it will find the particular requirements of God's will in its regard.[37]

The application of the senses provides a means by which the physical and the spiritual are joined together in deepening the exercitant's capacity for, and experience of, union with God in ways that make personal history a part of salvation history. This union results in a greater spiritual sensibility amid the physical world and thus a better understanding of how the exercitant participates in Christ's divine mission in her or his own time and place. A similar spiritual sensibility is cultivated by practicing the Ignatian examen: when our day is reviewed with God's assistance, we may become attentive to times we cooperated with or were blind to grace in the day past and so become more attentive to collaborating with God in the day ahead.[38]

[37] Ibid., 207.
[38] See Ignatius, *Spiritual Exercises*, 43.

Humility and Discernment

The Principle and Foundation suggests two key areas in which distinctions must be made in order to facilitate union and thus salvation: between God and the exercitant and between the rest of creation and the exercitant. Central to these distinctions is humility, or the true knowledge of oneself in relation to both God and creation. This knowledge includes the exercitant's awareness of the need for forgiveness and grace as well as the call to join in Christ's mission. Exercitants learn their true identities through the *Exercises* when they come to know their role in salvation history as both recipients and communicators of God's salvation. These two forms of humility, in receiving and communicating salvation, intersect with the exercitant's ability to distinguish between themselves, God, and creation in the *Spiritual Exercises*.

Humility in receiving salvation. The first week of the *Exercises* focuses on developing exercitants' humility in terms of their need for God's salvation. The first and second exercises of this week provide helpful examples of advancement in humility in relation to exercitants' discernment of God and creation.[39] In the first exercise, exercitants interact with salvation history through their memory, reasoning, and will in order to compare their own multiple sins with the singular sins of the angels, of Adam and Eve, and of particular people who have sinned mortally. Exercitants are to draw the contrast between the many ways in which they sin and the grave consequences that even one sin may entail.[40]

The exercise concludes in a colloquy, or dialogue, with Christ on the cross. Ignatius employs colloquies throughout the *Exercises* as invitations to conversation with Christ, as well as with others in salvation history. He intends these dialogues to reflect authentic relationships, describing them in terms of how friends speak to one another or how one might speak to another who has authority.[41]

---

[39] The first and second exercises of the first week may be found in Ignatius, *Spiritual Exercises*, 45–54; 55–61.

[40] Ibid., 50–52.

[41] Ibid., 54.

Through these conversations, the exercitant asks for assistance, admits to wrongdoing, shares anxieties, and seeks advice. If the questions asked in colloquies are merely rhetorical, there is nothing to be learned from another through the dialogue. Sincere questioning, however, indicates that insight or new understanding may be received by drawing on imagination and entering into dialogue. This implies that the exercitant must learn to listen well—to Christ, to one's self, to the retreat director—for the answers to questions.

The exercitant's conversation with Christ in this particular colloquy begins with questions asked of Christ that arise from wonder at the gifts of his incarnation and sacrificial death. Heightened awareness of all Christ has done and offered for our salvation leads the exercitant to a second set of questions: "In a similar way, reflect on yourself and ask: What have I done for Christ? What am I doing for Christ? What ought I to do for Christ?"[42] Questioning one's self in this way helps exercitants to see themselves as needing conversion. Asking what has been done for Christ implies an awareness of one's own participation in the history of sin, while considering what ought to be done for Christ indicates the possibility of distinguishing between one's past actions and future behavior in light of salvation history. Exercitants are moved toward conversion through these questions by coming to understand both intellectually and emotionally the sin that improperly separates them from God, blocking God's communication of love and preventing the exercitant from communicating love to others. Further, as these are questions posed in the midst of a colloquy with Christ, the exercitant ought to expect that authentic answers to these questions will come through Christ, who reveals both our sin and God's mercy. The humility born of this practice of discernment reunites exercitants with Christ by distinguishing between God, who brings salvation through the incarnation and passion, and the exercitant's own radical need of redemption.

[42] Ibid., 53.

Ignatius creates a connection between salvation history and one's own history, such that salvation history is part of the exercitant's memory, and the exercitant's personal history becomes part of salvation history through her or his response to Christ's call. Thus the second exercise of the first week begins in a similar vein to the first, though the remembrance grows more personal as each sin of the exercitant's life is considered.[43] As the exercise continues, exercitants are not to discern whether they possess humility but rather to use humbling examples to reflect on themselves.[44] Exercitants should compare themselves with all human beings and with the angels and saints and then contrast all creation with God to ask: Who am I? The initial responses to this question are dictated by the meditation, which directs exercitants to consider their bodies with abhorrence and to reflect on their sins as poison.[45]

The intended effect of this meditation is akin to a stunning depiction of the Milky Way's vastness with "You Are Here" printed next to an incredibly small dot on the galaxy's outer rim. The relationship between humility and external discernment in Ignatius's thought is particularly seen in the first few of these humbling examples. From self-comparison with other human beings, the angels, and saints, and all members of the created order, exercitants move to distinguishing creation as a whole from God and then distinguishing themselves from God. Interestingly, the questions posed in the exercise are existential: What am I? What are they? These are humbling inquiries because, through them, exercitants describe the differences between God and creation, and thus come to know more truly their own identity in light of their purpose of participation in the divine life. They gain a new perspective on their relationship to God and creation, and through this understanding of difference, they learn how to be united properly to both God and creation.

---

[43] Ibid., 56.
[44] Ibid., 58.
[45] Ibid.

The concluding prompts in this exercise, reflection on one's body and personal sins, are a reminder that Ignatius wrote during the sixteenth century, when Spanish art and spiritual writings tended to vivid, physical descriptions. Language that sounds florid or gruesome to us arose out of Ignatius's own time and culture, and we should be thoughtful about what we import to our own. Denigrating the body is theologically problematic for a faith that celebrates the incarnation and full humanity of Jesus Christ and may be damaging to individuals' understanding of the goodness of their embodied selves. These prompts ought to be reflected on with care but may help us to take seriously the impact of sin, to acknowledge the unchecked physical desires that lead us to serve ourselves and use others, and to accept personal responsibility for sin rather than seeking self-justification.

One last example of humility in receiving salvation is found in the fifth exercise of the first week, which centers on a meditation on the afterlife that is meant to be particularly evocative to the senses. Ignatius encourages the exercitant to see and hear in vivid detail the physical and emotional torment of those condemned to a fiery hell.[46] These severe and terrifying imaginings serve as a way of scaring the exercitant away from sin. They contrast with the end of the exercise, however, which concludes in a dialogue with Christ.[47] This colloquy might be expected to reinforce the exercitant's fears of the pains of hell by depicting Christ as a judge and uncompromising giver of the law; or, if undertaken shallowly, it might lead the exercitant to echo the Pharisee: "God, I thank you that I am not like the other people" (Luke 18:11). While the colloquy is indeed one of thanksgiving, the exercitant's gratitude is rooted in humble awareness of Christ's pity and mercy, which sustains them in life and brings salvation.[48] This exercise reinforces dependence on God, and gives hope that through this earthly life the exercitant will come to enjoy eternal life with Christ.

---

[46] Ibid., 69.
[47] Ibid., 65–72.
[48] Ibid., 71.

Humility in communicating salvation. Humility as true self-knowledge, and therefore as essential to discernment, is not reserved to the reception of salvation; it also appears under the auspices of the exercitant's ability to communicate salvific love to others and thus to cooperate in Christ's mission. This is first found in the opening lines of the Principle and Foundation, where human beings' purpose is described as worship and service of God, which is the path to salvation.[49] Here the emphasis is once again on the distinction between God and the exercitant as creator to creature, but the distinction is contextualized within the exercitant's purpose of adoration, devotion, and service. There is a strong sense that Christ's mission of salvation is one part of our redemption, and that the fullness of our salvation comes through our graced response to his mission. We embrace our redemption when the joy of salvation, learned through humility, leads us to join in Christ's mission. Salvation heals our sinfulness through our communion with God and others: we receive God's offer of mercy and forgiveness and respond by joining in Christ's mission ourselves.

Within the *Spiritual Exercises*, the way to join in Christ's mission is matter for the exercitant's further discernment. Whatever its particular course, however, Ignatius envisions the exercitant's purpose as apostolic. Through their spirituality, exercitants act as witnesses to redemption in Christ and respond to the call of God first known in the realization of their own need for salvation.[50] The second week of the *Exercises* begins with a focus on this call, first imagined as the call of a temporal king and then as the call

---

[49] Ibid., 23.

[50] "The whole church as the people of God is the universal sacrament of salvation. The apostolicity of the whole church is realized in an identity of faith and in the communication of this faith. This is true both for the church as a whole and for an apostolicity of ministry which cannot exist without this element. Universal apostolicity is fundamentally apostolicity of faith, but also includes such elements as service, witness, suffering and struggle." Timothy MacDonald, "Apostolicity," in *The New Dictionary of Theology*, ed. Joseph A. Komonchak, Mary Collins, and Dermot A. Lane (Collegeville, MN: Liturgical Press, 1987), 54.

of Christ the eternal king.[51] Ignatius uses martial imagery reflecting his early adulthood as a solider: Christ's desire is to bring salvation by conquering the world and entering victoriously into the Father's glory. Christ calls those who wish to join him in glory to share now in the painful labor of fulfilling this desire.[52] In the context of this exercise, humility consists in the willingness to take Christ's mission as one's own, rather than to follow one's own way, and thus to come to a more radical identity of intention and action with Christ.

In order to join Christ more completely, however, it is necessary for exercitants to continue distinguishing themselves from Christ, lest either their own thoughts or the influence of the bad spirit be confused with the motions of the good spirit. Ignatius envisions a union with God that still distinguishes between the creator and creature, and which is a process of spiritual development. Such spiritual maturity leads to a deepening trust in all we receive from God. These gifts are not taken for granted but rather are returned to God by increasingly giving ourselves.

Growing in capacity for self-gift may require abandoning physical pleasures and earthly affections so exercitants can authentically affirm: "I wish and desire, and it is my deliberate decision, provided only that it is for your greater service and praise, to imitate you in bearing all injuries and affronts, and any poverty, actual as well as spiritual, if your Most Holy Majesty desires to elect and receive me into such a life and state."[53] Here the connection between continual discernment and participation in Christ's communication of salvation is quite evident, as is the integration of will, intellect, and desire necessary to make an election. Exercitants who wish for a more perfect union with Christ's labor must act continually against those inclinations that oppose the recognition of creaturely identity and thus detract from the ability to serve, praise, and imitate Christ in the communication of salvation to the world.

[51] Ignatius, *Spiritual Exercises*, 91–94.
[52] Ibid., 95.
[53] Ignatius, *Spiritual Exercises*, 97–98. Ganss, *The Spiritual Exercises of Saint Ignatius*, p. 161, no. 59.

The opposition between pride and humility in connection with apostolic service is most dramatically presented through the meditation on the two standards (rallying flags) of Christ and Lucifer. It is noteworthy that this meditation comes just after Ignatius asks the exercitant to consider Christ's call to personal service, in other words, the particular way the exercitant will join Christ's mission through an election.[54] In the first part of the meditation, Lucifer opposes humanity's true purpose of worship and service as stated in the Principle and Foundation. Rather than overcoming themselves, Lucifer plans for human beings to be mired in their desire for wealth, worldly prestige, and pride.[55] Christ's address counters the call of Lucifer, directing his "servants and friends" to attract others by drawing them to desire poverty rather than riches, to choose censure and derision over worldly honor, and to cultivate humility rather than pride.[56] Thus the exercitant begins by meditating on the call of Lucifer, cast in terms of pride and the diminishment of the exercitant's human nature, which in turn leads others to disordered desires. Conversely, the meditation on Christ's call links the exercitant's humility with her or his ability to communicate salvific love by attracting others to grow in humility themselves. The exercitant's personal salvation is bound up with the salvation of others as well.

Indifference and Discernment

The connection between riches, worldly honor, and pride requires that a further distinction be made, not only between God and the exercitant, but also between other creatures and the exercitant, a discernment of indifference. The Principle and Foundation describes indifference as central to the exercitant's proper relationship to creation in light of their own creaturely purpose of worship and service.[57] Creation is cast in the role of being an aid to humans in reaching their true end and so is to be used or avoided to the

[54] Ibid., 135–48.
[55] Ibid., 142.
[56] Ibid., 146.
[57] Ibid., 23.

degree it advances or impedes humanity's purpose. Yet Ignatius does not ultimately promote a utilitarian relationship with creation but rather a relationship based on indifference. Ganss indicates that indifference means "undetermined to one thing or option rather than another; impartial, unbiased, with decision suspended until the reasons for a wise choice are learned; still undecided. In no way does it mean unconcerned or unimportant. It implies interior freedom from disordered inclinations."[58] Thus the exercitant's indifference should be neither a dismissal nor a denigration of creation. Rather, through indifference, the exercitant recognizes that creation is to be distinguished from God. Other creatures are not our ultimate purpose, nor do they necessarily contribute to our ultimate purpose.

Cultivation of indifference allows exercitants to resist a utilitarian relationship with other human beings as well as with the natural world. Exercitants distinguish other creatures from themselves in order to see all creation in proper relationship to God. Ignatius indicates that other creatures may help us toward our true purpose; however, this purpose is an apostolic service to God through reception and communication of Christ's salvation. Therefore indifference to other creatures allows exercitants to make choices that are for God's glory, rather than using other creatures for one's own ends through abuse, objectification, and manipulation.

Conversely, indifference confirms our creaturely dependence on the creator, thus reinforcing humility and discernment with regard to God's will. For example, in a meditation preceding the section on elections in the second week, Ignatius asks the exercitant to think of three persons who each have a large sum of money. They recognize the obstacle wealth poses to their true purpose and so desire to be rid of its spiritual load.[59] The first type of person does not take advantage of the means to be rid of their burden

---

[58] Ganss, *The Spiritual Exercises of Saint Ignatius*, p. 151, no. 20.
[59] Ignatius, *Spiritual Exercises*, 150.

despite their desire for peace in God.[60] The second type shares the desire for God's peace but wants to be unburdened of the attachment to wealth while keeping the money. They prioritize pleasing themselves over openness to God's will.[61] The third type represents those who have learned to be indifferent. This group of persons likewise wishes to be free of the attachment to wealth but is indifferent to the uses of the money itself and so wishes to retain or surrender it based only on discernment of God's will and determination of what is most for God's glory.[62] Through meditations such as this, Ignatius encourages exercitants to develop indifference as they discern the proper relationship between themselves, God, and the created world.

In the final section prior to beginning the specific work of making the election, which commits exercitants to their discerned response to God, Ignatius connects indifference with three ways of being humble. Ganss notes that Ignatius's description of these three modes is meant to bring the exercitants' affections into alignment with the indifference they first perceived intellectually. Love for Christ in the face of elections that may require sacrifice of exercitants' earthly desires is strengthened by joining the heart and head in a shared commitment.[63] Ignatius describes humility in its first mode as a requirement for salvation that enables one to be obedient to God. Humble persons commit to eschewing mortal sin by upholding divine and human laws at the expense of personal power, or even of their own lives.[64] The second mode of humility is of greater perfection than the first. Here humility is marked by the avoidance of even venial sin and indifference between choices that are of the same effectiveness in serving God. The third mode is the most perfect. In this way of humility, the exercitants remain indifferent to options that may equally praise

[60] Ibid., 153.
[61] Ibid., 154.
[62] Ibid., 155.
[63] Ganss, *The Spiritual Exercises of Saint Ignatius,* p. 200, no. 173.
[64] Ignatius, *Spiritual Exercises,* 165.

God but is willing to choose poverty, dishonor, and the appearance of foolishness in order to more fully imitate Christ's own earthly life.[65]

Movement toward the third, most perfect type of humility in imitation of Christ's self-emptying in the incarnation is facilitated in the final two weeks of exercises. In these weeks, the exercitant comes to greater union with God through reflections on the mysteries of Christ's life, death, and resurrection.[66] In light of these three modes of humility, Ganss recalls the account of Pedro Ortiz, whom Ignatius directed in the exercises. Ortiz describes the three ways of being humble as "three kinds and degrees *of love* of God and desire to obey and imitate and serve his Divine Majesty."[67] Humility is not self-annihilation for Ignatius but rather allows the exercitant to love most authentically through self-gift. Ganss indicates that placing these modes of humility prior to making an election situates indifference within the exercitant's deepening love of God.[68] The humility that distinguishes between the exercitant and God is tied to saving union with God, which is the result of the communication of the love between God and the exercitant. In turn, through this union, the exercitant seeks to communicate love to others in the way which most glorifies God by imitating Christ's communication of love.

Consolation, Desolation, and Discernment

The definition Ganss offers of the meaning of discernment in the *Spiritual Exercises* means Ignatius's two sets of rules for the discernment of spirits are part of a larger process of spiritual growth in which the exercitant learns to make distinctions in order to gain unity with God through Christ.[69] Central to these rules are

[65] Ibid., 167.

[66] See Ganss, *The Spiritual Exercises of Saint Ignatius*, pp. 173–74, no. 86.

[67] Ibid.; emphasis in original. Ganss believes Ortiz's notes likely correspond with conversations he shared with Ignatius on this section of the *Exercises*.

[68] Ibid.

[69] Ignatius, *Spiritual Exercises*, 313–27, 328–36.

experiences of "desolation" and "consolation." Spiritual consolation is when the soul is inspired interiorly to passionate love for
God. In consolation, the exercitant loves creation in relation to
God and is moved to grief for sin and its consequences as well as
to joy for service. Consolation expands the virtues of faith, hope,
and love and is marked by a peaceful calm as the exercitant is
drawn to God and salvation.[70]

In Ignatius's definition of consolation, we see again the theme
of indifference that provides the exercitant the freedom to receive
salvation and respond with a whole heart, as creation is loved in
light of the creator rather than in place of the creator.[71] Consolation
may be present when exercitants seek to acknowledge distinction
from and need for God through repentance and also when exercitants seek union with God through service and praise. Even
recognition of sin can be an experience of consolation, as through
it the exercitant may become aware of God's loving mercy. Finally,
Ignatius indicates that tranquillity and peace come from the proper
union of the exercitant with God as creature to creator; the redeem-
ing love of God and the exercitant's response to it unifies while
maintaining distinctions.

Desolation is described as a movement from spiritual grouchi-
ness to spiritual stagnation that dims the soul, drawing it to disordered desires and anxious tumult. In desolation, the exercitant
is moved away from indifference and toward an improper discernment, or distinction, between self and creation, which is contrary
to the exercitant's true purpose. Experiences of desolation have
repercussions for the exercitant's relationship with God as well.
As faith diminishes, hope and love dissolve into a separation
between the exercitant and God.[72] Rather than union with God
and movement toward sharing in Christ's work, in desolation the
exercitant is estranged from God. This is not a true distinction
between creature and creator allowing for mutual self-gift but is

[70] Ibid., 316.
[71] Ibid., 50.
[72] Ibid., 317.

"loved in the light of the Creator." [71]

rather a divorce between the exercitant and their ultimate purpose that blocks the mutual communication of love.

Finally, it is important for the exercitant to reflect carefully on experiences of desolation and consolation. For Ignatius, consolations and desolations come from outside the exercitant and therefore are to be distinguished from the exercitant's own thoughts. Further, the good spirit may allow desolation, while the bad spirit may bring false consolation. Thus desolation from the good spirit may be an occasion for the exercitant's further discernment of dependence on God and can be a reminder that consolations are themselves gifts of God that cannot simply be conjured at will.[73] Conversely, the bad spirit may induce consolation in order to build pride that separates the exercitant from union with God. Discerning consolations and desolations requires spiritual maturity and deep self-knowledge, including the exercitant's willingness to investigate the embodied integration of emotional and intellectual life with spirituality.

IV. A Spirituality of Discernment

This chapter began by exploring Philip Sheldrake's working definition of spirituality as a "conscious human response to God that is both personal and ecclesial" in order to set forth some of the constitutive aspects of spirituality.[74] Returning to this definition shows how the *Exercises* creates an Ignatian school of spirituality that forms the exercitant as a learner in a particular way.

The spirituality developed by the *Spiritual Exercises* incorporates each of the components in Sheldrake's definition. First, consciousness: Ignatian spirituality engages exercitants in a process of active reflection on their identity and role in the unfolding drama of salvation history. That reflection is not simply oriented to making a discernment but rather is itself a process of discernment. Further,

[73] Ibid., 322.
[74] Sheldrake, *Spirituality and History*, 45.

through discernment, the exercitant learns not only to distinguish emotions and desires but also to integrate them into an active reception of God's salvation and to respond through union with Christ's mission.

Second, the response to God: As discussed above, through the *Exercises* the exercitants are conscious not simply of the need to receive salvation but also of the call to communicate salvation to others. Exercitants learn to identify themselves as creatures in proper relationship to God, from whom they receive salvation in a communication of love. Proper relationships are established as well with other creatures, with whom exercitants share salvation as well as a salvific purpose. Discerned humility grounds the exercitants' response to God's saving work in the past and present and orients the exercitants to a future of greater collaboration with Christ's ongoing mission.

Further, through the imagination's integration of the intellect, emotions, and embodiment, the *Exercises* teaches exercitants to be spirituality sensible in the midst of the temporal world. This sensibility deepens their capacity to join in Christ's mission. Exercitants are better able to respond to God through their communication of salvation to others because their discernments have resulted in a greater understanding of God. This understanding transcends the world through union with God and thus transforms how the world is perceived: a new spiritual sensibility for creation's relationship to God and one's place within salvation history is gained.

Third, the *Spiritual Exercises* has both personal and ecclesial aspects. Exercitants grow in awareness of the link between the history of sin and themselves and discover a call to share in Christ's mission with a company of saints. Exercitants come to know God's offer of salvation through reflection on revelation as it is transmitted through salvation history. The discerning reception of this history in turn allows exercitants to collaborate with Christ by communicating salvation to others, thus creating ongoing histories of redemption.

Learning through a spirituality of discernment. The spirituality of the *Exercises* develops exercitants into persons of discernment through learning. Most fundamental for this formation is learning to cultivate humility and thus coming to know one's true identity in relationship to God and creation. By learning their identity as recipients of salvation, exercitants prepare to become communicators of salvation; they make decisions that correspond to their personal role in Christ's mission. While the *Exercises* is often undertaken in order to discern one's state in life, the broader meaning of discernment for Ignatius, of distinguishing and separating, means that discernment is more properly considered a habitual disposition than a project undertaken only for a particularly momentous decision. Discernment as a virtue is central to continually learning one's true identity, and thus to learning how to receive and communicate salvation habitually.

Further, the *Spiritual Exercises* accentuates learning in exercitants by emphasizing what is received from God and through others. Reception is spiritually prior to the exercitants' consideration of what they may in turn give to others in union with Christ. Reception in this spirituality is not passive; rather, the *Exercises* helps exercitants to actively receive Christ's communication of love by learning their sins and need for salvation. The exercitants' agency does not take away from the initiative of God in giving this gift; rather, the *Exercises* underscores the necessity of coming to a deeper knowledge of one's identity in the matrix of sin and grace that constitutes salvation history.

Discernment is not a private endeavor within the *Spiritual Exercises* and neither is learning. As suggested above, discernment itself concerns the relationship among the exercitant, God, and creation. The exercitant makes distinctions through colloquies with Christ, by considering the examples of angels, saints, and sinners, and with the aid of a retreat director. Thus the *Exercises* requires that the exercitant prayerfully listen to others and learn from exemplars. Further, this communal endeavor is undertaken not only for the sake of one's own salvation but also so that the exercitant might join in Christ's saving mission for the world. In this spirituality, learning has implications both for the exercitant's union with God and others and for the exercitant's ability to help others grow in union with God.

V. Conclusion

Learning is made explicit through a spirituality that consciously engages with the authentic, limited, communal, and transformative ways in which God's self-gift is received and responded to. Through the *Spiritual Exercises*, we can gain insight into what it means to learn discerningly in relation to these four elements and to become persons of discernment through spirituality.

Authentic discernment. The *Spiritual Exercises* promotes authentic discernment by developing the exercitant's ability to hear the call of Christ and respond through self-gift. This occurs through exercises that not only recount salvation history but also encourage reflection on how salvation is made present through the exercitant's personal history. Authenticity is vocational in the *Spiritual Exercises*. In other words, by coming to understand not only the need to receive salvation but also the call to share salvation with others, the exercitant grows in holiness and enters more deeply into true communion with God.

To describe authenticity as vocational is not to limit discernment to the determination of a particular calling. Rather, the *Exercises* provides a larger landscape for our call to join in Christ's mission: we discern our vocations in light of our final purpose, which is union with God and others. While our particular vocational path may be discerned, it is also necessary to learn how to walk this path in the way which responds most authentically to the salvation God offers us. An authentic response takes into account both the way that God saves—through the communication of love—and how we in turn are called to take part personally in the continuation of that communication through our vocation.

Limited discernment. Learning to distinguish is an essential aspect of discernment. Without the ability to distinguish between God, others, and ourselves, we lose the sense of the need to receive from others and to offer ourselves to others. Distinctions might appear at first to oppose communion. Yet in the *Spiritual Exercises* distinctions are necessary for communion, because it is only by recognizing the fact of our limitations that we are able to acknowledge our need for God's grace as it is communicated through salvation history. Distinctions help us realize not only our creaturely limitations but also the limitations that sin places on us. Through discernment we recognize our dependence on our creator, and the mercy extended to us by Christ.

We must also recognize our distinction from others in order to join with Christ in communicating salvation. Discernment helps us to perceive the differences between Christ's mission and our own hopes and intents and thus to reform our will to better correspond with Christ's calling. Central to making those distinctions is the discernment of spirits that helps us be attuned to our own choices and desires as well as to external forces that may bring us closer to or further from Christ.

Communal discernment. Joining in Christ's mission means that discernment is not undertaken simply for ourselves alone but for others' sake as well. Our path to holiness via our vocation is walked by sharing in the saving mission of Christ. Further, while this service is personal, it is not ours alone but rather a call to mission shared by all. Our discovery of Christ's mission and his invitation to join in it involves reflection on salvation history, as well as conversation with Christ as we open ourselves to learning our true identity and calling via dialogue. Hearing God's response also requires learning to trust through spiritual intimacy with others, such as the retreat director, who help us to pay attention and work through God's communication so that we may receive it as authentically as possible.

Further, when combined with the proper distinctions among God, ourselves, and others, the communal aspects of discernment mean that while our discernment serves others, it cannot simply take the place of others' discernments. Rather, if it is necessary for each person to make discernments, then we must take into account how others have learned to discern their reception and response to God's call in salvation history. To consider someone else as incapable of authentic discernment is to treat them as an object rather than as a subject with whom I am called to a shared mission. On the other hand, acknowledging our shared limitations as learners can lead us to communal engagement in discernment as a continuous process rather than as a singular event.

Transformative discernment. The authentic, limited, and communal discernments described above each contribute to discernments that transform our ability to imagine the world. This imaginative shift involves the ability to discover our vocational identity by perceiving more deeply our proper relationship to God and others. Through imagination, salvation history does not remain in the distant past but instead becomes a part of our own memory, even as our present moment becomes a part of this history's continuation.

Once we are able to discover the "now" of salvation history, the world around us ceases to be opaque but instead mediates the presence of God and discloses how we may join in Christ's mission in our own time and place. This transformed view of the world means we may learn authentically from all creation. Training ourselves to see the world as authentically communicating God's self-gift requires the distinctions that acknowledge our limitations, while the communal aspects of discernment both form and help us to be open to authentic reception and response. When our ability to perceive God at work is transformed, so too is our ability to cooperate with God's salvific mission by acting within salvation history in ways that not only constitute our own holiness but also are transformative for others as well.

The final chapter will develop in further detail the potential fruits of this spirituality for the bishop's ministry of discerning the *sensus fidelium.* Before doing so, however, it is necessary to address a second way in which our ecclesial imagination is still shifting from institutionalism to a vision of the church as apostolic communion. Spiritualities of discernment will have limited impact without structures of discernment, the topic of the next chapter.

Chapter 4

The Society of Jesus: Structures of Discernment and Processes of Authentication

> *The Society is made up of persons. This is one of the greatest spiritual experiences a General can have: that of understanding spiritually, as it were "from within," so many members of the Society—to enter into contact with them in very varied ways and circumstances, directly and indirectly.*[1]
>
> —Fr. Pedro Arrupe, SJ
> Superior General of the Society of Jesus, 1965–1983

How does a spiritual understanding of others "from within" come about? Surely spiritual understanding is rooted in spiritualities in which our personal and ecclesial response to God is made conscious.[2] The previous chapter looked particularly to Ignatius's *Spiritual Exercises* as formation in such a spirituality. The purpose of the *Exercises* is to form us into persons of discernment—persons who discern habitually and are therefore continually learning to receive and respond to God's self-gift. The discernment fostered

---

[1] Pedro Arrupe, *Essential Writings*, ed. Kevin Burke (Maryknoll, NY: Orbis Books, 2004), 70.

[2] Philip Sheldrake, *Spirituality and History* (Maryknoll, NY: Orbis Books, 1998), 45.

by the *Spiritual Exercises* is one in which distinctions are made among ourselves, God, and others. These discernments, or distinctions, are made in recognition of our personal limitations so that we may more authentically receive God's self-gift, which is our salvation. In our reception of that gift—mediated through others—we grow in familiarity with God through a communication of love that calls us in turn to participate more deeply in Christ's salvific mission of forgiveness and mercy and so enter into a communion of love with God and others.

Yet in order for a spirituality to be sustained and thus be truly transformative, it must also have structures. At times, charism, the gifts of the Spirit for building up the church, and institutions, the church's organizational structures, are seen as opposing one another. The freedom afforded by the Spirit to explore new paths seems hampered by the heavy ballast of the church's institutions, or the exercise of institutional authority may be experienced as narrow, arbitrary, or even vindictive. Conversely, church members may be concerned that those who claim the authority of the Spirit are navigating without the guidance of the community's authoritative tradition, and those in authority may feel pressure from many directions to make a clear decision in the face of complex situations that do not admit of simple answers and that have profound consequences on people and their communities. In the midst of these tensions, it is helpful to view spirituality and structures as mutually dependent on one another. In Genesis 2, God's Spirit is breathed into an earthen body to create human life. Not only individually but also as a church, we need structures of grace to embody the Spirit.[3] These structures may not only support a spiritual understanding of others from within but also hold us accountable so that, like Pedro Arrupe, we may grow in a spiritual understanding.

To explore how structures embody spirituality, this chapter considers the Society of Jesus' structures in relation to the discernment

---

[3] See Kevin Ahern, *Structures of Grace: Catholic Organizations Serving the Common Good* (Maryknoll, NY: Orbis Books, 2015).

of a person formed by years within the Society, whose spirituality is based in the *Exercises* and who has been given an authoritative position within the order: the Jesuit superior.[4] In the Society, all superiors share in the authority of the superior general; their ministry is a delegation of the superior general's ministry on behalf to the Society's members (known as companions). Superiors have authority over a broad variety of communities, from the superior general who is responsible for the flourishing of the Society's mission around the world, to provincial superiors who govern the Society's apostolate in a region, to superiors who minister within smaller, local communities of companions.

As with the last chapter, the ultimate goal of this exploration is not to impose either the Society's spirituality or structures on the larger church; rather, it is to envision potential ecclesial structures to support the bishop's ministry of discernment. Significant differences exist between the ministries of a local church's bishop and a Jesuit community's superior.[5] For our purposes, it is suffi-

---

[4] Unless otherwise noted, the term "superior" in this chapter refers to all those within the Society of Jesus who hold that office, and not only to the superior general. "It is thus from the general as head that all authority of the provincials should flow, from the provincials that of the local superiors, and from the local superiors that of the individual members." The Society of Jesus, *The Constitutions of the Society of Jesus and Their Complementary Norms: A Complete English Translation from the Official Latin Texts*, ed. John W. Padberg (St. Louis, MO: Institute of Jesuit Sources, 1996), [666]. In citations from this work, numbers with brackets refer to sections from *The Constitutions*; without brackets to *The Complementary Norms*. See also John Carroll Futrell, *Making an Apostolic Community of Love: The Role of the Superior in the Society of Jesus According to St. Ignatius of Loyola* (St. Louis, MO: Institute of Jesuit Sources, 1970), 9. Futrell writes that the role of the superior general "is shared vicariously with all the subordinate superiors, since this role is identical on the various levels of its exercise—general, provincial, or local."

[5] To sum up these differences briefly: the bishop's ministry is sacramentally based, and so through his ordination the bishop receives the grace to authoritatively teach, govern, and sanctify. He exercises his ministry in hierarchical communion with the episcopal college and its head, the pope; the bishop's authority, however, is not a participation in or delegation of either collegial or papal authority. Further, the bishop's ministerial authority endures even if he is no longer the local ordinary, for instance, should he retire. In contrast, the Jesuit superior's authority is for governance, and while it may be described as a ministry it is not sacramentally conferred. The superior's authority is a delegation of the superior

cient to note that both ministries involve authoritative discernment to foster an apostolic communion: a community that receives God's self-gift together and responds to God's self-gift through shared mission. As discerners of God's self-gift through and with their communities, the bishop and superior face similar realities: they seek to authentically receive God within history and do so in the face of their personal limitations; they learn about God's self-gift through others, and this communal learning process is potentially transformative for their personal ability to minister for the union and mission of their community.

This chapter unfolds in three parts. First, "Structures Arising from Spirituality" will consider how the *Spiritual Exercises* and a spirituality of discernment are foundational for the Society of Jesus. Ignatian spirituality is integral to the Society's shared life and mission, and the origin and purpose of the Society as well as the role of the superior took shape through communal discernment. Next, "Structuring Mutual Discernment for Shared Mission" discusses the purpose of obedience and authority in the Society as part of a process of authentication leading to the union of wills for a common mission. Finally, "Structural Supports for Authentic Discernment" describes particular aids Jesuit superiors receive in order to minister personally with a discerning love.

I. Structures Arising from Spirituality

The companions in the Society of Jesus share a spiritual heritage fostered by the *Spiritual Exercises*. The *Spiritual Exercises'* significance is codified in *The Constitutions of the Society of Jesus* and the *Complementary Norms* that govern the Society's life. These documents are both concerned with the individual companion's spiritual growth and with advancing the Jesuit's common apostolate, or mission. The *Constitutions* and *Norms* arise from the experiences of Ignatius, the Society's founding companions, and

---

general's authority and continues only as long as he remains assigned to that office.

the generations of companions who followed them.[6] Thus, while these texts express the ideals and best intentions of the Society, they also attempt to actualize these ideals by addressing a range of topics, from forming individual companions, to describing the purpose of the apostolate, to detailing the Society's governance practices.[7]

While the Constitutions include regulations that are of a more formal, juristic tenor, they also convey the spiritual principles that are indispensable to the Society's goals.[8] Antonio de Aldama indi-

---

[6] The number of works included within *The Constitutions of the Society of Jesus* requires some distinctions to be made, both for the sake of clarity and to avoid needless repetition. Within this book, when *Constitutions* is used, the five documents included in *The Constitutions of the Society of Jesus* are being referenced as a whole: Formula of the Institute, General Examen, Declaration on the General Examen, Constitutions, and Declarations on the Constitutions. Constitutions, without italics but with a capital, refers to the fourth document, which is composed of individual constitutions composed by Ignatius as first superior general. This system seems best suited to the needs of this project; other ways of communicating these differentiations may be chosen. See especially Ganss's translation and commentary in George Ganss, trans., *The Constitutions of the Society of Jesus* (St. Louis, MO: Institute for Jesuit Resources, 1970), 356–57. *The Complementary Norms* are meant to be read with the *Constitutions* and make up the second part of the Society's governing law. They were developed from general congregations.

[7] Antonio M. de Aldama, *An Introductory Commentary on the Constitutions*, trans. Aloysius J. Owen (St. Louis, MO: The Institute of Jesuit Sources, 1989), 12. "It is true that the Constitutions are the fruit of experience (what human law is not?), but not of experience alone. To experience must be added reflection on the demands of this vocation and on the specific end of the Society, and spiritual illumination. . . . The Constitutions lead to experience. These laws are not philosophical propositions written for intellectual speculation; they are made for practice, to be observed. Likewise we grant that the observance of these laws (again as in the case of any other law) need not be literal, only conformed to the mind of the legislator. Equally, we grant that it is characteristic of the Ignatian Constitutions (as we shall discuss later) not to be merely procedural, but along with this to furnish a motive, and through it a spirit with which the procedures are to be observed."

[8] The *Spiritual Exercises* is certainly not the only spiritual resource within the Society: "All, even those who have already completed their formation, should strive constantly to nourish and renew their own spiritual lives from those sources that the Church and the Society give us (biblical study, theological reflection, liturgy, Spiritual Exercises, recollections, spiritual reading, and the like)."

cates that in order to interpret the Constitutions well we must keep in mind the relationship between the Society's spirituality and its organizational structures. He describes the Society's mission as its life and indicates that the Constitutions "show us how the body, in which such a life is to be enfleshed, is organized; the manner of structuring the religious order in which [that life] has to be realized."[9] The *Spiritual Exercises* is the privileged source of Jesuit spirituality; its spiritual practices form the companions in love of God and neighbor through humility and a commitment to sharing in Christ's mission of salvation. The organizational structures and practices described in the *Constitutions* and *Norms* are means of consciously choosing the personal and communal response to God that shapes the Society's life and mission.

The *Norms* repeatedly describe the *Spiritual Exercises* as essential to the Society. First, the experience of the exercises is a catalyst to action. As noted in the previous chapter, the various exercises include a call for the exercitant's conversion. This conversion is not only away from sin but is also a conversion—or transformation—toward deeper union with Christ's mission. The Society's "character and charism . . . arise from the Spiritual Exercises," and the experience of the *Exercises* leads to joining in Christ's mission: the salvific communication of love.[10]

Second, the *Spiritual Exercises* is not only a point of departure for the Society's mission but is also essential for sustaining the companions in mission. The *Spiritual Exercises* is the source of the Society's spiritual gifts that allows it to achieve its end, as well as "the living expression of the Ignatian spirit that must temper and interpret all our laws."[11] While the *Exercises* is foundational for a novice's vocational discernment, it is also an ongoing means of

---

Society of Jesus, *Complementary Norms*, 241. Ibid., 227, §1: "Every community of the Society is a faith community that comes together in the Eucharist with others who believe in Christ to celebrate their common faith. More than anything else, our participation at the same table in the Body and Blood of Christ makes us one companionship totally dedicated to Christ's mission in today's world."

[9] Aldama, *An Introductory Commentary*, 14–15.

[10] Society of Jesus, *Complementary Norms*, 2, §1.

[11] Ibid., 8.

each companion's spiritual growth.[12] Since the experience of the need for Christ's salvation and the call to join Christ's mission is discerned habitually, the companions' spirituality is both grounded and dynamic. As the means for the Society's "refreshment and renewal," and for "carrying out of our apostolic mission in a more profound way," the *Exercises* is normally to be undertaken by each companion for eight days each year.[13]

Discernment, so constitutive of the *Spiritual Exercises*, is translated through the *Constitutions* and *Norms* to the Society's structures in order to promote a common mission, or apostolic unity. The fundamental example of discernment within the Society is also revelatory of the Jesuit's spirit of organization and may be discovered in the "Deliberation of the First Fathers." This text records the communal process undertaken in 1539 by the companions as they discerned together: "There was unity of mind and purpose: to seek the gracious and perfect will of God according to the scope of our vocation; but there were various opinions concerning the more effective and more successful means both for ourselves and for our fellowmen."[14] Their discussion, contextualized in days spent in prayer, came to center around two questions. An affirmative answer to the first question, whether the companions should be formally and permanently united, necessitated the second question, whether the companions should make a vow of obedience to one of their members.

The purpose of the vow of obedience was "in order that we might carry out the will of our Lord God more sincerely and with greater praise and merit and, at the same time, carry out the will and command of His Holiness to whom we had most willingly offered our all: will, understanding, strength, and the rest."[15] To

---

[12] Ibid., 46, §2.

[13] Ibid., 231, §1.

[14] "The Deliberation of the First Fathers," in appendix of John Carroll Futrell, *Making an Apostolic Community of Love: The Role of the Superior in the Society of Jesus According to St. Ignatius of Loyola* (St. Louis, MO: Institute of Jesuit Sources, 1970), 1. Numbers reference sections of this text rather than the pages of Futrell's book.

[15] Ibid., 4.

resolve the question of whether to make this vow, the companions chose to practice communal discernment in order to seek the will of God in both prayer and reason.[16] On successive nights, the companions came together to present reasons against and for the vow of obedience. Their discussion flowed from "our usual exercises of prayer, meditation, and reflection" and led to the unanimous decision to vow obedience to a superior "in order that we might better and more exactly fulfill our principal desires of accomplishing the divine will in all things, and in order that the Company might be more surely preserved in being, and finally, that all individual matters that might occur, both spiritual and temporal, might be provided for properly."[17]

This statement of the companions' original reasons for vowing obedience to a superior is important for understanding the superior's role in the Society today. While the passage above refers to the particular decision to have a superior general, the superior general's ministry is shared by local superiors throughout the world. Therefore, the task of a superior is oriented to both communion and mission. Yet the Deliberations' concluding paragraph demonstrates that the decision to vow obedience to one member of the Society did not preclude the ongoing need for communal discernment:

> Retaining the same method of discussion and procedure in all remaining questions, always proposing both sides, we continued in these and other deliberations for nearly three months from the middle of Lent through the feast of John the Baptist. On this day everything was terminated and concluded joyfully and in complete concord of spirit—not without having previously engaged in many vigils and prayers and labors of mind and body before we had deliberated and made our decisions.[18]

---

[16] Ibid., 5. Mutual discernment inclusive of all the companions was not happenstance; the text describes several different possibilities for addressing the question of obedience.

[17] Ibid., 7–8.

[18] Ibid., 9.

In these final paragraphs of the Deliberation, an orientation within the Society to communal discernment is made manifest. With a common apostolic calling in place, individual prayer and reflection are brought together with extensive dialogue as well as obedience and authority in order to discern the will of God for the continuation of that shared mission. While the "Discernment of the First Fathers" may provide a romantic view of the Society's origins, it also offers an originating vision of two complementary aspects of the Society: the discernment necessary for unified apostolic work and the role of the superior in fostering union for mission.

II. Structuring Mutual Discernment for Shared Mission

The Society's early discussions formed how the companions viewed obedience and authority in relation to the mission of their new order, as well as the importance of union for their continued existence and apostolic work. In the *Spiritual Exercises*, union with God is facilitated by making proper distinctions that better allow the exercitant to receive God's salvific communication of love and to communicate that love to others in turn. These discernments cultivate the humility necessary for knowing one's need for God's saving self-gift and one's call to communicate salvation to others. Similarly, apostolic union in the Society is founded on discernment and right relationships in order for communication among the companions to flourish in charity and trust: "If we are thus to hear and respond to the call of God in this kind of world, we must have a discerning attitude both individually and in community. We cannot attain this discerning attitude without self-abnegation, which is the fruit of our joy at the approach of the Kingdom and results from a progressive identification with Christ."[19] Without

---

[19] Society of Jesus, *Complementary Norms*, 223, §4.

communication rooted in ongoing discernment, the companions' joint and ultimate goal of uniting their vocations to Christ's salvific mission will be compromised.

The Constitutions describe a number of situations calling for discernment, from the process undertaken by a novice and the community about his state of life to the discretion called for in determining how to live the vow of poverty.[20] Each discernment, whether mundane or momentous, is ordered toward union with God that is at once personal, communal, and apostolic. Multiple attestations in the *Constitutions* and *Norms* point to the importance of the *Exercises* in creating persons of discernment who are continually coming to know themselves and others in proper relationship to God.

A companion's discernment is undertaken in order to unite his apostolic endeavors to the mission of others in the Society. As noted in chapter 3, such union requires communication, an action that Ignatius closely associates with love.[21] Love is not equivalent to communication but is, for Ignatius, inseparable from communication: love necessitates communication. In the *Spiritual Exercises*, discernments are made in order to receive God's communication of love through others; conversely, in receiving and responding to God's self-gift, we transcend, or go beyond, ourselves by communicating God's love to others in return. Through the communication of love, the Society's shared life and mission is not a fusion but is rather a communion of discerning persons for whom the communication of love is both life and mission. To be in a communion of love is to know God in an authentic, communal, and transformative way, even as we must still acknowledge the limitations placed on knowledge by human finitude and sin.

The communication of love that discernment enables is prescribed by the *Constitutions* and *Norms* in order to make clear the

---

[20] See Society of Jesus, *Constitutions*, [154] and [287].

[21] Ignatius of Loyola, *Spiritual Exercises*, in *Ignatius of Loyola: The Spiritual Exercises and Selected Works*, ed. George E. Ganss, Classics of Western Spirituality (New York: Paulist Press, 1991), 231.

particular occasions and methods by which communication is undertaken for mutual discernment of a shared mission:

> Whatever helps toward the union of the members of this Society among themselves and with their head will also help much toward preserving the well-being of the Society. This is especially the case with the bond of wills, which is the mutual charity and love they have for one another. This bond is strengthened by their getting information and news from one another and having much intercommunication, by their following one same doctrine, and by their being uniform in everything as far as possible, and above all by the bond of obedience, which unites the individuals with their superiors, and the local superiors among themselves and with the provincials, and both the local superiors and provincials with the general, in such a way that the subordination of some to others is diligently preserved.[22]

The goal of unity in mission, here described as the "bond of wills," provides the context for obedience and authority within the Society. Obedience and authority serve the union of wills through what chapter 1 described as a process of authentication.[23] Processes of authentication recognize that no one person or group has access to all truth to the degree that others may be ignored. Rather, these processes promote mutual reception and discernment of the truth through honest dialogue in which church members learn the truth from one another.

In a process of authentication, the truth does not remain external to the one receiving it, as it may when one is obedient to official power rather than to the truth communicated through ministerial office. Instead, truth is received mutually and internally so it can

---

[22] Society of Jesus, *Constitutions*, [821].

[23] In the following consideration of obedience and authority, the intent is to consider what Lash might call the process of "authentication" between the superior and the companion as two authorities within the Society. While obedience and authority are questions within the church as a whole, an exact similarity does not exist between the type of obedience vowed by the companions and the type of obedience that might be generally predicated of all Christians.

be a communal and transformative source of faith and action. The "bond of wills" in the Society is more than a shared agreement; it relies on a shared understanding and perception—a common discernment—of God's presence and call. Ultimately this shared understanding aims at a bond of wills not simply between the superior and a companion, nor even within the Society, but rather between the companions and God. The following sections explore how discernment for obedience and discernment for authority mutually contribute to this union of wills through the communication of love, and how, in turn, this communication of love becomes a process of authentication.

Discerning obedience. Just as humility in the *Exercises* is about the capacity to know oneself in order to foster union with God and others, obedience in the Society is undertaken for unitive, rather than ascetical, purposes. This is shown in the descriptions of obedience. For example, the preface to the first edition of the Constitutions, traditionally attributed to Pedro de Ribadeneira, states: "In matters falling under obedience, not only must our action be guided by the superior's command and our will by his will, but even—something much more difficult—our understanding by his understanding."[24] This statement is rooted in one of the Declarations on the Constitutions:

> The command of obedience is fulfilled in regard to the execution when the thing commanded is done; in regard to the willing when the one who obeys wills the same things as the one who commands; in regard to the understanding when he forms the same judgment as the one commanding and regards what he is commanded as good. And that obedience is imperfect in which there does not exist, in addition to the execution, also that agreement in willing and judging between him who commands and him who obeys.[25]

[24] Pedro de Ribadeneira, "Preface to the First Edition of the Constitutions," in Society of Jesus, *Constitutions of the Society of Jesus and Their Complementary Norms,* xix.

[25] Society of Jesus, *Constitutions,* [550].

Obedience is therefore not simply formal, manifested by following what the superior wills and fulfilling the superior's command. Rather, it requires a communication of love so complete as
to move the companions toward a shared understanding and
vision.

The importance of obedience that is not merely external but
rather internal is echoed in the Constitutions:

> It is very helpful for making progress and highly necessary
> that all devote themselves to complete obedience, recognizing
> the superior, whoever he is, as being in the place of Christ
> our Lord and maintaining interior reverence and love for him.
> They should obey entirely and promptly, not only by exterior
> execution of what the superior commands, with due fortitude
> and humility and without excuses or complaints, even though
> things are commanded which are difficult and repugnant to
> sensitive nature, but also by striving interiorly to have
> genuine resignation and abnegation of their own wills and
> judgments, bringing their wills and judgments wholly into
> conformity with what the superior wills and judges in all
> things in which no sin is seen, and regarding the superior's
> will and judgment as the rule of their own, so as to conform
> themselves more completely to the first and supreme rule of
> all good will and judgment, which is the Eternal Goodness
> and Wisdom.[26]

Taken alone, this passage from the Constitutions conveys an
uncompromising obedience: the superior's will and judgment is
likened to that of God. The basis on which such a comparison may
be made will be discussed further below. Here, it is important to
note that the goal of obedience is to unite one's will and action
with God's. The purpose of the companion's prompt and complete
obedience in conformity with the superior's will is not to promote
a servile spirituality but rather to actively recognize the distinctions between God's will and his own and so to overcome these
distinctions in a way that parallels the purpose of the *Spiritual
Exercises*. In this sense, the will of the superior acts as a rallying

[26] Ibid., [284].

point for the companions as they seek to act in accord with the will of God and in union with each other.

A similar understanding of obedience that moves beyond the particular authority of the superior is echoed in the General Examen:

> [G]enuine obedience considers, not the person to whom it is offered, but Him for whose sake it is offered; and if it is exercised for the sake of our Creator and Lord alone, then it is the very Lord of everyone who is obeyed. In no manner, therefore, ought one to consider whether it is the cook of the house who gives the order or its superior, or one person rather than another. For, to consider the matter with sound understanding, obedience is not shown either to these persons or for their sake, but to God alone and only for the sake of God our Creator and Lord.[27]

Here it is clear that obedience is related to the companion's humble discernment of his identity in relationship with God. The companion is encouraged to consciously discern the truth of God's self-gift mediated through others, whatever their official degree of authority within the Society's hierarchy.

Seeking union with the will of the superior requires ongoing discernment if obedience is to be transformative of the companion's understanding as well as of his will and actions.

> Therefore, if we are to receive and fulfill our mission through obedience, we must be faithful to that practice of spiritual apostolic discernment, both personal and in community, so central to our way of proceeding, as rooted in the Spiritual Exercises and the Constitutions. This discernment grows and gains strength by the examination of conscience, personal prayer and brotherly dialogue within our community, and the openness to superiors through the account of conscience that inclines us to obedience.[28]

[27] Ibid., [84].
[28] Society of Jesus, *Complementary Norms*, 150, § 2.

Rather than an imposed, ascetic practice, obedience is related to a companion's discernment that is at once spiritual and apostolic, personal and communal. Obedience is discerned in order to gain the understanding that is necessary for a union of wills and so to join in salvific mission with Christ and one's companions. In addition to prayer, dialogue and opening up personal discernments to others is essential for both discernment and obedience.

Conscience places limits on the vow of obedience. This underscores that obedience is not a matter of extinguishing the spiritual agency necessary for discernment but of activating it. If obedience and authority were a zero sum game in the Society, then a companion would be either obedient or disobedient to the will of his superior. Instead, the Constitutions outlines something quite different: a formal way forward that goes beyond exhortations to discern in order to create a process of authentication. If a companion cannot in conscience conform himself to his superior's will—a bond of wills fails to form through discerned, shared understanding of God's will—what we find built into the Society's structure are the next steps in a process of authentication. First, "prayer and contemplation" precede the companion's "sincere dialogue" with his superior, in which the companion can communicate his reasoning.[29] Should this dialogue not lead to a conclusion and if the superior's will is unchanged, then the companion has recourse to higher superiors. If the difficulty in forming a bond of wills still remains, others from outside the Society may be invited by the companion and the superior to "form the individual's conscience more clearly."[30] The Constitutions note: "This procedure cannot be imposed on either the superior or the member. It is entirely voluntary and unofficial, and is nothing more than a new effort to find the divine will."[31] Finally, should the superior and companion remain at an impasse, the superior may consult with other superiors about how to deal with the matter in a way

[29] Ibid., 154.
[30] Ibid.
[31] Ibid.

that shows deference both for the companion's conscience and for the good of the Society as a whole.[32]

If obedience is primarily an ascetical practice, then dialogue toward obedience is not necessary; asceticism is found in obeying and not necessarily in discerning. As a means of unity, however, obedience may well necessitate dialogue—a process of authentication—that aims at creating a shared understanding. In the Society, a discerned obedience is not the end of discussion but rather opens communication. Further, while dialogue aims at the formation of the companion's conscience, the process of dialogue is "a new effort to find the divine will," which suggests this dialogue is not simply a tool a superior uses to facilitate the exercise of his authority but is, rather, an authentically mutual attempt to further receive the mystery of God in ways that may be transformative both for the superior and the companion.[33]

Discerning authority. The superior's exercise of authority is meant to serve unity, not by fiat, but through careful discernment. Such discernment is not primarily of principles but of persons and contexts. It is based in coming to know another not as a projection of oneself but rather as a distinct "thou." Such discernment is necessary in order to gain spiritual understanding of others, which Pedro Arrupe speaks of at this chapter's beginning. In a similar vein, the *Complementary Norms* characterizes the superior's ministry as a spiritual authority made manifest through discerning love:

> After the example of Christ, whose place they hold, superiors should exercise their authority in a spirit of service, desiring not to be served but to serve. Government in the Society should always be spiritual, whereby superiors direct our

---

[32] While this process of authentication is considered to be a norm for dealing with situations in which a bond of wills between superior and companion cannot be reached, the Constitutions also note that a regular opposition between conscience and obedience to the superior's authority may mean vocational discernment on the companion's part is necessary.

[33] Society of Jesus, *Constitutions*, [154].

members with discerning love rather than through external laws, conscious before God of personal responsibility and of the obligation to rule their subjects as sons of God and with regard for the human personality. Government should also be strong where it needs to be, open and sincere.[34]

Exercising authority through discerning love requires the superior to have knowledge of his companions, a knowledge that grows from the seed of the superior's prior, loving self-commitment to his companions and their well-being. Ignatius notes the necessity of the superior's love in a declaration: "Very especially helpful, among other qualities, will be [the superior's] credit and prestige among his subjects, as well as his having and showing love and concern for them, in such a way that the subjects hold the opinion that their superior has the knowledge, desire, and ability to rule them well in our Lord."[35] The love the superior manifests for the companions creates relationships that are crucial for his ability to discern in the service of unity and mission.

Through their relationships with him, the companions are able to share their discernments and convey their consciences to the superior. The account of conscience is not equivalent to an examination of conscience in the sacrament of reconciliation; rather, it is an opportunity for the companions to communicate their discernments to their superior. Again, this disclosure is not envisioned as a tactic used by those in authority to better gauge their "target audience." Rather, receiving his companion's discernments is essential for the superior's capacity to discern authentically:

> The account of conscience, by which the superior becomes able to take part in each one's discernment and to help him therein, is to retain intact its value and vitality as an element of great moment in the spiritual governance of the Society. Therefore, all should give an account of conscience to their superiors, according to the norms and spirit of the Society,

---

[34] Society of Jesus, *Complementary Norms*, 349, §1.
[35] Society of Jesus, *Constitutions*, [667].

inspired by charity, with any obligation under pain of sin always precluded. In addition, the relationships between superiors and their brethren in the Society should be such as to encourage the manifestation of conscience and conversation about spiritual matters.[36]

Hearing his companions' accounts of conscience and participating in others' discernment places the superior in the position of reception necessary for spiritual governance. Forthright manifestations of conscience will include a companion's spiritually discerned experience of both sin and grace, better allowing the superior to care for the companion's flourishing and facilitating the companion's ability to join in communicating salvific love in union with the Society's apostolate.[37] Further, in the *Spiritual Exercises*, the exercitant's reception of salvation is integrally related to the exercitant's ability to join in the communication of salvific love to others. As the recipient of his fellow companions' reflections, the superior learns how God is at work throughout the Society and therefore how to discern the union of wills within the companions he serves.

---

[36] Society of Jesus, *Complementary Norms*, 155, § 1.

[37] "Likewise, the more thoroughly they are aware of the interior and exterior affairs of their subjects, with so much greater diligence, love, and care will they be able to help the subjects and to guard their souls from the various difficulties and dangers which might occur later on. Later, in conformity with our profession and manner or proceeding, we must always be ready to travel about in various parts of the world, on all occasions when the supreme pontiff or our immediate superior orders us. Therefore, to proceed without error in such missions, or in sending some persons and not others, or some for one task and others for different ones, it is not only highly but even supremely important that the superior have complete knowledge of the inclinations and motions of those who are in his charge, and to what defects or sins they have been or are more moved and inclined; so that thus he may direct them better, without placing them beyond the measure of their capacity in dangers or labors greater than they could in our Lord endure with a spirit of love; and also so that the superior, while keeping to himself what he learns in secret, may be better able to organize and arrange what is expedient for the whole body of the Society." Society of Jesus, *Constitutions*, [92].

In his position of authority, the superior's decision represents the unifying will of God as he discerns it with the aid of his companions' discernments. The superior's authoritative discernment is privileged, but not because he has private access to a revelation of God's will that others do not. Rather, the superior's discernment becomes authentic through the depth and breadth of his discernment, undertaken through dialogical engagement with his companions, which aims at discovering the divine will. Trust in the spiritual work of discernment is so strong that when the companions offer their obedience to their superior, they can as well be said to offer God their obedience and thus unify themselves to enact God's will.

Further, the superior contributes to an environment of mutual learning and exchange within the Society: "The superior should endeavor to make his mind clearly known to his confreres and understood by them; and he should take care that they, according to the nature and importance of the matter and in proportion to their own talents and duties, share more fully in his knowledge and concern both for the personal and community life of our members and for their apostolic labors."[38] Again, obedience is not only mandated but also worked toward through the superior's communication of his own discernments and reasoning in relation to the companions' context. Neither obedience nor authority is meant to remain formal and external but rather becomes internal and transformational through the authentic communication of love that unites the companions with Christ and each other.

The superior's ability to enter into this communication is based on his own spiritual advancement as a person of discernment: "In the exercise of authority, the gift of discretion or of discerning love is most desirable. To acquire this virtue, the superior should be free from ill-ordered affections and be closely united and familiar with God, so that he will be docile to the will of Christ, which he should seek out with his subjects and authoritatively make manifest to them."[39] The superior's own ability to discern ought to have

---

[38] Society of Jesus, *Complementary Norms*, 353.
[39] Ibid., 352. See also 350, §1.

been fostered throughout his time in the Society through the *Spiritual Exercises*, spiritual direction, fraternal correction, and experiences of communal discernment. While the superior should be a spiritual exemplar for others, however, he is still developing in his own spiritual response to God and must be challenged to grow in making distinctions among God, others, and himself. Docility—or a willingness to learn—from the will of Christ is embodied in his relationships with other companions and translates to a discerning love through which the superior learns to see the world through God's eyes and to respond as God does through self-gift. Seeking God's will *with* his companions helps the superior to authentically know God's will *for* his companions.

The distinctions the superior makes between himself and his companions are founded on the distinction between himself and God. These distinctions better allow the superior's own humble discernments to be trusted. The superior's recognition of his need of God's saving self-gift identifies him first as the recipient and only second as the co-communicator of salvation. This recognition reinforces the superior's equality with his companions in relation to God: the superior is not alone in receiving and communicating salvific love. Further, it is through others that the superior has received salvific love, and it is through others that the superior can learn more of God's will. Imposition of the superior's will onto God is a violation of humility and marks a lack of discernment; projection of the superior's will onto his companions likewise indicates a lack of discernment between himself and others. When the superior's capacity to make these distinctions is evident to his companions, the decisions he is authorized to make become more easily authenticated and internalized as shared discernments of the will of God. The superior's reception of his companions' discernments through processes of authentication is essential for the kind of obedience and authority that is not merely superficial but instead creates the union of wills necessary for shared mission.[40]

---

[40] "Superiors should readily and often ask for and listen to the counsel of their brethren, of a few or of many, or even of all gathered together, according to the importance and nature of the matter, and even by means of spiritual discernment

III. Structural Supports for Authentic Discernment

In addition to the spirituality in which he is formed throughout his time in the Society, superiors are also aided by the Society in particular ways. These aids reflect the importance of the superior's spirituality for the Society's union and mission, as they are structures that promote the integration of the superior's person and ministry. The superior's dialogically based discernment for unity is not simply meant to be an ideal but rather is the practical means by which a union of love with God and among the companions preserves the companions in their apostolic work. The Society's documents describe five structural aids: the manifestation of conscience and the roles of the consultors, collateral, admonitor, and assistants for provident care.

Manifestation of Conscience. As noted above, the superior must receive his companion's communications of love in order to discern well. To that end, each of the companions has the responsibility to manifest his conscience to the superior:

> Likewise, it should be strongly recommended to all that they should have and show great reverence, especially interior reverence, for their superiors, by considering and reverencing Jesus Christ in them; and from their hearts they should warmly love their superiors as fathers in him. Thus in everything they should proceed in a spirit of charity, keeping nothing exterior or interior hidden from the superiors and desiring them to be informed about everything, so that the superiors may be the better able to direct them in everything along the path of salvation and perfection. For that reason, once a year and as many times more as their superior thinks good, all the

---

carried out in common (according to no. 151, §2). They should gratefully welcome suggestions that their brothers offer spontaneously, but the duty of superiors themselves to decide and enjoin what ought to be done remains intact." Ibid. 354, §1. "Although in regard to these choices and other important or doubtful matters [the superior] may hear the advice of other persons he considers in the Lord will judge soundly, the power to decide will ultimately be his." Society of Jesus, *Constitutions*, [761].

professed and formed coadjutors should be ready to manifest their consciences to him.[41]

In a related section of the *Norms*, the manifestation of conscience's purpose is tied to the Society's mission: "Obedience is always an act of faith and freedom whereby the religious recognizes and embraces the will of God manifested to him by one who has authority to send him in the name of Christ. But both the superior who sends and the companion who is sent gain assurance that the mission is really God's will if it is preceded by special dialogue."[42]

The regular representation of conscience is important for the superior because without it his reception of God's self-gift through others is reduced. Lack of communication means a companion has somehow failed in his own calling to communicate love to others and, of course, this failure is not one-sided if the superior's ministry has not cultivated an environment of reception. Without the manifestation of conscience, the superior is hindered in his ability to know his companions and to gain the "spiritual understanding" to which Pedro Arrupe refers. This in turn results in a reduction of the superior's ability to make authoritative decisions that unify the Society in its apostolic work.

Consultors. In addition to conferring more generally with the companions and receiving their manifestations of conscience, superiors are aided by consultors "that they may more easily discover the will of God."[43] While the advice or consent of the consultors is not generally required for the superior to act, the *Norms* states that "superiors should not act against the unanimous advice of their consultors without the approval of their major superior."[44] Consultors are most often appointed for a superior by the next superior in the Society's hierarchy. When the major

[41] Society of Jesus, *Constitutions*, [551].
[42] Society of Jesus, *Complementary Norms*, 150, §1.
[43] Ibid. 355, § 1.
[44] Ibid. 355, § 2.

superior visits a Jesuit community he is to elicit feedback from the companions regarding current consultors and gain a sense for who might serve well as a consultor in the future. Conversely, superiors of local communities are to forward to the superior general their opinions of provincial consultors after consultation on this matter with their own, local consultors.[45]

The consultors do not replace the need for the superior to consult broadly within his community, yet their institution reinforces the importance of discerning dialogue. Further, aside from the superior general, superiors do not appoint their own consultors. While power dynamics may always be in play, this practice may prevent the superior from limiting those with whom he dialogues to those with whom he already agrees (or who agree with him). While the consultors do not have a deliberative, or determining, vote in the superior's discernment, the fact that the superior cannot act against their unanimous advice means that as a group they have significant authority within the community. Thus they are a means by which the Society moves beyond acknowledging the importance of dialogical discernment to embodying that spirituality in its way of life.

The collateral. A second aid to the superior was conceived in the early days of the Society, though as a structure it has fallen into disuse. This is the position of "collateral," a companion assigned to a mission with a superior who is not under that superior's authority. The collateral was intended to be of service to both the superior and the community of companions by facilitating understanding between the two.

The collateral's role in the community is to act as a counselor to the superior, unconstrained by direct obedience to that superior, though still obligated by his obedience within the Society to act for its united benefit.[46] The superior may ask the collateral to take

[45] Ibid. 356, § 1–2.

[46] "Our community is the entire body of the Society itself, no matter how widely dispersed over the face of the earth. The particular local community to which one belongs at any given moment is, for him, simply a concrete—if, here and now, a privileged—expression of this worldwide brotherhood." Ibid., 314 §2.

on particular tasks; whether he is asked or not, however, it is also the collateral's role to "faithfully" and with "Christian freedom and modesty" communicate to the superior any concerns about the superior's person or office.[47] The collateral is not meant to stand in opposition to the superior; if he and the superior disagree, he is to unite himself to the superior's will unless he is convinced of a wrong, in which case the collateral is to inform the next superior in the Society's hierarchy. Further, the collateral is also to work with the companions to bring about unity among them with regard to decisions of the superior, as well as to promote "esteem and love" of the superior.[48]

In a declaration on the Constitutions, Ignatius indicated two instances in which the collateral should be assigned: either to support a superior who lacks experience or needs additional assistance or to provide a companion to assist the superior in his role on behalf of the community.[49] George Ganss reasons that assigning a collateral was discontinued because, in practice, it did not serve the function it was created to perform.[50] Aldama offers a contrasting view and writes:

> In conceiving of this quite original office of collateral, Ignatius revealed his profound intuition concerning the loneliness which the office of superior entails. It is not enough for the superior to have someone or several individuals to advise him in dubious cases; such advisors can readily be found among the subjects. He needs to have at his side a confidant to whom he can open his heart, overburdened perhaps by the weight of his office, a friend from whom he can receive not only light and counsel but also relief and fraternal help and eventually admonition, not to speak of his pacifying action

---

[47] Society of Jesus, *Constitutions*, [661].

[48] Ibid.

[49] Ibid.

[50] George Ganss, trans., *The Constitutions of the Society of Jesus* (St. Louis, MO: Institute for Jesuit Resources, 1970), 286–87n3. Ganss cites the narration of Juan Alfonso de Polanco (d. 1576) that indicates " 'experience showed that an office of this kind tended more to enervate the practice of obedience than to give any great help to the rector or the subjects' (*PolChron*, II, 457)."

in moments of trouble. All this he will best find in one who is not a subject, but a friend and companion.[51]

Aldama's interpretation is supported by Ignatius's declarations, which describe how the superior ought to interact with the collateral. For instance, Ignatius writes that the superior "ought to have and show special love and respect for [the collateral], conversing familiarly with him so that he in turn may have more courage and ease in expressing his opinion and may see more clearly the matters where he can render help."[52] The superior should encourage the collateral to share his opinions honestly about matters that concern the superior. The superior, however, should also desire that the collateral independently bring to their discussions concerns about the superior's person and office. By personally encouraging the collateral to fulfill his duties, the superior is called to "look and rely upon the collateral as another self, in unity of spirit in our Lord."[53]

In his declarations, Ignatius underscores the importance of the collateral for the superior's discernment. The superior ought to cultivate a relationship with the collateral that allows both the superior and the collateral to hear one another's concerns and insights. Their relationship is one of mutual, humble discernment, in which the superior can be honest about situations he finds perplexing, while the collateral is empowered to raise his own concerns not only about the community in general but also, more particularly, about how the superior is personally ministering to that community. By describing the collateral as "another self,"

[51] Antonio M. de Aldama, *An Introductory Commentary on the Constitutions*, trans. Aloysius J. Owen (St. Louis, MO: The Institute of Jesuit Sources, 1989), 271. Like Ganss, Aldama cites Polanco, but with a different view: "In fact, according to Polanco's testimony, practice showed that it was very useful and even necessary; and a few months before his death Ignatius manifested a desire that each provincial and rector have a 'collateral,' 'even though not all of them had need of it.' MI Epp, X, 129."

[52] Society of Jesus, *Constitutions*, [661].

[53] Ibid.

Ignatius proposes a relationship with the collateral in which the superior can see not only other members of the Society more clearly but also himself. Through their relationship, the superior may come to a more authentic understanding of God, himself, and others.

As noted above, while the office of the collateral has never been formally repealed, it is a structure no longer used by the Society today. John Carroll Futrell indicates, however, that the "greatest human risk of a superior is that he might unwittingly close himself within his own judgment and preconceptions, and nothing would be more fatal to true union with the companions in his community. By having 'another self' with him at all times, he is given the means to attain the spiritual liberty necessary for truly making a community of love."[54] While the collateral could negatively impact the power dynamics of the community, it seems the contributions this ministry could make to the union of the Society should also be given consideration. Though superiors throughout the Society share in the authority of the superior general, the general also receives certain aids for his ministry that are not always extended to the other superiors. In particular, therefore, having a collateral with the freedom and courage to communicate both concerns and affirmations about the superior's "person and office" could help reduce temptations to misuse authority throughout the many centers of the Society's apostolate.

The admonitor. The Society extends "provident care" to the superiors general to ensure his personal well-being in relation to his ministry. This care is more than simply a way to help the superior general achieve a work-life balance (though it does include concern for the general's health). Rather, the Constitutions describe provident care as an "authority" that the Society has in relation to the general.[55]

One structure of authoritative care is the role of admonitor, a ministry that may be made available to other superiors as well.

[54] Futrell, *Apostolic Community of Love*, 78.
[55] Society of Jesus, *Constitutions*, [766].

154 A Ministry of Discernment

The admonitor is to have regard for the superior's soul. For instance, in a section describing the admonitor's relationship with the superior general, the admonitor is required to be attentive to limitations within the superior "regarding his person or his office," to prayerfully consider the matter and, if necessary, to reprove the superior "with due modesty and humility" in order to encourage the superior to better serve and glorify God.[56] As was the case with the collateral, here again we see a structure in the Society that reinforces authenticity as the superior's person and ministry are linked: concerns about either the superior's person or his ministry may be addressed by the admonitor. Unlike the collateral, however, the admonitor is not thought of as another self who helps the superior to bear his responsibilities to the community. Rather, he may either be the superior's confessor or someone else the Society appoints, and he fulfills his role when he perceives that the superior's spiritual integrity is being lost.[57] Thus he acts as an important bulwark against the natural limitations of sin that erode spiritual integrity and authentic union with God and others.

Assistants for provident care. A second structure of the Society's authoritative care for the superior general is the ministry of the assistants for provident care. These four members of the superior general's council are chosen through a general congregation. Assistants are to exemplify a rich combination of pastoral and administrative abilities and be men "adept at conserving peace and union among themselves and with the general," whose love for the order makes them "best equipped to proffer counsel on behalf of the entire Society."[58]

---

[56] Ibid., [770].

[57] "The general's admonitor, who can be chosen freely from the assistants for provident care or from other members of the Society, must be professed of the four solemn vows. He should be a man who is a good religious, familiar with God in prayer, advanced in age, or sound and mature judgment, well-versed in the Institute and matters of the Society, possessing great zeal for the Institute joined to discretion and prudence, not at all credulous or timid; rather he should be such as would be thought acceptable to the superior general and not apt to betray his office or the good of the Society because of human respect." Society of Jesus, *Complementary Norms*, 379 §1.

[58] Ibid., 364, §2–§3.

The superior general's ministry is to ensure "the good government, preservation, and growth of the whole body of the Society."[59] Through his assistants, the Society provides structural supports for the superior general's personal fulfillment of his office. Beyond helping the general with his administration duties, the assistants are also expected to address with the superior general any concerns they may have: "Every third month, the assistant who has been professed for the longest time should convoke the others, and they should consider among themselves whether it seems that the general should be warned about any matter, whether in regard to his own person or to his governance; they should caution him if at least half of them so judge."[60] The admonitor is apt to be the superior general's confessor, and thus their relationship is primarily spiritual rather than administrative; their relationship evolves in relation to the superior's own awareness of faults. In contrast, the assistants observe and experience firsthand how the superior general personally governs the Society and are thus better enabled to judge how the superior general's manner of governance could better serve the Society's preservation in unity. This structure reinforces the Society's sensibility of the integral link between the general's person and office to such a degree that the assistants are also empowered to begin the process of removing the superior general from his ministry should he be unable to fulfill its duties.[61]

IV. Conclusion

In the Society of Jesus, obedience and authority are characterized by discernment for unity. The unity of the Society is for the sake of both the individual companion's salvation and the Society's apostolate, their mission of communicating to others the salvation they have received through God's self-gift in Christ. The Society's

[59] Society of Jesus, *Constitutions*, [719].
[60] Society of Jesus, *Complementary Norms*, 365.
[61] Ibid., 366.

structure was conceived in a process of prayer and dialogical discernment, and its governing documents establish both the centrality of the *Spiritual Exercises* and the necessity of discernment and communication for the order's unity.

Obedience and authority in the Society arise within the discernment of unity and mission. Through processes of authentication, obedience and authority are mutually conditioning aspects of the discernment process in which the companions and their superior come to know and understand the situation, mind, and will of the other. Undertaken in the midst of years of formation in the *Spiritual Exercises*, with its emphasis on discerning one's need for and call to communicate salvific love, these dialogues lead to mutual spiritual development. In turn, dialogue fosters the ability to know and respond to God's will, both for the individual companion and for the Society's common apostolate.

The companion and the superior have responsibility for discerning well "within" themselves and for communicating their discernments to each other in order to enable a shared response to God's will. The superior's spirituality of discernment is particularly influential, as his authoritative decisions serve as a locus for the order's unity. The Society's governing documents suggest the superior's discernment for unity is most fruitful when his spirituality is complemented by particular qualities, most particularly his own ability to communicate love to the companions in such a way that they can confidently share their own discernments with him and in turn trust that the superior's authoritative discernments incorporate what he has learned through his companions. Thus the superior's authority is aided through his commitment to ongoing spiritual growth into a person of discernment who actively receives God's self-gift through his companions.

In developing his ability to offer himself in love to his companions and in deepening his commitment to spiritual growth, the superior is aided by his own spiritual practices as well as by his interactions with his companions. First, and perhaps most evident, is the superior's own ability to be described as a person of discernment. As suggested in the previous chapter, through humility, people of discernment know themselves as creatures of God amid a greater creation, as sinners in need of salvation, and as people whose redemption is caught up in communicating Christ's salvation to others.

The superior's process of coming to learn who he is in relation to God and others should, of course, be fostered throughout his time in the Society. Given the additional weight with which his discernments are invested through his ministry, and in light of his essential role in uniting and preserving the Society, the superior's advancement in discernment must be continually cultivated. The Constitutions indicate that the general, and by extension, all superiors, "ought to employ the time which his health and energies allow him, partly with God, partly with the aforementioned officials and helpers in conferring now with some and now with others, and partly with himself in reflecting privately and thinking out and deciding what should be done with the help and favor of God our Lord."[62] The administrative demands on the superior are great and time consuming; dedicating time to growing in the personal capacity to discern, however, is essential to his good governance of the Society.

The superior's authority and discernment are advanced through "discerning love" or "discrete charity," which are frequently referenced in the *Constitutions* and *Norms*. These phrases describe both the purpose and manner with which discernment is undertaken in relation to the superior's discernment with his companions. Discerning love requires the superior's expression of love for his companions, a love whose reception is greatly aided by the companions' sense of their superior as a person whose commitment to them expresses a genuine desire to come to know them as they are and to govern the Society for the common good. Love for his companions is the precondition of the superior's ability to come to know and understand them; thus it is a love that expresses the willingness to receive and learn from the other. This love better

---

[62] Society of Jesus, *Constitutions*, [809].

enables the superior to assist the individual companions in their spiritual growth as well as to gauge how each companion may shape and contribute to the Society's common mission.

Further, the analysis of the *Spiritual Exercises* in the previous chapter indicated that true communications of love—and thus of the knowledge that love imparts—require distinctions. To communicate is to go beyond one's self and requires that the person we are in dialogue with is truly seen as an "other," a "thou," and thus as a mystery who may never be used as a means to an end. Without such a distinction, and its implicit recognition of the other as another creature in relationship with God, the companion is at risk of becoming a screen upon which the superior's own needs, hopes, frustrations, and motivations are projected. Thus the superior's commitment to his companions is characterized by a discerning love that allows him to come to know God at work in another and which is dependent on his ability to make distinctions between himself and his companions.

The superior learns to discern dialogically through the lessons the *Spiritual Exercises* offers in imaginative dialogue, which prepare and advance the superior's continued growth in discernment. The "other" in the dialogues of the *Exercises*, often Christ, calls exercitants both to conversion and to participation in a salvific mission. The exercitants' attention to their emotional and intellectual responses to these calls is essential for greater union with God. While his companions do not replace Christ in the dialogue, as one who receives others' self-communications, the superior must also pay attention to his interior responses to what he learns from his companions. In other words, while learning about others is an essential part of mutual discernment, it is not sufficient. Rather, the superior's dialogues for discernment are also opportunities for his personal transformation in light of what is received from the other. This conversion may in turn result in a renewed awareness of his own and the order's call to participate in Christ's mission. Transformation is part of what makes the superior's participation in such dialogue truly spiritual and not simply juridical: it is formative of his "conscious human response to God that is both personal and ecclesial."[63] The superior's attentiveness to his response to what he receives from his companions ultimately makes his response to God more conscious and thus deepens his spirituality. The superior's ability to acknowledge his limitations in openness to receiving God authentically through the community of companions makes transformation possible. The possibility of transformation through authentic reception of God's self-gift in turn allows for the Society's union in mission to advance.

The superior's authority and discernment are aided through particular members of the Society. A companion's intent in manifesting his conscience need not be the conversion of his superior; rather, it should be a genuine manifestation of his own discernment in the midst of his experiences of sin and grace. It is a mark of the superior's commitment to his own spiritual growth that he may receive through his companions a personal word of conversion or call to participation in Christ's mission. In addition, the superior is unable to discern well without receiving his companions' honest manifestations of conscience, since he is to discern with and through, and not simply for, others.

Finally, as noted above, some in the Society are charged not only with manifesting their consciences with regard to themselves but also with regard to their perception of the superior's personal spiritual integrity in relation to his office. Even if the position of collateral remains unfulfilled, the consultors, the admonitors, and, in the case of the superior general, the assistants for provident care have both responsibility and authority for helping the superior to retain his spiritual integrity in the context of his ministry. Here we find again the integral connection between the superior's spiritual vitality and his ability to unite the Society.

It is possible to engage in the *Spiritual Exercises* and not become a person of discernment. The presence of structures is no guarantee that the spirituality they are meant to embody will be lived out. Without romanticizing either Ignatian spirituality or Jesuit structures of discernment, however, it is possible to draw from

[63] Sheldrake, *Spirituality and History*, 45.

both these resources inspiration for our ecclesial imagination of the church as an apostolic communion. The final chapter considers how this spirituality and the accompanying structures may be adapted to the bishop's ministry of discernment in the local church.

Chapter 5

Discerning the *Sensus Fidelium*: Episcopal Spirituality and Diocesan Structures

> *I am the good shepherd. I know my own and my own know me, just as the Father knows me and I know the Father. And I lay down my life for the sheep.*
>
> —John 10:14-15

In addresses to seminarians, priests, and bishops, Pope Francis has encouraged pastors to take on "the smell of the sheep," a striking metaphor for describing how pastors ought to be personally impacted by their ministry.[1] He has alluded as well to the idea that pastors minister by accompanying their people "who have a flair for finding new paths."[2] Francis's acknowledgment of that "flair" encourages us to reexamine the "sheep" of the church as more than just a passive herd that needs tending. Rather, bishops shepherd the people of God who are empowered by the Holy

[handwritten: # why is this new?]

---

[1] For example, see Francis, "Homily for Chrism Mass," http://www.news.va /en/news/pope-homily-for-chrism-mass-full-text.

[2] Antonio Spadaro, "A Big Heart Open to God," *America* 209, no. 8 (September 13, 2013), http://americamagazine.org/pope-interview.

Spirit through their baptism to receive God's loving self-gift and to respond with love in return.

The dynamism of self-gift is both the church's communion and the church's mission. As love is communicated for union and mission through histories and cultures, the sense of the faithful becomes an authoritative source for knowing God's revelation in the apostolic tradition. Through the Spirit, we authentically receive God's self-gift both through and despite our limitations of finitude and sin. We receive God's gift communally as it is shared with us through others, and by receiving and responding to that love we are transformed personally, collectively, and for mission. God's gift and our response creates the communion through which we enter into the divine life and are made holy.

Through his baptism, the bishop is a part of the people of God; he is one of the sheep guided and accompanied by Christ, and he is one of the people empowered by the Spirit to receive and respond to God's saving self-gift. Through his ordination, the bishop authoritatively teaches the people of God. Yet at points in the church's history, emphasis was placed so strongly on hierarchical authority that God's self-gift was viewed as trickling down from God to bishops, from bishops to priests and religious, and finally to the laity. This conception of the church, which influenced practice, meant that the church was divided between the hierarchy, empowered by the Spirit to teach, and the laity, rendered docile by the Spirit to learn. Bishops were the successors to the apostles, and the sheep could have little to teach the shepherd about the church's apostolic tradition.

Vatican II began to shift our ecclesial imagination away from the limits of institutionalism to a vision of the church as an apostolic communion. Viewing the church as an apostolic communion means the church as a whole is both learner and teacher.[3] The

---

[3] Francis Sullivan, "The Bishop's Teaching Office," in *Unfailing Practice and Sound Teaching: Reflections on Episcopal Ministry*, ed. David A. Stosur (Collegeville, MN: Liturgical Press, 2003), 72–73. Sullivan writes: "Before a bishop can teach what the Church has handed on to him, he must first listen to it; before he can belong to 'the teaching church' (*Ecclesia docens*) he must belong to the 'learning Church' (*Ecclesia discens*)."

Spirit's activity throughout the church requires us to acknowledge the diverse "knowers" within the church; we must be willing to truly learn from one another in authentic, limited, communal, and transformative ways. Learning requires dialogue, and that we both ask questions and admit we sometimes get the answers wrong. As members of an apostolic communion, all are called to trust the Holy Spirit at work in our learning so that through grace and one another we may faithfully fulfill the purpose to which God calls us.

If through the Holy Spirit the *sensus fidelium* is an authoritative source of the church's knowledge of God, then the bishop must discern, or learn from, the *sensus fidelium* so that his own teaching may be shaped by the local church. How then is the bishop's discernment of the *sensus fidelium* not only a requirement of his office but also formative of his personal holiness? How does the bishop's personal holiness allow him to receive and represent the *sensus fidelium* of the local church? Church documents from Vatican II and following the council begin to address these questions. They describe the local church as fully church and not simply as "a piece" of the universal church; they note the need for a close bond between the bishop and the local church in order for the bishop's ministry to be most pastorally effective; they recommend a number of personal qualities and virtues to help the bishop fulfill his office; and they point to particular occasions when dialogical discernment may be undertaken.

While these church documents embody a shift away from the institutionalism of previous centuries, they do not yet fully envision the link between the bishop's person and ministry within an apostolic communion at the level of the local church. Three absences in these documents are particularly critical areas for further development if the bishop's discernment of the *sensus fidelium* is to contribute to his growth in holiness in such a way that he comes to personally symbolize the faith of the local church. First, episcopal learning is narrowed to best practices in pastoral application rather than viewed as pastoral reception. In other words, the *sensus fidelium* is used as a gauge of teaching effectiveness rather than as a living source of the apostolic tradition that ought to guide the bishop's teaching. Second, the documents tend to emphasize the local church's reception of the universal church over the universal church's reception of the local church. This translates to a lack of sensibility for how the bishop comes to personally symbolize the *sensus fidelium*—to take on the smell of the sheep, in Francis's words—and thus represent the local church's sense of faith within the universal church. Third, the documents do not adequately envision the bishop's formation in holiness through his reception of the *sensus fidelium* or how virtues may be cultivated through his ministry of discernment.

A way to address these critical absences is to consider how spirituality forms the bishop into a person of discernment in relation to his ministry and how diocesan structures embody spirituality by creating processes of authentication to facilitate and strengthen discernment through accountability. This is not to presume that in practice particular bishops do not already engage in discernment and dialogue in order to receive the *sensus fidelium*. It is rather to acknowledge that learning through reception of the *sensus fidelium* has to become a conscious part of the bishop's ministry, and that such learning is not yet fully developed in the practices prescribed by magisterial documents and canon law.

If our ecclesial imagination is to expand to view the bishop as a person of discernment in relation to his ministry, then we must inquire into practices of discernment that cultivate his capacity to know God more authentically by acknowledging limitations, learning communally, and being transformed personally. Such practices place the bishop in a posture of learning and questioning in order to teach and govern well. Organizational structures reinforce and facilitate these practices. Investigating the practices of discernment in the *Spiritual Exercises* provides insight into a spirituality that makes discernment a conscious and continual process of receiving and responding to God. The structures of the Society of Jesus demonstrate how this spirituality is embodied organizationally to support discernment. Through these two sources, we gain a sense of what discernment is and how the bishop might grow personally through discernment, as well as how discernment grounds authority and obedience in a shared understanding, communion, and mission. Processes of authentication and particular persons who aid discernment are also essential for linking the bishop's personal discernment with his ministry.

In order to draw together the bishop's ministry as discussed in chapters 1 and 2 with the insights from the *Spiritual Exercises* and Society of Jesus in chapters 3 and 4, this concluding chapter aims to create a comparative model of discernment and the structures that support it. The first two chapters attempted to build a rich understanding of the church as an apostolic communion and of the bishop's ministry in the local church. The next chapters entered deeply into the spirituality of discernment promoted by the *Exercises* and how this spirituality is built into the structures of the Society of Jesus with particular regard for the superior's discernment. Now we return again to the bishop in the local church to ask what insights from Ignatian spirituality and Jesuit structures may be helpful for the bishop's development into a person of discernment, as well as how to construct local church structures that aid, sustain, and hold the bishop accountable for such development. The goal of this comparative model is not simply to prescribe either Ignatian spirituality to the bishop or Jesuit structures to the local church; rather, it is an exercise in re-imagining the local church and the ministry of the bishop in order to envision what may help the church to better live as a faithful apostolic communion, both in our theories and in our practices.

A blueprint for constructing this model is provided by the first chapter's description of how we receive God's self-gift, or revelation. Our reception of God's self-gift is authentic, limited, communal, and transformative. A person of discernment engages in spiritual practices that cultivate authentic reception, or knowledge, of God by acknowledging limitations, learning communally, and being transformed personally into one who receives and responds well to God. Structures of discernment support and strengthen these spiritual practices for both individuals and communities. To determine how the bishop may learn to receive God more authentically through the *sensus fidelium*, this chapter considers in detail the spiritual practices and structures that help him grow in holiness by becoming a person of discernment through his ministry of discernment. The first section, "Limitations Leading to Union," explores in detail how discerning personal limitations within his ministry may lead the bishop to more deeply receive and respond to God's self-gift and so be united with God and others. "Communal Reception and Processes of Authentication" describes the need for collaborators in discerning dialogue and suggests ways of renovating and constructing diocesan structures. Finally, "Transformative Reception through Diocesan Structures" identifies persons within the local church who may aid the bishop's transformation through the integration of his person and ministry.

I. Limitations Leading to Union

As chapter 2 illustrated, the church asks much of our bishops. The high degree of these expectations alone highlight the limitations bishops—and all ministers—bring to their service. These expectations can also work against the acknowledgment of limitations when combined with other factors. For instance, a genuine desire to serve the church may be coupled with overconfidence in one's self, and blindness to personal sin affects us all. Yet conscious awareness of limitations is essential both to growth in holiness and to the integrity of the bishop's ministry in the local church.

The limitations the *Spiritual Exercises* asks us to acknowledge are at work both in how we receive others' communications of love and in how we respond. For Ignatius, to discern is to make distinctions in order to see more clearly so that we may enter into communion with others more deeply. This parallels the unity of the Trinity: three distinct persons who are one in a communion of love. In human terms, to distinguish ourselves from others is to acknowledge our limitations, which take a variety of forms. Our minds and bodies are finite and thus limited. Our perspectives and experiences provide insight but also limit our vision due to our positions within our cultures and societies. Our sins act as limits on our capacity for love and communion. When Ignatian spirituality encourages us to acknowledge these limitations, to become aware of what distinguishes us from God and others, it is not seeking merely to move around these limitations as obstacles but instead to move through these limitations as we receive and respond to the communication of love.

For Ignatius, the communication of love is both the source of salvation and a call to mission. In the communication of love, we "overcome" ourselves in order to enter into authentic union with God and others, which is our salvation and holiness. Such self-transcendence has two aspects. On the one hand, it requires discernments that allow us to receive the communication of God's love as it is mediated through others; on the other hand, it requires discernments that allow us to respond by communicating God's love as mediators ourselves. In Ignatian spirituality, an inauthentic transcendence occurs when I do not acknowledge the distinctions between myself, God, and others. This is a blindness to my limitations. These limitations both put me in need of God's self-gift and are also obstacles hindering me from receiving God's self-gift.

Only by joining in the communication of love can I overcome myself, and only by acknowledging limitations can I join in the communication of love. Avoiding acknowledging limitations means I am not able to overcome myself but am rather trapped within myself; it is not to be united with others but rather to impose myself upon God and others; it is not a communication of love that builds communion through mutual reception and response but is rather a monologue that drowns out my ability to both truly learn and teach. In order to make these limitations a conscious part of receiving and responding to God, a spirituality of discernment is necessary.

Chapter 3 explored five aspects of discernment within the *Spiritual Exercises*: distinctions made between external and internal thoughts to aid the communication of love; the use of imagination to see the intersection of our personal history with salvation history; the development of humility in receiving and responding to

Christ's mission of salvation; indifference as the capacity to answer Christ's call as fully as possible; and attentiveness to consolations and desolations as markers of growth in becoming persons of discernment. These elements are not linear and discrete steps toward becoming a person of discernment; rather, they are ongoing and intersecting spiritual practices which form persons in habitual discernment. Each of these areas will be considered in the following sections in order to see how discernment of limitations may translate to the bishop's reception of and response to the local church's *sensus fidelium*.

Discerning External and Internal Thoughts

As the bishop is present to the faithful of the local church through his ministry, he must be attentive to many things. The gifts, experiences, and needs of the faithful take shape within the local church's histories and cultures and raise pressing theological, pastoral, and administrative questions. Many are looking to the bishop for answers, and as a minister who desires the good of the local church, it may be tempting, or simply seem most efficient, for him to draw on his own knowledge and intuitions in order to provide immediate solutions. Yet, the bishop is better prepared to make the decisions required by his ministry if he has been consciously growing in his ability to acknowledge the limitations of his own perspective and his need to be guided by the Holy Spirit.

Through limitations, Ignatian spirituality promotes a discerning self-knowledge: a way of knowing ourselves in relationship to others without becoming complacent by thinking that we have already learned everything we need to know about either ourselves or others. Being conscious of our limitations is complex, and for Ignatius it involves making further distinctions between our own internal thoughts and those arising externally from us, which may be from either the good or the bad spirit. Authentic communications of love depend on the ability to distinguish between the thoughts that arise from within ourselves and those thoughts which come externally through the good and bad spirit.

Whether these external thoughts are acknowledged or not, they interact with and shape our internal thoughts, uniting with our will to form our thinking, perceiving, and acting. Acknowledging these distinct types of thoughts and their interactions should allow us to be guided more deeply by the good spirit and to recognize and avoid the guidance of the bad spirit. This very acknowledgment is a recognition of limitation—we can't perceive the path to communion clearly on our own and are susceptible to being taken to a very different destination. There is vulnerability to this acknowledgment, but it is by becoming aware of our vulnerability that we may learn to choose well which paths to follow; without acknowledging limitations, we may navigate haphazardly and risk using faulty coordinates.

The bishop's discernment of external and internal thoughts. By the sacramental character of his office, the bishop is one with the local church. The further question, however, is how the bishop personally enters into communion with the local church both through and for his ministry. The *Spiritual Exercises* suggests a spirituality in which the bishop is formed in acknowledging his limitations and distinguishing himself from God and others. Such acknowledgment is essential for this communion. In acknowledging these distinctions, the bishop can come to perceive the faithful of the local church as his teachers, mediators of the Holy Spirit through whom he may learn to know himself more authentically by receiving their communications of love, which are God's self-gift and the embodiment of the apostolic tradition.

Drawing inspiration from the *Exercises'* use of distinctions, we may analogously describe the *sensus fidelium* as "external" to the bishop, a "thought" that arises from the Holy Spirit. By being attentive to the interaction between his own thoughts and perceptions and those he receives through the *sensus fidelium*, the bishop is able to be guided personally by the Holy Spirit, mediated through the local church's communications of love. Of course, in addition to receiving the *sensus fidelium*, the bishop may also receive other impressions and opinions, some of them from the bad spirit, some neutral or not essential for the communication of love.

The range of external thoughts the bishop receives means that distinguishing thoughts and acknowledging limitations is not a spiritual project to be completed but is rather a spiritual process that must continue in order for the bishop's personal ministry for communion to be most fruitful. Even as the bishop more deeply unites his own faith with that of the local church, these distinctions remain necessary.

Given his position of power and authority within the church, the bishop will need to seek a way to be transparent about his limitations. As the Jesuit superior is to cultivate relationships with his companions that encourage them to disclose themselves to him, so too must the bishop find ways to be transparent about his need to receive the local church. These limitations were ritually symbolized by Archbishop Diarmuid Martin and Cardinal Sean O'Malley when together they washed the feet of victims of sexual abuse and laid prostrate on the floor of Dublin's Pro-Cathedral during a Liturgy of Lament and Repentance in 2011.[4] More recently, Pope Francis has several times publicly acknowledged his personal limitations. For instance, speaking to the crowds on the night of his election, he focused on his ministry as Bishop of Rome and asked for the people's prayers and blessing before he blessed them.[5] In response to an interviewer asking, "Who is Jorge Mario Bergoglio?" Francis responded, "I am a sinner. This is the most accurate definition. It is not a figure of speech, a literary genre. I am a sinner."[6] In the same interview he spoke about his ministry as a Jesuit superior: "I did not always do the necessary consultation. And this was not a good thing. My style of government as a Jesuit at the beginning had many faults." When pressed by a reporter to respond to criticisms of the economic implications of his teaching, Francis replied, "If I have not had a dialogue with those who criticize, I don't have the right to state an opinion, isolated

---

[4] Lisa Wangsness, "Words of Pain, Contrition in O'Malley's Irish Service," *Boston Globe* website, http://www.boston.com/news/local/massachusetts/articles/2011/02/21/words_of_pain_contrition_in_omalleys_irish_service.

[5] Francis, "Pope Francis: His First Words," The Vatican Today website, http://www.news.va/en/news/pope-francis-his-first-words.

[6] Spadaro, "A Big Heart Open to God."

from dialogue, no?" And when a reporter asked why he had not addressed the needs of the middle class, he replied, "It's a good correction, thanks. You are right. It's an error of mine not to think about this."[7] Through their words and actions, Archbishop Martin, Cardinal O'Malley, and Pope Francis convey awareness of their limitations and their willingness to engage with and learn from others.

Making limitations transparent to the faithful both flows from and reinforces the bishop's self-awareness. Acknowledging limitations and the need to distinguish one's self from God and others, both privately and publically, place the bishop in a position of vulnerability—of not personally knowing all the answers and perhaps of needing to admit some of his past answers have been mistaken. Vulnerability is not a posture many of us assume easily or willingly, which is why it is important that spirituality helps to make awareness of limitations conscious and ongoing, so that the bishop remains open to receiving the local church's communication of love by continually fostering relationships to encourage this communication. The bishop's vulnerability itself calls for faith; its great hope is that by acknowledging limitations, he will come not only to know himself but also God.

Imagination and Salvation History

Recent research suggests that even when using a hands-free device, drivers who are speaking on the phone are susceptible to "inattentional blindness."[8] Caught up in their conversation, drivers still see other vehicles and road signs but are either slow to process or do not remember them. There is an analogy between these findings and what may happen in ministry. Driving along

[7] Gerard O'Connell, "Pope Says He Will Give More Attention to the Middle Class (Full Transcript of Pope's Press Conference)," *America*, "Dispatches," July 13, 2015, http://americamagazine.org/content/dispatches/pope-says-he-will -give-more-attention-middle-class-full-transcript-popes-press.

[8] For example, see David L. Strayer, Frank A. Drews, and William A. Johnston, "Cell Phone–Induced Failures of Visual Attention during Simulated Driving," *Journal of Experimental Psychology: Applied* 9, no. 1 (2003).

the road of the church's historical pilgrimage, the bishop may become so caught up in the demands of doing ministry that, ironically, his ability to minister is diminished. Of course, sometimes the adrenaline rush of a "near miss" on the road can recall a driver to heightened attention; similarly the bishop may experience an extraordinary encounter with another who startles him into a renewed perspective. Yet the bishop is called to more than an occasional awareness of the faithful's presence but rather to a habitual attentiveness to how the Holy Spirit is at work through their lives. Imagination fosters this attentiveness both intellectually and emotionally so the bishop learns to perceive the local church's pilgrimage of faith as part of salvation history.

Imagination is not daydreaming (a way of escaping from reality) but rather is a way of entering into others' experiences and of viewing our own lives from God's perspective. It transforms our vision so that we may be attentive to the Holy Spirit. Our new way of seeing may bring not only joy but also a sense of shock as we perceive God's presence in ways that may not only surprise us but also trouble our assumptions about God's self-gift and what it means to respond faithfully. Imagination is integral for discernment because our imaginations shape what we can perceive, including the ability to see from others' perspectives by moving beyond the boundaries of our own. Further, our intellect, emotions, and physical senses are drawn together through imagination so we may come to know more fully.

The *Spiritual Exercises* encourages us to use our imaginations in two ways: to explore salvation history, and to learn how our own lives are becoming a part of the story of salvation. First, imagination helps us to overcome the "gaps" between ourselves and our ancestors in faith as we enter more deeply into the reality of their stories and encounter God with them. Imaginative engagement with Scripture and tradition is a training ground for recognizing and receiving God's salvation as it has been communicated to diverse people through their histories and cultures. Imagination is also a way of participating in their responses to God's offer of conversion and communion and of considering the shape our own response might take. Second, in Ignatian spirituality, imagination helps us see that salvation history has not ended. Rather, seeing ourselves from God's perspective invites us to envision our lives as the next chapters of this history. Through imagination, we become aware of how God's communication of love is being offered to us within our own time and place, of our need for God's love and mercy, of how we are or are not responding with our own communications of love.

Imagination is a step toward acknowledging limitations authentically because it tells us that we do not have the full picture but must instead learn to see ourselves in new ways and with the aid of others' perspectives. Imagination also reinforces that our salvation is not abstracted from our histories, cultures, and our very bodies but is known through history, culture, and embodiment. Salvation is neither only intellectual nor only emotional but calls us to recognize the relationship between our intellectual and emotional lives in order to receive God's gift and respond to it more entirely by loving with all our heart, mind, soul, and strength (Luke 10:27). Further, through imagination we not only gain a new self-perception but also come to see other creatures as mediators of grace, as those from whom we can receive love and to whom we are asked to respond with love.

Imagination and salvation history in the local church. As the faithful receive and respond to God's saving self-gift incarnated within history and culture, the *sensus fidelium* becomes the story of salvation in the local church. Aided by imagination, the bishop can learn to perceive himself in new ways by entering into the stories of the faithful. This entry is both intellectual and emotional. Imagination cultivates the bishop's understanding and empathy, which are necessary to know others' encounters and responses to God and which increase with practice. Distinctions remain important for the bishop: imagining salvation history is a spiritual process of entering into others' experiences rather than imposing himself on others, of taking seriously others' contexts and perceptions, and of learning others' experiences, emotions, and ways of thinking. Imagination also calls for the bishop's physical entrance into the way faith is incarnated within culture, of attending to the richness of the local church's expressions of faith in art, food,

o becoming a part of that Church.
on their that level.

dance, liturgy, music, social action, and popular piety. Through his senses, the bishop perceives the many mediations of God's presence within the local church.

\ After trying to enter imaginatively into others' experience, the bishop is better prepared to imagine his own life from God's perspective. This is a means for the bishop to see more clearly how God is offering him salvation through the mediation of others. It is particularly an opportunity to grow in his sensibility for how the story of salvation is unfolding in his own life as a member of the local church. Viewing his life from God's perspective is not a narrow vision. Rather, it places the bishop in the larger context of salvation history in which he can see not only himself but also the mediation of God's love to him. The *sensus fidelium* is one form of God's mediation of love to the bishop, and so this exercise in imagination helps the bishop perceive the ways he is being offered salvific love through the local church. Using his imagination to see himself from God's perspective is an affirmation of the bishop's limitations as well as an opening to learning how to authentically overcome those limitations by receiving the *sensus fidelium* as God's saving self-gift.

Humility in Receiving and Responding to Salvation

In the Gospel of Mark, Jesus asks his disciples about his identity: Who do they think he is? While Peter arrives at the right term—"You are the messiah"—it quickly becomes clear he and the other disciples do not understand what it means to be the messiah; they consistently reject Jesus' teaching that suffering and death will precede glory (Mark 8:27-33). Since the disciples misunderstand what it means for Jesus to be the messiah, they misunderstand as well who they ought to be as Jesus' disciples. Instead, it is those who receive healing from Jesus, such as the hemorrhaging woman and blind Bartimaeus, who are aware of their need for salvation and reach out to Jesus in hope and trust. Similarly, we may misunderstand what it means to call Jesus "teacher" if we do not acknowledge that he learned as well, not only as a child, but also through his ministry. When Jesus encounters a Syrophoenician woman, he learns that the kingdom of God goes beyond the Jewish people to include the Gentiles as well (Mark 7:25-30). In a parallel way, the bishop's participation in Christ's teaching ministry not only includes learning from others but also requires it. In his role as teacher, the bishop invites people to know for themselves the love of God through the mercy of Christ and the intimacy of the Holy Spirit. His teaching is empowered by his own knowledge of God's love, not as an abstract idea, but rather as the gift he learns to receive personally as the source and sustenance of his salvation. By receiving and responding to God's gift, the bishop not only comes to know God but also himself and others.

In Ignatian spirituality, distinguishing among ourselves, God, and others and learning to perceive salvation history in a new way contribute to the formation of humility as a virtue. Humility—authentic knowledge of ourselves in relation to God and others—is necessary both to receive others' communications of love and to respond by joining in Christ's salvific mission. Through this humility we learn to overcome ourselves in order to enter more fully into union with God and all creation. The humility that comes from making distinctions—realizing who I am and who I am not—can transform limitations into illuminations of our need for God and others and enlighten our response.

The *Spiritual Exercises* asks exercitants to reflect on "examples that humble," snapshots of salvation history, in order to better understand themselves. In order to emphasize the need to receive God's salvation, these examples are meant to evoke our awareness of both our creaturely and sinful limitations as well as God's love and mercy. The examples themselves draw on the imagination in order to compel us to ask questions that are not merely rhetorical but are instead deeply personal, in particular the question "Who am I?" Further, the *Exercises* encourages seeking the answer to this question in colloquies, or dialogues.

Learning to answer authentically the question "Who am I?" goes beyond a shallow and abstract concession of limitations: of course,

God is God and I am not; of course, I am both part of creation and distinct from other creatures; of course, I am a sinner in need of God's mercy. To deepen and concretize our self-knowledge, the *Exercises* develops awareness of limitations on both the intellectual and emotional levels so that thinking and feeling may consistently shape being and acting. Discernment is not simply something that is "done" but instead who a person of discernment is: a person whose conscious awareness of limitations opens the door to God and others. More particularly, through the *Exercises* this person of discernment asks questions honestly about themselves and searches for answers in dialogue with others.

Answering the question of who we are, not as creatures and sinners generally, but in the particularities of our personal limitations, is to come to know ourselves as well as the God who creates us and offers us the mercy of salvation. By receiving God's salvation we learn to respond in kind by offering ourselves to others. Through our response of self-gift we both accept and participate in Christ's mission of salvation. In the *Spiritual Exercises* this response requires the humility of knowing our limitations: the mission we are called to join is Christ's and not our own; the communication of love we offer is a response to what we have received and not a message of our own devising. Yet in a way our response is distinctive. It marks a transition from our reception of salvation to our personal response, or vocation, which may be shared by others but which we must live uniquely, given our own discernments and our contexts. In other words, the communication of love is a common vocation, but the form of communication our lives take is invested with our particularity.

The bishop's humility. Just as those engaged in the *Spiritual Exercises* cultivate humility by asking questions and engaging in dialogue, so too can the bishop ask questions of others through dialogues. The purpose of these dialogues is to receive and enter into the *sensus fidelium* as salvation history. Here the bishop's prior transparency with the faithful about his own limitations is necessary so they may receive his questions as genuine inquiries rather than an episcopal version of the Socratic method. Rooted in transparency and his genuine desire to learn and understand, the bishop might ask questions, such as: "Will you share with me how you have known God's love?" "Who is Christ for you?" "How do you live out your faith in your daily life, in your family, friendships, work, and community?" "What gives you hope, and what causes despair?" "How is God's mercy at work in your life?" "What is the experience of God's forgiveness like for you? How do you respond?" "What nourishes your faith life?" "What does it mean to live in communion with God and others?" "How do you pray?" "Can you describe for me what God's love is and how to share it with others?" Receiving answers from the faithful may lead to other questions for the bishop's self-reflection: "Who am I in relation to the faithful of the local church, as one called by baptism to be one of the faithful myself?" "How do I know myself as a creature and sinner through the faithful's examples of holiness and brokenness?" "What is God teaching me about my own need for conversion through the witness of the faithful?" "How are God's love and mercy manifest in their lives, and how are they communicating God's love and mercy to me personally in my limitations?"

By making dialogue with the faithful and self-reflection a spiritual exercise in humility, the bishop learns authentically about his need for God's communication of love. He also learns what God's love "looks like," not in an abstract way, but as it is being incarnated within the time and place of the local church, and how this love is tied to his own salvation through the local church. In the Society of Jesus, when the superior receives his companions' discernments, he comes to a greater depth of understanding about both God and how God is at work among the companions. Similarly, when the bishop receives the *sensus fidelium* he comes to know more about God through the faithful's embodiment of the apostolic tradition and gains a sensibility for the Spirit's activity among the people. Reception and the learning that accompanies it is not just "data" coming in; rather, this knowledge of God and sensibility for God's presence is part of the bishop's authentic reception of and conversion to God mediated through others.

As he grows in becoming a person of discernment through his ministry, the bishop's reception of the local church's *sensus fidelium* in turn shapes his own communication of love. His response is itself grounded in acknowledgment of his limitations, through which he comes to learn God's love and mercy. The love of God we receive is the love we are called to return, and here the bishop integrates his personal call to conversion with his vocational response to Christ—his ministry. Of course, the bishop's teaching is not rooted in the *sensus fidelium* alone; however, what he has learned through the *sensus fidelium* about the apostolic tradition incarnated in the local church ought to shape his ministry of teaching, just as learning from the *sensus fidelium* has shaped him personally. Receiving the faithful's sense of how the Spirit is at work leads him to further understand how the faithful may themselves be further united into a missionary communion.

Cultivating Indifference

Among the many qualities of bishops prescribed by *Apostolorum Successores* is personal hospitality for the poor. This hospitality should be embodied in the bishop's way of life, from the clothing he wears, to the place he dwells, to the company he keeps. Yet to truly embrace a simple lifestyle that breaks down barriers between the bishop and those who are often pushed to edges of our communities requires conversion of identity and desire. In other words, personal hospitality to the poor is linked to a deepening identity with Christ that shapes how we choose to live. In the letter to the Galatians, Paul writes: "I have been crucified with Christ; and it is no longer I who live, but it is Christ who lives in me" (2:20). Paul's claim is that through baptism, his identity has been radically reconfigured to Christ so that by participating in Christ's death he participates in Christ's life as well. Living out this baptismal identity involves an ongoing conversion of desire in order to imitate Christ more completely, including his material poverty and solidarity with those who are marginalized. Such a conversion is not merely external, making the bishop more approachable, but is also internal, affecting the way the bishop perceives his ministry, encounters others, and makes decisions.

In the *Spiritual Exercises*, learning to receive and respond to God's communication of love requires the cultivation of indifference. As chapter 3 noted, indifference is not a lack of caring for one's self or others but is rather to become free of attachments that prevent us from responding fully to God. Indifference resists a relationship with other creatures that either utilizes them for our own purposes or idolizes them as our purpose.

Indifference is also important for continual growth in responding to God. It is a reminder that in our limitations we are to entrust ourselves to God. Humility develops indifference because this virtue helps us recognize our creaturely dependence on God as well as how to relate to other creatures as co-communicators of love and collaborators in Christ's mission. Conversely, indifference calls for a deepening humility manifested in a capacity to give ourselves more completely by trusting that all we have and are is from God. To grow in indifference is to love more entirely and thus to overcome ourselves more completely and be joined with Christ's mission more authentically. For Ignatius, progressing in humility through indifference is to move past our own preferences to an openness to the will of God and ultimately to an imitation of Christ's poverty.

The bishop's cultivation of indifference. The need for indifference reminds the bishop that the pastoral virtues outlined by ecclesial documents in chapter 2 are not simply strategies for effective ministry, even though these virtues are essential for ministry. Without indifference, these virtues risk becoming mere tactics for ministerial "success," fostering relationships based in utility rather than in the mutual communication of love. Employing virtues as tactics will personally affect the bishop, but not necessarily in a way that leads to his personal conversion to Christ or helps him overcome himself in order to enter more fully into the local church's communion. Indifference also helps the bishop to trust God, who works through his limitations rather than despite them, and to see others not as competitors but rather as graced communicators of God's love.

Further, as indifference expands the bishop's humility, acknowledging limitations and learning from others can become a continual part of the bishop's personal ministry. Becoming habitually conscious of limitations and of one's authentic relationship to God and others means there is always more to learn about God's communication of love: the bishop is never done discerning the *sensus fidelium* or with coming to more personally symbolize the local church's faith. The ongoing nature of discernment becomes less daunting the more the bishop can perceive through indifference the abundance of God's self-gift, making it easier to surrender himself in response. Conversely, as the bishop learns to receive others and to offer himself more entirely in love, his capacity to imitate and thus "take the place of Christ himself, teacher, shepherd, and priest, and act in his person" grows as well (LG 21).

Ecclesial documents indicate the bishop is to have particular care for the poor and those on the margins of society and of the church. Indifference aids dialogue with and reception of the faithful who have been pushed from the center of their communities, as it contravenes the worldly association of wealth and power with influence. Imitation of Christ's poverty is learned through union with people experiencing poverty. Their knowledge of Christ has a preferential claim on the bishop's reception and teaching of the apostolic tradition.

Indifference helps the bishop to know as well the trappings of ecclesial power and to overcome the limits of his circle of care while preventing the poor and marginalized from becoming a window dressing for charity or justice. By growing in humility through indifference, and coming to a greater personal imitation of Christ's material and spiritual poverty, the bishop may personally minister for justice and solidarity in the local church's communion and mission. Indifference allows the bishop's tutelage by impoverished persons to take root in his own response to God. This may include advocacy with the poor through his teaching, as well as consideration of how best to use diocesan resources for the common good and ways of working for justice within and beyond the church.

Consolations and Desolations

The Holy Spirit's call to grow more deeply in receiving and responding to God's self-gift, and thus to grow in holiness, is embedded in the bishop's own *sensus fidei* (sense of the faithful person). Yet acknowledging limitations, engaging the imagination, and cultivating humility and indifference require making choices about how to respond to God. In the midst of ministry, these choices are not always clear, and it may be difficult for the bishop to know whether his choices are transforming him more deeply into a person of discernment or are simply ratifying comfortable habits that replace the tasks of discernment with the ease of assumptions. While the bishop may be able to look back to see how he has grown spiritually, the demands of ministry also call for a self-awareness in the present moment to help the bishop examine his personal willingness and resistance that may signal either spiritual growth or entropy. Although the spiritual growth needed for discerning the *sensus fidelium* may be difficult, even painful, the *sensus fidelium* is God's revelation received and embodied within history; to discern it is to receive the Good News more fully and to enter into the joy of the Gospel.

Consolations and desolations in the spiritual life help us navigate our limitations by gauging how well we are learning to receive and respond to Christ's salvation. The *Spiritual Exercises* notes that consolations can be present when we recognize our sinfulness and turn to God in conversion, and that desolations can be markers of a spiritual torpor in which we rest not in God but rather within ourselves. Alternatively, Ignatius realizes that consolations may be false and that desolations may provoke us to greater trust in God. Discerning consolations and desolations necessitates awareness of both our limitations and of our growth in learning to overcome ourselves. The counsel of others who can help us see ourselves more clearly is particularly important for this discernment.

Consolations and desolations in the bishop's ministry. As the bishop learns to receive and to respond to the *sensus fidelium*, he may know both consolations and desolations. Desolations may come because personal conversion through reception of the *sensus fidelium* is not an easy path and is one that is walked in the midst of a number of demands. Clergy in diocesan ministry may be particularly susceptible to burnout.[9] Having the counsel of others is particularly important for the bishop both personally and ministerially and will be considered more fully in relation to the bishop's transformative ways of receiving the *sensus fidelium*. Here it can be noted that providing opportunities for the bishop's prayer and spiritual renewal is important for his ability to perceive the call to conversion in desolation, as well as to transform desolation into a call to entrust himself more deeply to God's abundant mercy.

The freedom to acknowledge his limitations and to learn from others may be consoling for the bishop as well, as Augustine himself knew. Knowing God's self-gift through and with the faithful allows the bishop's limitations to become pathways for mercy and vehicles for overcoming himself in union with God and others. And, certainly, should the bishop see the fruits of his labors both personally and ministerially, consolations help to reinforce that he is responding well to God's offer even as humility keeps the continual need for conversion in sight. Consolations may cause difficulty, too, if they become occasions for self-congratulation rather than for humility, or if they encourage the bishop to become complacent in the ongoing process of learning from the faithful.

---

[9] Antony Raj and Karol E. Dean, "Burnout and Depression Among Catholic Priests in India," *Pastoral Psychology* 54, no. 2 (November 2005): 157–71. "The findings revealed that diocesan/secular priests experienced significantly more burnout and depression than religious order priests. These findings are consistent with Virginia (1998), who discovered a significant difference between these two groups in the United States. In addition to reasons previously discussed (e.g., the job of priests is never finished, priests are confronted with people's expectations) the diocesan priests have multiple responsibilities and feel pulled in many directions to perform everything equally well, without being able to set priorities. This tends to lead to more burnout and depression" (166). While the study does not conclude that social support is a significant factor in burnout and depression, the similarity of findings across cultures indicates that "structural and administrative systems can lead to burnout and depression" (168).

Here again, the bishop's own self-awareness of his limitations coupled with the counsel of others is of essential importance.

II. Communal Reception and Processes of Authentication

As one of the baptized, the bishop's faith is communal. Throughout his life and in various ways, he has received and learned to respond to God's self-gift through and with others. The Holy Spirit dwells in this community and makes it one with Christ; the authority of the people of God in the *sensus fidelium* flows from their shared and intimate union with God, arising from their reception and response of self-gift. In ordination, the bishop's authority is not abstracted from that of the people of God; rather, his vocation is a particular type of authority within the people of God. Without continuing to have his own *sensus fidei* shaped by the local as well as the universal church, however, in practice the bishop's authority for teaching, governing, and sanctifying begins to be divorced from the very communion that ought to give it life and purpose. Therefore the bishop's authority is not in competition with the *sensus fidelium* but rather requires engagement with the *sensus fidelium* in order to be fruitful for his ministry. By discerning the *sensus fidelium* of the local church, the bishop listens for, and is obedient to, the Holy Spirit who works within the local church for the union and mission of God's people. Conversely, the bishop's teaching, governing, and sanctifying ministry may be received more authentically by the local church when his authoritative decisions are shaped by discernment.

The history and structures of the Society of Jesus root obedience and authority within a spirituality of discernment. In founding the order, after a process of prayer and dialogue, the first companions came to a shared determination that through the vow of obedience they could more completely fulfill their purpose: to join together in responding to Christ's call to mission. As discussed in chapter 4, however, deciding to have a superior did not end the need for discernment in the Society; rather, communal discernment became a fundamental way of seeking to know and respond to the divine will. The Jesuit superior's authority ideally gains authenticity as it arises out of dialogical discernment, and so his authority is neither a substitute for dialogue nor is dialogue reduced to a tactic.

The superior's discernment is communal in two senses. First, he receives the discernments of his companions through dialogue. This reception is a structure of discernment because it attempts to embody organizationally the principles of spirituality that enliven the Society of Jesus. These dialogues, or manifestations of conscience, are the superior's opportunity to receive his companions' discernments. Through his companions' discernments, the superior learns how they perceive Christ calling them to join in his salvific mission. Manifestations of conscience occur regularly—at least once a year if not more often—and can be part of a process of authentication. A process of authentication is a shared way of seeking the divine will and internalizing it so that God's will becomes one's own will. In the Society, this process is aided by continual formation in a spirituality of discernment through the *Spiritual Exercises*, which each member of the Society is to engage in once a year.

There is a mutuality to the process of authentication: the superior receives his companions' discernments, and through that reception, better comes to know God's call to the Society, both for its members individually and as a whole. Conversely, because his own discernment is informed by his companions' discernments of God's will, the authenticity of the superior's authoritative discernment becomes more easily trusted and received by his companions. Through authentication, authority is more than command, and obedience more than external acquiescence to that command. Rather, obedience is more radical because it is the response to a gift that has been internalized, that has shifted from being another's truth to a shared truth. Conversely, authentication means authority gains resonance because its truths have not been arrived at singly but rather communally. Here there is a parallel between the external thoughts from the good spirit uniting with the exercitant's internal freedom through discernment. The process of authentication allows discernments "external" to the superior or companions to become "internal" in such a way that a union of wills is created within the community.

This union of wills is a second way in which the superior's discernment is communal—in its practical effect. Ultimately, the companions do not merely unite their will with the superior's will; rather, obedience to the will of the superior is characterized as union with God's will. The superior's will has been formed through discerning reception of his companions' discernments, and so his will becomes the effective symbol of God's will. In the Society, God's will is understood as the call to join in Christ's salvific mission by extending the communication of love to others. The superior's discernment is communal in this second sense because it leads to joint discovery of the ways the community will unite with God's will by answering the call to mission.

The Bishop's Communal Discernment

Chapter 2 described several particular opportunities for the bishop to enter into dialogue with the local church: diocesan synods, pastoral visitations, the presbyteral council, the finance council, the pastoral council, coadjutor and auxiliary bishops, and the diocesan curia. To varying degrees, these structures have potential to become structures of discernment as well. They are described in ecclesial documents as opportunities for dialogue about pastoral action as well as about governance of the local church. Yet renovation of these structures is necessary if they are also to become part of a process of authentication in which the bishop discerns the Spirit at work within the local church, comes to symbolize and teach the local church's faith, and engages the local church in mission. Three primary obstacles must be overcome in order for these structures to support processes of authentication. First, discernment of the apostolic faith must be part of dialogue's purpose in the local church. Second, spiritual formation of collaborators in discernment is necessary. Third, processes of authentication require time and sustained relationships to unfold. These obstacles and ways of addressing them are discussed below.

The Purposes of Dialogue

The ecclesial documents reviewed in chapter 2 promote dialogue through diocesan structures; through dialogue the local church is known. The tension in these documents is that dialogue tends to be a well-intentioned strategy whose purpose is unidirectional: the bishop dialogues so that the people of the church will better receive him and, presumably, will also receive the universal church, which the bishop symbolizes through his hierarchal communion with the college of bishops. Dialogue in this sense helps the bishop better know the people so they may receive what he has to offer.

The bishop's ministry of mediating the universal church to the local church through his knowledge of the faithful is essential. It is, however, not sufficient for the church as an apostolic communion. Certainly the bishop has much to learn from the local church about the best approaches to pastoral application. Yet the *sensus fidelium* is more than the local church's Spirit-given disposition to receive the bishop's teaching; it is also the Spirit-empowered capacity of the local church to live the apostolic faith. Thus the bishop can learn more than pastoral application from the *sensus fidelium*: he can learn the apostolic faith itself as it is being lived concretely within the local church.

It is this aspect of the bishop's learning—of the faith that he must also teach—that particularly requires a process of authentication in order for the bishop's personal sense of faith to be shaped by the local church's *sensus fidelium*. As his *sensus fidei* is formed by the *sensus fidelium* through processes of authentication, the bishop becomes a personal symbol of the local church's faith. Since the *sensus fidelium* is the incarnation of faith within history and culture, the bishop is simultaneously becoming more knowledgeable about the context of the local church. Thus the bishop is learning both about the apostolic tradition and about how to teach this tradition in ways that can be meaningfully received by the faithful in both substance and form.

Forming Collaborators in Discernment

The Jesuit superior benefits from being deeply formed in a spirituality of discernment, a spirituality he shares with his companions: there are discernments for him to receive. Certainly the bishop can receive much from members of the local church who have not consciously made discernment a part of their spirituality. For instance, the questions suggested earlier in the chapter for the bishop to pose to the faithful do truly help the bishop learn how the apostolic faith is understood and lived by the faithful. Through these communications of love, the faithful are sharing more than practical advice but also their understanding of God's self-gift. Practice in discernment and in reflection on their lives of faith, however, facilitates the faithful's contributions to the dialogue so they may more fully explain the reasons for their hope (1 Pet 3:15).

In order to become collaborators in discernment, the faithful will need opportunities to grow in discernment themselves through their spirituality. To address this need well, we need not presume the faithful must be formed in the practices of discernment cultivated by the *Spiritual Exercises;* just as the bishop's own practices of discernment need not be formed by Ignatian spirituality, neither must his collaborators. While a shared spirituality of discernment provides a common language and even experience to draw on, the diverse spiritualities of the Christian tradition may offer a variety of approaches to discernment that enrich dialogue. Whether one spirituality or many, prayerful and thoughtful reflection on faith may increase both the likelihood and the fruitfulness of discerning dialogue within the local church. If the bishop is himself a person of discernment, then providing opportunities for the faithful to be formed in discernment can be part of the gift his ministry offers to the local church.

Beyond direct dialogue with the bishop, the faithful's discernment ought to aid them personally by helping them embrace faith more deeply, contribute more fully to parish life, and advance the church's mission more entirely by responding to the needs of the world. In other words, the resources required to develop spiritualities of discernment with the faithful have benefits beyond the need of the bishop to learn from the faithful. To be clear, it is not only the lay faithful who may need formation into persons of discernment. For example, inviting seminarians to explore spiritualities of discernment may lead to a shift from discerning the "big choices" to discernment as a way of life and ministry. The spiritualities seminarians develop may translate to their future roles within the church as persons of discernment whose ministry is characterized by discernment.

Time and Sustained Relationships

While a local church filled to the brim with persons of discernment would itself be a good, on a more practical level, processes of authentication also benefit from sustained personal relationships and regularity. The bishop and his collaborators in discernment must have time and opportunity for building relationships, including not only discerning dialogues but also sharing prayer and open conversation to ground them in worship, mutual respect, and friendship. In order to build up the mutual trust and exchange required by processes of authentication, communal, dialogical discernment must occur regularly and with the bishop present. This is not the case for several of the structures described in chapter 2. Diocesan synods and pastoral visitations are not held frequently; pastoral councils are not canonically required, and where they are established they must meet only once a year; and the frequency of the presbyteral council's meetings depends on statutes drawn up by council members and approved by the bishop. Further, the bishop may send delegates to take his place on visitations and at pastoral council meetings.

Adjusting the expectations for regular meetings as well as the bishop's attendance at those meetings does mean a greater commitment to communal discernment is required of both the bishop and the faithful. This time commitment is a practical obstacle.[10] Yet if structures are to embody spirituality, then those structures ought to reinforce the significance of dialogical discernment for the bishop personally and ministerially as well as help recognize the beneficial impact the faithful's discernment may have for the church's life and mission.

Renovating and Constructing Diocesan Structures

Both renovating diocesan structures and constructing new ones provide better venues for the bishop to engage in processes of authentication with his collaborators in discernment. As with any building project, there are some benefits in starting from scratch: getting to choose the design, being unconstrained by what was built in the past, and tailoring the construction to meet specific needs and fulfill particular hopes. On the other hand, renovating may be beneficial because we don't have to put the time and resources into building new structures but can rather work within the structures we have. Changing existing structures can be difficult but may ultimately help us to retain the benefits of those structures while achieving new goals. Given the presence of several structures with good potential within the church, the following sections suggest renovations of the diocesan pastoral and presbyteral councils and of diocesan synods and pastoral visitations to incorporate discernment and processes of authentication. Conversely, the changing role of laity in the church generally, and more particularly in the United States, after Vatican II requires building a new structure of discernment with lay ecclesial ministers and lay theologians.

---

[10] William D. Borders, "The Bishop as Builder of Community," in *The Ministry of Bishops: Papers from the Collegeville Assembly* (Washington, DC: United States Catholic Conference, 1982), 38. "How does a bishop fulfill these roles of his vocation in a practical way? In a small diocese he can relate with his people on the same personal level that the Apostles did. . . . But a personal model such as that portrayed in Scripture, is hardly possible in a larger diocese."

Renovating the pastoral and presbyteral councils. The pastoral council provides an example of a possible renovation. According to canon law, diocesan pastoral councils are to be established "to the extent that pastoral circumstances suggest it."[11] Given the importance of dialogue with the faithful and the requirement that bishops establish opportunities for the faithful to collaborate in his ministry, it is difficult to imagine a diocese in which pastoral circumstances do not necessitate the establishment of this council, or something similar to it.[12] Canon law also indicates the council "investigates, considers, and imposes practical conclusions about those things which pertain to pastoral works in the diocese."[13] As noted above, this function is important but needs to be expanded if the pastoral council is to fulfill a larger purpose. Should the geographical and/or demographic size of the diocese require it, the council could meet regionally either biannually or quarterly, so the bishop would meet relatively frequently with each of the regional groups that together compose the full council. Not only does this help to build up relationships over time, but as a structure that shapes the bishop's allocation of time, it also keeps the bishop involved in ongoing reception of and discernment with the faithful.

Pastoral council members should be formed in practices of discernment rooted in spiritualities that correspond well to them personally. This will require the bishop to make resources available to members of the council, such as funding for retreat opportunities and ongoing spiritual direction, tuition for theological study, books, videos, and presenters from diverse Catholic spiritual traditions. The purpose of these resources is to help the faithful move from their experience of faith to thoughtful reflection on the substance of their faith. Of course, it may be that the bishop

[11] John P. Beal, James A. Coriden, and Thomas J. Green, eds., *New Commentary on the Code of Canon Law* (New York: Paulist Press, 2000), c. 511.

[12] It may be the case that in particular circumstances the pastoral council's meetings are impeded; those same impediments, however, would exist for the presbyteral and finance councils, which are both mandated by canon law.

[13] *New Commentary on the Code of Canon Law*, c. 511.

needs formation in discernment as well and so could join with the pastoral council members in learning a particular spirituality of discernment.

Care ought to be taken in the composition of the pastoral council. Canon law already indicates that people chosen for the council should represent the demographics of the diocese, including various geographical regions, socioeconomic backgrounds, and vocations.[14] Certainly faithful representing the ethnicities and races constituting the diocese should be included as well, particularly those who are marginalized or oppressed either socially or within the church itself. Further, the preferential option for the poor articulated in Catholic social teaching means persons who are materially poor or marginalized ought to be strongly represented on the council. While canon law indicates members of the pastoral council should be in full communion with the church, in renovating the council to include discernment, space within the council should be open to those whose relationship with the church is more tenuous. Receiving the discernments of those who may be on the church's margins presumes that as a person of discernment, the bishop is able to receive God's communication of love, which is always mediated through his and others' limitations. Finally, the length of an individual's participation in the council needs to strike a balance between the extended time it takes to engage in communal discernment and the opportunity for new voices to take part in the dialogue.

Chapter 4 described particular steps in a process of authentication between a superior and companion that are to be followed should an initial union of wills not be formed between the two. In contrast, the suggested goal of a renovated pastoral council is not for the bishop to direct individual members toward their particular role in the church's mission (though as will be discussed later, mission is an outcome of processes of authentication). Rather, ecclesial documents speak about a union of minds within the local church, a shared understanding, a common sense of the faith. This,

---

[14] Ibid., c. 512, §2.

instead of directing a particular person's vocational path, is the initial purpose of the revised council suggested here. This difference in purpose between the Society and the local churchs' processes of authentication does not, however, remove the need for transparent processes within the council. Without attempting to provide an exhaustive list of these processes, certain principles undergirding them may be identified, such as shared prayer; freedom for disagreement without ecclesial sanctions; the opportunity for all council members to directly communicate their discernments to the bishop and to receive his discernments; and a format for communal dialogue among the council members allowing for respectful mutual exchange and learning. As Pope Francis noted in his opening address to the Extraordinary Synod on the Family, "[I]t is necessary to say all that, in the Lord, one feels the need to say: without polite deference, without hesitation. And, at the same time, one must listen with humility and welcome, with an open heart."[15]

Renovating other diocesan structures with an eye to forming collaborators for discernment is possible and holds promise for the diocese as a whole. For example, forming the presbyteral council members in spiritualities of discernment may translate back to parishes. This would expand the circle of discernment: parish pastors would be in a better position to invite parishioners into discernment for the life and mission of the parish. Conversely, by receiving the discernments of their parishioners, the discernment of these priests is in turn enriched for their work with the presbyteral council and its formation of the bishop. Further, the bishop's college of consultors is drawn from the presbyteral council, thus providing the bishop with another group capable of collaborating with him in discernment. As one of the presbyteral council's tasks

---

[15] Francis, "Greeting of Pope Francis to the Synod Fathers during the First General Congregation of the Third Extraordinary General Assembly of the Synod of Bishops," October 6, 2014, Vatican website, http://w2.vatican.va/content /francesco/en/speeches/2014/october/documents/papa-francesco_20141006 _padri-sinodali.html.

is discernment of the Holy Spirit, renovating this structure would further focus its purpose by intentionally forming its members in discernment of the apostolic tradition present in the *sensus fidelium*.[16] As in other structures of discernment, a prayerful environment coupled with relationship building and the freedom for honest dialogue will be necessary.

Renovating diocesan synods and pastoral visitations. Other diocesan structures may also provide greater numbers of the faithful with a means of entering into processes of authentication with their bishop. Diocesan synods offer a substantial, if irregular, occasion for this dialogue. Ecclesial documents describe the synod as requiring both spiritual and intellectual formation of the faithful. This preparation, coupled with dialogue at the synod itself, is an opportunity for shared investigation of the apostolic tradition as it is being lived out within the local church. This may include prayer on the central issues at hand; the ability to ask further questions in order to better grasp the meaning, intent, and implications of both the *sensus fidelium* and magisterial teaching; and determining points of shared understanding or areas of divergence that require renewed efforts to discern the apostolic tradition and foster a union of minds.

Pastoral visitations offer a more intimate opportunity for this process of authentication to occur within the context of parish life, as well as for the bishop's continued learning from the faithful. The pastoral visitation is particularly important in order for the bishop to receive the *sensus fidelium* in context. For many Catholics, the parish is the center of faith. Catholics are gathered together through their parish to celebrate the sacraments, to be formed in faith, and to be nourished for mission. Yet celebration, formation, and mission are themselves influenced by the larger context in which the faithful live and work. Even within the local church, the discernments of the faithful from a suburban parish may take

[16] Sacred Congregation for Bishops, *Apostolorum Successores*, 182, Vatican website, http://www.vatican.va/roman_curia/congregations/cbishops/documents/rc_con_cbishops_doc_20040222_apostolorum-successores_en.html.

on different qualities and emphases than those of faithful who live in a city center or rural community. In addition, parishes themselves often include faithful of diverse backgrounds and experiences. Differences in ethnicities, races, and cultures, as well as socioeconomics and local histories, influence how the apostolic tradition is both received and expressed. Thus, it is only by undertaking discernment within our histories and cultures that the church can perceive both our communion and our mission. Without a sense for these cultures and histories, the bishop risks missing insights into the apostolic tradition or misinterpreting others' expression of this tradition.

Furthermore, for the bishop, the pastoral visitation becomes an occasion for entering personally into the context of the *sensus fidelium* by joining physically in the faithful's existential experiences. In this way, he may better understand how reception of and response to God's self-gift is taking shape in this time and place. Through the visitation, his own capacity for imagining how salvation history is made present through the local church is formed. This means the pastoral visitation is too narrowly conceived if it remains limited to rituals and meetings within a church building. Rather, visitations must go beyond the church grounds in order for the bishop to gain insight into the daily existence of the faithful within their neighborhoods, schools, places of employment, cultural milieus, and political structures.

In turn, such a visitation requires a preparation of the faithful that goes beyond catechesis about the role of the bishop and nature of the church, as described in *Apostolorum Successores*. Rather, preparation must include aids for the faithful to reflect on their faith in relation to their daily lives, their hopes, frustrations, joys, and concerns. Such preparation may help the faithful introduce their bishop to the intersection of faith, culture, and history that is present in the *sensus fidelium*. Renovating the visitation in this way requires the presence of both the bishop and the faithful for an extended time. In addition to providing the bishop with greater insight into the *sensus fidelium*, however, it also allows for relationships to be built between the people and their bishop, and so for processes of authentication to develop. The bishop experiences the lives of the faithful and so may better inquire about the meaning they invest in their faithful actions; conversely, the faithful may also ask the bishop to explain his own sense of faith.

Remodeled structures incorporating processes of authentication help the bishop to discern well by engaging in dialogue with the faithful. Mutual self-communication fosters discerning love, which is necessary in order for the bishop to learn the apostolic tradition from the faithful who incarnate this tradition in their lives through the Spirit. This learning in turn allows him not only to perceive how to teach in ways that foster communion within the church but also how to further direct the local church's mission. Here there is a movement from the "union of minds" with regard to God's revelation to a "union of wills" for mission that more closely parallels processes of authentication in the Society of Jesus. If the church's mission is its response to God's self-gift, then through reception of the *sensus fidelium*, the bishop also learns more about how to minister for the local church's communication of love to others. Certainly the bishop must consider other factors in addition to the *sensus fidelium* in discerning the next steps in the church's missionary pilgrimage. Yet his sensibility for how God's self-gift is being made manifest by the church is an essential way in which he learns how the local church is called to mission in response to God.

Both the diocesan synod and pastoral visitations can be more broadly understood as occasions for advancing the church's mission. The local church's "union of minds" has a larger purpose, as through the Spirit this union of minds is a sharing in the mind of Christ. In his letter to the Philippians, Paul exhorts the faithful to share the mind of Christ, who does not rest in communion with God but rather lives out that communion through mission (2:1-11). Through synods and visitations, both bishop and faithful can discern how their union of minds calls the local church to share the communication of love and so to write the next chapters of salvation history—for themselves and for others. These two structures are also opportunities for the bishop to promote subsidiarity in the local church's mission as he learns more about the particular spiritual and human resources within the local church. Since the bishop is not receiving the local church *en masse* but rather the particular discernments of the faithful, he also has the opportunity to learn through these dialogues how to facilitate the faithful's personal contributions to the local church's shared mission.

Creating structures for lay ecclesial ministers and theologians. The increasing number of lay ecclesial ministers as well as lay theologians in many dioceses suggests a new diocesan structure is needed.[17] Of course, lay ministers and theologians, like pastors, might participate in several structures outlined above. Yet engaging in processes of authentication with laity who exercise a great deal of leadership within the local church seems an exceptional opportunity for the bishop to learn the apostolic faith as well as to understand further the life of parishes and Catholic institutions. Bringing these lay faithful into conversation with one another may also provide for mutual exchange of theological theory and pastoral practice in ways that benefit the local church's communion and mission.

In addition to general discernment, this gathering of lay faithful with pastoral and theological expertise may direct its attention to particular questions regarding the local church's *sensus fidelium*. Nevertheless, expertise in a particular field is no guarantee of being a person of discernment. Thus, as in the pastoral and presbyteral council, formation of lay ministers and theologians in spiritualities of discernment will be important, as will regular meetings and time to build up relationships with one another and with the bishop. Here again, given the bishop's power and authority within the local church, as well as the relative vulnerability of lay ministers and theologians, strong principles for transparent processes will need to be in place in order for discerning dialogue to flourish in honesty and trust.

---

[17] See Amanda C. Osheim, "The Local Church in Dialogue: Toward an Orthopraxis of Reception," in *Visions of Hope: Emerging Theologians and the Future of the Church*, ed. Kevin J. Ahern (Maryknoll, NY: Orbis Books, 2013), 181–89.

III. Transformative Reception through Diocesan Structures

Becoming a person of discernment and engaging in communal processes of authentication is transformative for the bishop's person and ministry; in other words, discernment and dialogue change the way the bishop knows and understands God's self-gift, as well as how he responds in faith through his own self-gift. As a person of discernment, he is in a continual state of acknowledging limitations, learning to receive others' communications of love, and discovering how to respond vocationally through his own self-gift. In processes of authentication, the bishop's own sense of the faith continues to be formed through the *sensus fidelium* so that he may become a symbol of the local church's faith, and so that his teaching may be received more readily by the faithful. Being shaped by and offering himself to the local church are essential parts of the bishop's response to Christ; through the self-gift of his ministry, he is continually transformed and enters more completely into Christ's mission.

In Ignatian spirituality, conversion cannot be undertaken alone, nor is conversion for ourselves alone. Rather, growth in holiness, which begins by accepting the communication of love in the midst of our limitations, is expressed by learning to join in Christ's mission for and with others. In a parallel way, as the bishop grows in habitual discernment, his personal conversion and response are transformative not only for himself but also for the local church. By inviting the faithful to teach him and to be collaborators in discernment with him, the bishop provides the faithful with opportunities for further reflection on God's self-gift and new occasions for becoming conscious of their own response and how that response is part of the local church's mission.

The original meaning of the word "pastor" is "to feed."[18] In a church imagined as an apostolic communion, the bishop feeds the faithful not only through his direct teaching but also by providing

---

[18] *Webster's New Collegiate Dictionary*, s.v. "pastor."

them with the encouragement, formation, and opportunity to engage in discernment of the Spirit's work. Thus the bishop's ministry, shaped through his personal conversion, may be transformative of the local church too: by growing in holiness through discernment, the bishop also learns how to pastor the people of God so they may grow in holiness as well. This potential for transformation of both the bishop and of the local church means it is not the bishop alone who has responsibility for his personal transformation. Rather, the local church also has a responsibility to care for the bishop's growth into a person of discernment through structures that aid the integration of the bishop's person and ministry.

In the Society of Jesus, particular persons are assigned to help ensure the superior's person and ministry are integrated. These positions are structures that function in various ways to promote the superior's discernment, to help the superior perceive areas of disintegration between his person and ministry, and to ensure the superior is ministering for the good of the Society and its mission. The superior's consultors do not take the place of other companions in the superior's discernment, but the consultors are meant to help the superior discover God's will. While no longer assigned, the collateral was to act as the superior's second self, a confidant not under the superior's authority who had care both for the superior and his companions. The admonitor attends to the superior's spiritual life in particular and is often his confessor. Finally, the assistants for provident care are to pay careful attention to the integrity of the superior general's person and ministry. Apart from the consultors, persons in each of these positions are not only empowered but are also required to raise up to the superior's attention any obstacles to the personal fulfillment of his ministry.

Transformative structures in the local church. Similar structures to aid the bishop in personally fulfilling his ministry do not exist within the local church. The structure that comes closest is the finance council, which is mandated by canon law to help ensure the bishop's integrity with regard to diocesan business affairs; yet this council's scope is limited to administration and does not speak directly to the bishop's personal ministry of discernment. Ecclesial documents and practices have given relatively more attention to what the bishop is empowered to do through his office than to how the bishop may also learn to personally fulfill his office. This is in part due to trust in the sacramental character of episcopal ministry as well as the influence of an ecclesiology inclined to institutionalism. Though conciliar and postconciliar documents give greater attention to the bishop's personal qualities in relation to his ministry, local church structures have yet to embody the mutuality of an apostolic communion in which the bishop does indeed have pastoral care for the faithful but the faithful of the local church also provide pastoral care for their bishop. Some structures in the local church may be developed to begin fulfilling this need: the college of consultors, auxiliary and coadjutor bishops, spiritual direction, and the diocesan curia. The goal of these structures is twofold. First, to continually support the integration of the bishop's person and ministry so his growth as a person of discernment may continually transform his ministry, and so his ministry is an ongoing source of transformative personal growth. Second, through these structures people are empowered to act for the well-being of the local church, whose members are impacted by the bishop's integration of his person and ministry.

The college of consultors. The college of consultors (usually about six to twelve priests) is appointed by the bishop from the presbyteral council, which is in turn made up of priests elected from across the diocese, *ex officio* members, and any additional priests appointed by the bishop. While its name is similar to the Jesuit superior's group of consultors, the diocesan college's function is currently more administrative than oriented to discernment, and it has a particular role to fulfill when an episcopal see is vacant in order to ensure the continued functioning of the local church until a new bishop is in place.

The previous section on the bishop's communal way of receiving God's self-gift indicated the presbyteral council as a whole could be collaborators in the bishop's discernment of the *sensus fidelium*. Should they be formed as persons of discernment through participation in the presbyteral council, members of the college of consultors could be empowered to aid the bishop in two further ways. First, as the college members are collaborators in discernment with the bishop who have engaged with him in processes of authentication, they may also be empowered to raise to the bishop's attention incongruence between the bishop's person and ministry. Second, the college could also assist newly appointed bishops by introducing them to the diocese's past practices of discernment and by helping to ensure the bishop has adequate resources for developing a spirituality of discernment that intersects with his ministerial responsibilities in the local church.

Auxiliary and coadjutor bishops. Auxiliary and coadjutor bishops may fulfill in the local church a function similar to that of the collateral in the Society of Jesus. Part of the collateral's role was to encourage good relationships between the superior and companions, and his freedom to fulfill that role rested on the collateral not being under obedience to the superior. As one who was part of the community, the collateral could assist with communication between the companions and the superior, potentially serving as a linchpin within the community. Conversely, as one who was not under the superior's obedience, the collateral could be looked on by the superior as a second self and confidant and could aid the superior not only in knowing his companions but also in knowing himself. The transformative potential of the relationship between superior and collateral is demonstrated in the mutuality of the relationship, conceived by Ignatius as a friendship rooted in honesty, in which the superior can be transparent about his own limitations, and the collateral can be proactive about raising concerns for the superior's consideration.

Canon law describes auxiliary and coadjutor bishops as assisting with the diocesan bishop's governance, consulting with him, sharing in his pastoral care for the local church, and ministering in harmony with him. The auxiliary and coadjutor bishops are not described as being under obedience to the diocesan bishop; rather, sacramentally, through their ordination, all bishops promise obedience to the pope, who is the head of the college of bishops. *Apostolorum Successores* does indicate the auxiliary ought to be obedient to the bishop; given how both Catholic ecclesiology and canon law understand the episcopal vocation, however, it is reasonable to interpret obedience as a recommended attitude the auxiliary fosters toward the bishop rather than a canonical requirement (AS 70). Thus both auxiliary and coadjutor bishops are uniquely placed to aid mutual reception between the local church and diocesan bishop in a way parallel to the Jesuit collateral. They have a particular freedom for acting as another self to the diocesan bishop who can raise concerns with him about the integration of his personal and ministerial transformation and are confidants with whom the bishop can discuss his problems. Of course, an auxiliary or coadjutor bishop must also discern the *sensus fidelium* of the local church. Even if an auxiliary or coadjutor bishop is appointed from within his home diocese, learning to receive the local church will be necessary and, of course, his own personal conversion ought to be ongoing. The need for the auxiliary and coadjutor bishops as well as the diocesan bishop to engage in discernment represents an opportunity for fraternal accountability among the bishops within the local church in order to mutually encourage one another to grow as persons of discernment.

Spiritual director. Another means for the local church to offer pastoral care for the bishop in transformative ways is to provide a spiritual director who helps the bishop to reflect critically and prayerfully on his spiritual life as it relates to his ministry. The process of conversion required to be a person of discernment is a continual challenge; growth in the spiritual life may be facilitated by others with whom the bishop can share himself honestly in order to acknowledge his limitations and to work through those limitations to receive God's offer of loving mercy. A spiritual director—lay, ordained, or religious—who is not only familiar with spiritualities of discernment but also a witness to the bishop's ministry within the local church can help the bishop integrate his person and ministry in transformative ways through ongoing conversion.

Curial assistants. If the spiritual director assists the bishop to move from personal to ministerial transformation, the bishop's assistants in the diocesan curia can also be empowered to evaluate

202 A Ministry of Discernment

the bishop's ministry of discernment and point out areas where further personal transformation is needed to fulfill that ministry. These assistants are daily witnesses to the bishop's teaching and pastoral decision making and thus have a high degree of insight into the practical exercise of his ministry. They can to some degree parallel the functions of the superior's assistants, who on a quarterly basis are to consult with each other to determine whether they perceive lack of personal integrity in the superior's ministerial practices.

When the bishop's assistants confer about the integration of the bishop's person and ministry, it need not be seen as a fault-finding expedition. Rather, it is an acknowledgment that integrity between spiritual intent and ministerial practice is not always easy to maintain, particularly given the demands inherent in episcopal ministry. These assistants may act as a means of reinforcing the bishop's need to tend to his spirituality in order to minister well and of underscoring how particular aspects of his ministry could benefit from further discernment. While certain members of the diocesan curia are clergy members (such as the vicar general), a mixture of lay, religious, and ordained assistants could be designated to fulfill this role on behalf of the local church.

Adaptations to the local church's structures such as those suggested above are not intended to inhibit the bishop in exercising his ministry. Rather, these adaptations recognize additional relationships are required for the bishop's personal transformation to be integrated with his office. While aspects of these relationships may be fulfilled informally by others in the bishop's life, these positions are also opportunities for the local church to offer formal care and assistance to the bishop as one of the faithful who in turn ministers for the well-being of his brothers and sisters in Christ. The Society of Jesus' "providential care" for its superiors general offers insight into the local church's responsibility for its bishop: in an apostolic communion the bishop does not only manifest God's love to the local church but also receives love from the faithful. This mutual love ought to be embodied in diocesan structures.

IV. Conclusion

Constructing a model of episcopal discernment by drawing on the *Spiritual Exercises* and the Society of Jesus provides a way of reimagining the bishop's ministry in the local church to reflect the mutual reception and learning of an apostolic communion. Whether this particular model is fruitful for local churches can only be verified through practice, which is also a means of refining our theology and norms for the local church. Much as the *Exercises* and structures of the Society arose through experience, so must the theories and practices of the bishop's ministry of discernment within the local church. A model can illuminate the way forward, but the bishop and faithful must be the ones to walk the path. The practical wisdom derived from their experiences in turn becomes a means of enlightening others in the church's communion and of advancing the church's missionary pilgrimage.

While this book has explored the implications of one way the bishop may grow into a person of discernment and so better fulfill his ministerial responsibilities with respect to the *sensus fidelium*, the church's rich heritage suggests other spiritualities have potential contributions to make as well. For instance, spiritualities expressed through popular piety offer the opportunity to know the faith of the people at the intersection of their prayer and daily lives. The Benedictine emphasis on hospitality may help us better imagine the bishop's reception of others, while the spiritual dynamism of prayer and work may provide insight into the union of the bishop's person and ministry. The devotion to the humanity of Christ and commitment to poverty in the spiritualities of Clare and Francis of Assisi lead to discernment of the Holy Spirit, "the Father of the poor," with those who are impoverished materially.[19] As Pope Francis wrote in *Evangelii Gaudium*, those in poverty

---

[19] "*Veni Sancte Spiritus*," in *New St. Joseph Sunday Missal: The Complete Masses for Sundays, Holydays, and the Easter Triduum* (Totowa, NJ: Catholic Book Publishing Corp., 2011), 494.

"have much to teach us."[20] Further, new spiritualities may also develop, which are rooted in the church's tradition, reflective of the present situations of the faithful, and responsive to the need for communal discernment in the local church.

Spiritualities of discernment require structures in order to be embodied. In his celebration of the fiftieth anniversary of the synod of bishops as a permanent structure of dialogue within the universal church, Pope Francis described the synodal church as one "which listens, which realizes that listening 'is more than simply hearing.' It is a mutual listening in which everyone has something to learn. The faithful people, the college of bishops, the Bishop of Rome: all listening to each other, and all listening to the Holy Spirit."[21] Francis noted as well that this synodal church begins with listening to the people of God. For this structure of the universal church to flourish, local structures are needed as well.

Diocesan structures are needed to provide accountability for both individuals and communities and to ensure that discernment is undertaken continually. They also provide clear expectations and processes of authentication to strengthen mutual trust and communication and to facilitate the ways we receive and respond to God's self-gift. Finally, structures help allocate diocesan resources for formation in discernment, as well as the time and commitment needed for personal and communal discernment to flourish. While the Society of Jesus provides insight into reforming diocesan structures, structures for dialogue and accountability may also be adapted to the local church from the practices of many religious orders, lay movements and associations, Catholic non-profits, and other groups who seek to embody their spiritualities in their organizational structures and who value dialogical discernment for union and mission.

[20] Francis, Apostolic Exhortation *Evangelii Gaudium* (The Joy of the Gospel) (Washington, DC: United States Conference of Catholic Bishops, 2013), 198.

[21] Francis, "Ceremony Commemorating the 50th Anniversary of the Institution of the Synod of Bishops," October 17, 2015, Vatican wesite, http://w2.vatican.va/content/francesco/en/speeches/2015/october/documents/papa-francesco_20151017_50-anniversario-sinodo.html.

Ultimately, while the bishop's ministry is one of discernment, it is not the bishop alone who must discern the *sensus fidelium*. Rather, the Spirit's indwelling within the church is a call for all the faithful to grow through reflection on God's self-gift and to examine our responses in order to enter more deeply into the divine life. As an apostolic communion, the Spirit prompts us to grow in learning to receive the invitation God offers us. By receiving God's self-gift, we learn how to give ourselves in return, so God may be all in all (1 Cor 15:18).

Bibliography

1985 Extraordinary Synod of Bishops. *The Final Report*. *AFER* 28, nos. 1–2 (February–April 1986): 81–94.

Ahern, Kevin. *Structures of Grace: Catholic Organizations Serving the Common Good*. Maryknoll, NY: Orbis Books, 2015.

Aldama, Antonio M. de. *An Introductory Commentary on the Constitutions*. Translated by Aloysius J. Owen. St. Louis, MO: The Institute of Jesuit Sources, 1989.

Alszeghy, Zoltán. "The *Sensus Fidei* and the Development of Dogma." In *Vatican II: Assessment and Perspectives*, vol. 1, edited by R. Latrourelle, 138–56. New York: Paulist Press, 1988.

Aquinas, Thomas. *Summa Theologica*. Translated by Fathers of the English Dominican Province. Notre Dame, IN: Christian Classics, Ave Maria Press, 1981.

Arrupe, Pedro. *Essential Writings*. Edited by Kevin Burke. Maryknoll, NY: Orbis Books, 2004.

Augustine. "On the Anniversary of His Ordination. P.L. 340." In *Selected Sermons of St. Augustine*, translated and edited by Quincy Howe, Jr., 214–16. New York: Holt, Rinehart and Winston, 1966.

———. *On the Trinity*. In *A Select Library of the Nicene and Post-Nicene Fathers of the Christian Church*, vol. 3, edited by Philip Schaff. Grand Rapids, MI: Wm. B. Eerdmans Publishing Company, 1988.

Austen, Jane. *Pride and Prejudice*. In *The Complete Novels of Jane Austen*. The Modern Library. New York: Random House, n.d.

Baldisseri, Lorenzo. Letter to Cardinal Timothy Dolan. October 18, 2013. scribd.com/doc/180575701/Vatican-questionnaire-for-the-synod-on-the-family.

Beal, John P., James A. Coriden, and Thomas J. Green, eds. *New Commentary on the Code of Canon Law*. New York: Paulist Press, 2000.

Boff, Leonardo. *"Ecclesia Docens* and *Ecclesia Discens."* In *Who Has a Say in the Church?*, edited by Jürgen Moltmann and Hans Küng, 47–51. New York: Seabury Press, 1981.

Borders, William D. "The Bishop as Builder of Community." In *The Ministry of Bishops: Papers from the Collegeville Assembly*, 37–41. Washington, DC: United States Catholic Conference, 1982.

Brown, Raymond E. *The Churches the Apostles Left Behind*. New York: Paulist Press, 1984.

———. *An Introduction to the New Testament*. New York: Doubleday, 1997.

Catholic Common Ground Initiative. *The Second Cardinal Bernardin Conference*. New York: The Crossroad Publishing Company, 1999.

Congar, Yves. *I Believe in the Holy Spirit*. Vol. 2. New York: The Crossroad Publishing Company, 1983.

———. *Tradition and Traditions*. London: Burns and Oates, 1966.

———. *True and False Reform in the Church*. Translated by Paul Philibert. Collegeville, MN: Liturgical Press, 2011.

Congregation for Bishops and Congregation for the Evangelization of Peoples. *Instruction on Diocesan Synods*. Vatican website. http://www.vatican.va/roman_curia/congregations/cbishops/documents/rc_con_cbishops_doc_20041118_diocesan-synods-1997_en.html.

Coriden, James. "Panel Discussion: James Coriden, Avery Dulles, Joseph Komonchak, and Philip Selznick." In Catholic Common Ground Initiative. *Church Authority in American Culture. The Second Cardinal Bernardin Conference*, 74–101. New York: The Crossroad Publishing Company, 1999.

Crowe, Frederick. "The Church as Learner: Two Crises, One *Kairos.*" In *Appropriating the Lonergan Idea*, edited by Michael Vertin, 370–84. Washington, DC: The Catholic University of America Press, 1989.

———. "The Magisterium as Pupil: The Learning Teacher." In *Developing the Lonergan Legacy: Historical, Theoretical, and Existential Themes*, edited by Michael Vertin, 283–91. Toronto: University of Toronto Press, 2004.

Crowley, Paul G. "Catholicism, Inculturation and Newman's *Sensus Fidelium.*" *The Heythrop Journal* 33, no. 2 (April 1992): 161–74.

Cusack, Barbara Anne. Commentary on "Title III: The Internal Ordering of Particular Churches [cc. 460–572]." In *New Commentary on the Code of Canon Law*, edited by John P. Beal, James A. Coriden, and Thomas J. Green, 610–66. New York: Paulist Press, 2000.

"The Deliberation of the First Fathers." In appendix of *Making an Apostolic Community of Love: The Role of the Superior in the Society of Jesus According to St. Ignatius of Loyola* by John Carroll Futrell. St. Louis, MO: Institute of Jesuit Sources, 1970.

Dillard, Annie. *The Writing Life*. New York: Harper and Row Publishers, 1989.

Dulles, Avery. *Models of the Church*. Garden City, NY: Image Books, 1978.

———. "Second General Discussion." In Catholic Common Ground Initiative. *Church Authority in American Culture: The Second Cardinal Bernardin Conference*, 118–53. New York: The Crossroad Publishing Company, 1999.

Espín, Orlando O. "Tradition and Popular Religion. An Understanding of the *Sensus Fidelium*." In *The Faith of the People*, 63–90. Maryknoll, NY: Orbis Books, 1997.

Francis. "Ceremony Commemorating the 50th Anniversary of the Institution of the Synod of Bishops." October 17, 2015. Vatican website. http://w2.vatican.va/content/francesco/en/speeches/2015/october/documents/papa-francesco_20151017_50-anniversario-sinodo.html.

———. *Evangelii Gaudium* (The Joy of the Gospel). Washington, DC: United States Conference of Catholic Bishops, 2013.

———. "Greeting of Pope Francis to the Synod Fathers during the First General Congregation of the Third Extraordinary General Assembly of the Synod of Bishops." Vatican website. http://w2.vatican.va/content/francesco/en/speeches/2014/october/documents/papa-francesco_20141006_padri-sinodali.html.

———. "Homily for Chrism Mass." The Vatican Today website. http://www.news.va/en/news/pope-homily-for-chrism-mass-full-text.

———. "Pope Francis: His First Words." The Vatican Today website. http://www.news.va/en/news/pope-francis-his-first-words.

Futrell, John Carroll. *Making an Apostolic Community of Love: The Role of the Superior in the Society of Jesus According to St. Ignatius of Loyola*. St. Louis, MO: Institute of Jesuit Sources, 1970.

Gaillardetz, Richard R. "The Office of the Bishop within the *Communio Ecclesiarum*: Insights from the Ecclesiology of Jean-Marie Tillard." *Science et Esprit* 61, Fascicle 2–3 (September 2009): 175–94.

———. "Power and Authority in the Church: Emerging Issues." In *A Church with Open Doors: Catholic Ecclesiology for the Third Millennium*, edited by Richard R. Gaillardetz and Edward P. Hahnenberg, 87–111. Collegeville, MN: Liturgical Press, 2015.

———. "The Reception of Doctrine: New Perspectives." In *Authority in the Roman Catholic Church*, edited by Bernard Hoose, 95–114. Burlington, VT: Ashgate, 2002.

———. *Teaching with Authority: A Theology of the Magisterium in the Church.* Collegeville, MN: Liturgical Press, 1997.

Ganss, George, trans. *The Constitutions of the Society of Jesus.* St. Louis, MO: Institute for Jesuit Resources, 1970.

———. *The Spiritual Exercises of Saint Ignatius.* Chicago: Loyola University Press, 1992.

Granfield, Patrick. "The Church Local and Universal: Realization of Communion." *The Jurist* 49 (1989): 449–71.

Grogan, Brian. "The One Who Gives the Exercises." In *The Way of St. Ignatius of Loyola: Contemporary Approaches to the Spiritual Exercises*, edited by Philip Sheldrake, 179–90. Bristol: SPCK, 1991.

Gutierrez, Gustavo. "The Option for the Poor Arises from Faith in Christ." *Theological Studies* 70 (2009): 317–26.

Hahnenberg, Edward. "Through the Eyes of Faith: Difficulties in Discerning the *Sensus Fidelium*." Paper presented at the annual meeting of the Catholic Theological Society of America. Milwaukee, WI. June 2015.

Himes, Michael J. "The Development of Ecclesiology: Modernity to the Twentieth Century." In *The Gift of the Church*, edited by Peter Phan, 45–67. Collegeville, MN: Liturgical Press, 2000.

———. "The Ecclesiological Significance of the Reception of Doctrine." *Heythrop Journal* 33, no. 2 (April 1992): 146–60.

———. "A Theology for Law." In *The New Canon Law: Perspectives on the Law, Religious Life, and the Laity*, 1–14. St. Louis, MO: The Catholic Health Association of the United States, 1983.

Hinze, Bradford E. *Practices of Dialogue in the Roman Catholic Church*. New York: Continuum, 2006.

Hume, George Basil. "Spiritual Foundations of a Bishop's Ministry." In *The Ministry of Bishops: Papers from the Collegeville Assembly*, 49–63. Washington, DC: United States Catholic Conference, 1982.

Hurbon, Laënnec. "The Slave Trade and Black Slavery in America." Translated by John Bowden. In *1942–1992: The Voice of the Victims*, edited by Leonardo Boff and Virgil Elizondo, 90–100. London: SCM Press, 1990.

Ignatius of Loyola. *Ignatius of Loyola: The Spiritual Exercises and Selected Works*. Edited by George E. Ganss. New York: Paulist Press, 1991.

Imperatori-Lee, Natalia. "Latina Lives, Latina Literature: A Narrative Camino in Search of the *Sensus Fidelium*." Paper presented at the annual meeting of the Catholic Theological Society of America. Milwaukee, WI. June 2015.

International Theological Commission. "Theology Today: Perspectives, Principles, and Criteria." Vatican website. http://www.vatican.va/roman_curia/congregations/cfaith/cti_documents/rc_cti_doc_20111129_teologia-oggi_en.html.

John Paul II. *Centesimus Annus*. Vatican website. http://w2.vatican.va/content/john-paul-ii/en/encyclicals/documents/hf_jp-ii_enc_01051991_centesimus-annus.html.

Kaslyn, Robert J. Commentary on "Book II. The People of God [cc. 204–746]." In *New Commentary on the Code of Canon Law*, edited by John P. Beal, James A. Coriden, and Thomas J. Green, 241–90. New York: Paulist Press, 2000.

Kasper, Walter. *An Introduction to Christian Faith*. New York: Paulist Press, 1980.

Kelly, J. N. D. " 'Catholic' and 'Apostolic' in the Early Centuries." *One in Christ* 6, no. 3 (1970): 274–87.

Kennedy, Robert T. Commentary on "Book V: The Temporal Goods of the Church [cc.1254–1310]." In *New Commentary on the Code of Canon Law*, edited by John P. Beal, James A. Coriden, and Thomas J. Green, 1451–526. New York: Paulist Press, 2000.

Lash, Nicholas. *Voices of Authority*. Shepherdstown, WV: Patmos Press, 1976.

MacDonald, Timothy. "Apostolicity." In *The New Dictionary of Theology*, edited by Joseph A. Komonchak, Mary Collins, and Dermot A. Lane, 52–54. Collegeville, MN: Liturgical Press, 1987.

Maida, Adam J. "The Spirit of the New Code of Canon Law." In *The New Canon Law: Perspectives on the Law, Religious Life, and the Laity*, 68–71. St. Louis, MO: The Catholic Health Association of the United States, 1983.

Mazza, Enrico. *The Celebration of the Eucharist: The Origin of the Rite and the Development of Its Interpretation*. Translated by Matthew J. O'Connell. Collegeville, MN: Liturgical Press, 1999.

McDonnell, Kilian. "The Ratzinger/Kasper Debate: The Universal Church and Local Churches." *Theological Studies* 63 (2002): 227–50.

———. "Walter Kasper on the Theology and Praxis of the Bishop's Office." *Theological Studies* 63 (2002): 711–29.

Müller, Hubert. "The Relationship between the Episcopal Conference and the Diocesan Bishop." In *The Nature and Future of Episcopal Conferences*, edited by Hervé Legrand, Julio Manzanares, and Antonio García y García, 111–29. Washington, DC: The Catholic University of America Press, 1988.

Newman, John Henry. *An Essay on the Development of Christian Doctrine*. 1888. Reprint, Whitefish, MT: Kessinger Publishing, 2006.

———. "On Consulting the Faithful in Matters of Doctrine." In *Conscience, Consensus, and the Development of Doctrine*, 392–428. New York: Doubleday, 1992.

Norris, Frank B. "The Bishop: First Liturgist of the Local Church." In *Shepherds and Teachers: The Bishop and Liturgical Renewal*, 39–42. Chicago, 1980.

O'Connell, Gerard. "Pope Says He Will Give More Attention to the Middle Class (Full Transcript of Pope's Press Conference)." *America Magazine* website. http://americamagazine.org/content /dispatches/pope-says-he-will-give-more-attention-middle-class -full-transcript-popes-press.

Osheim, Amanda C. "The Local Church in Dialogue. Toward an Orthopraxis of Reception." In *Visions of Hope: Emerging Theologians and the Future of the Church*, edited by Kevin J. Ahern, 181–89. Maryknoll, NY: Orbis Books, 2013.

Padberg, John W. General Introduction. In *Ignatius of Loyola: The Spiritual Exercises and Selected Works*, edited by George E. Ganss, 9–63. New York: Paulist Press, 1991.

Paul VI. *Mysterium Fidei*. Vatican website. www.vatican.va/holy_father /paul_vi/encyclicals/documents/hf_p-vi_enc_03091965 _mysterium_en.html.

Pew Research Center. *"Nones" on the Rise: One in Five Adults Have No Religious Affiliation*. Pew Forum website. http://www.pewforum .org/files/2012/10/NonesOnTheRise-full.pdf.

Prusak, Bernard P. *The Church Unfinished: Ecclesiology through the Centuries*. Mahwah, NJ: Paulist Press, 1989.

Quinn, John R. *Ever Ancient, Ever New: Structures of Communion in the Church*. New York: Paulist Press, 2013.

Rahner, Hugo. *Ignatius the Theologian*. Translated by Michael Barry. New York: Herder and Herder, 1968.

Raj, Antony, and Karol E. Dean. "Burnout and Depression among Catholic Priests in India." *Pastoral Psychology* 54, no. 2 (November 2005): 157–71.

Rausch, Thomas. "Reception Past and Present." *Theological Studies* 47 (1986): 497–508.

Ribadeneira, Pedro de. "Preface to the First Edition of the Constitutions." In Society of Jesus, *The Constitutions of the Society of Jesus and Their Complementary Norms: A Complete English Translation from the Official Latin Texts*, edited by John W. Padberg, xv–xx. St. Louis, MO: Institute of Jesuit Sources, 1996.

Ruddy, Christopher. *The Local Church: Tillard and the Future of Catholic Ecclesiology*. New York: The Crossroad Publishing Company, 2006.

Rulla, Luigi M. "The Discernment of Spirits and Christian Anthropology." *Gregorianum* 59, no. 3 (1978): 537–69.

Rush, Ormond. "Determining Catholic Orthodoxy: Monologue or Dialogue." *Pacifica* 12, no. 2 (June 1999): 123–42.

———. *The Eyes of Faith: The Sense of the Faithful and the Church's Reception of Revelation*. Washington, DC: The Catholic University of America Press, 2009.

Sacred Congregation for Bishops. *Apostolorum Successores.* Vatican website. http://www.vatican.va/roman_curia/congregations/cbishops /documents/rc_con_cbishops_doc_20040222_apostolorum -successores_en.html.

———. *Directory on the Pastoral Ministry of Bishops.* Ottawa, Ontario: Publication Service of the Canadian Catholic Conference, 1974.

Second Vatican Council. *Apostolicam Actuositatem; Christus Dominus; Dei Verbum; Lumen Gentium; Sacrosanctum Concilium; Unitatis Redinte-gratio.* In *Vatican Council II: The Basic Sixteen Documents.* Edited by Austin Flannery. Collegeville, MN: Liturgical Press, 2014.

Selznick, Philip. "Second General Discussion." In Catholic Common Ground Initiative. *Church and Authority in American Culture. The Second Cardinal Bernardin Conference,* 118–53. New York: The Crossroad Publishing Company, 1999.

Sheldrake, Philip. *Spirituality and History.* Maryknoll, NY: Orbis Books, 1998.

Society of Jesus. *The Constitutions of the Society of Jesus and Their Complementary Norms: A Complete English Translation from the Official Latin Texts.* Edited by John W. Padberg. St. Louis, MO: Institute of Jesuit Sources, 1996.

Southern, R. W. *Western Society and the Church in the Middle Ages.* London: Penguin Books, 1970.

Spadaro, Antonio. "A Big Heart Open to God." *America* 209, no. 8 (September 13, 2013), *America Magazine* website. http://america magazine.org/pope-interview.

Stagaman, David J. *Authority in the Church.* Collegeville, MN: Liturgical Press, 1999.

Strayer, David L., Frank A. Drews, and William A. Johnston. "Cell Phone–Induced Failures of Visual Attention during Simulated Driving." *Journal of Experimental Psychology: Applied* 9, no. 1 (2003): 23–32.

Sullivan, Francis A. "Authority in an Ecclesiology of Communion." *New Theology Review* 10, no. 3 (August 1997): 18–30.

———. "The Bishop's Teaching Office." In *Unfailing Practice and Sound Teaching: Reflections on Episcopal Ministry,* edited by David A. Stosur, 67–86. Collegeville, MN: Liturgical Press, 2003.

————. *From Apostles to Bishops: The Development of the Episcopacy in the Early Church*. New York: The Newman Press, 2001.

————. "Magisterium." In *The New Dictionary of Theology*, edited by Joseph A. Komonchak, Mary Collins, and Dermot Lane, 617–23. Collegeville, MN: Liturgical Press, 1987.

————. *Magisterium: Teaching Authority in the Roman Catholic Church*. Eugene, OR: Wipf and Stock Publishers, 1983.

————. "The Sense of Faith." In *Authority in the Roman Catholic Church*, edited by Bernard Hoose, 85–93. Burlington, VT: Ashgate, 2002.

Sullivan, James S. "Called to Holiness. The Bishop as Sanctifier." In *Servants of the Gospel: Essays by American Bishops on the Their Role as Shepherds of the Church*, edited by Leon J. Suprenant, Jr., 59–63. Steubenville, OH: Emmaus Road Publishing, 2000.

Tillard, J.-M. R. *Church of Churches: The Ecclesiology of Communion*. Collegeville, MN: Liturgical Press, 1992.

————. "Reception-Communion." *One in Christ* 28, no. 4 (1992): 307–22.

————. "*Sensus Fidelium*." *One in Christ* 11, no. 1 (1975): 2–29.

————. "Tradition, Reception." In *The Quadrilog: Tradition and the Future of Ecumenism*, edited by Kenneth Hagen, 328–43. Collegeville, MN: Liturgical Press, 1994.

"*Veni Sancte Spiritus*." In *New St. Joseph Sunday Missal: The Complete Masses for Sundays, Holydays, and the Easter Triduum*, 494. Totowa, NJ: Catholic Book Publishing Corp., 2011.

Wangsness, Lisa. "Words of Pain, Contrition in O'Malley's Irish Service." *Boston Globe* website. http://www.boston.com/news/local/massachusetts/articles/2011/02/21/words_of_pain_contrition _in_omalleys_irish_service.

Wood, Susan K. *Sacramental Orders*. Collegeville, MN: Liturgical Press, 2000.

Zanca, Kenneth J., ed. *American Catholics and Slavery, 1789–1866: An Anthology of Primary Documents*. Lanham, MD: University Press of America, 1994.

Index

Code of Canon Law, 45–46, 49, 55, 58,
64, 68–69, 71, 74–75, 77–79, 164,
188, 190–91, 198, 200–201
communication, 2, 76; bishops, 34,
169, 171, 177, 178, 180, 195, 197;
discernment, 137–39, 143, 146,
148–49, 158, 180, 185; communication of love, xvi, xix, 104, 106–7,
112, 120, 122–25, 133, 136–37, 139,
146, 158, 166–69, 171, 173, 175,
176–77, 179–80, 187, 191, 195, 197;
communion, 4, 16, 23, 25, 29,
106–7, 129, 140, 146, 156, 185, 195,
200, 204; mutual reception and
response, 4, 6, 23, 25, 30, 37, 39,
93, 106, 120, 122, 125–26, 129,
136–38, 149, 166, 167, 176, 179,
195, 197; overcoming-self,
self-transcendence, 107, 137, 158,
167, 175; salvation, 116, 118, 123,
125, 129, 133, 136, 145, 167, 185,
195; *see also* revelation
communion. *See* apostolic communion, bishop, communication,
Trinity
companion(s): apostolic unity, shared
mission, 136–37, 139–43, 145, 148,
153, 156, 177, 185; discernment,
135, 141–47, 156–58, 177, 184, 187;
manifestation of conscience, 148–
49, 159, 184; obedience, 139–43,
146; process of authentication, 142,
191; Society of Jesus, xix, 90, 130–
34, 144, 151
Congar, Yves, 11, 13–15, 26–28
Congregation for Bishops and Congregation for the Evangelization
of Peoples, 75
consensus fidelium, 15, 17–18
consolation, desolation, xix, 94, 104,
120–22, 168, 181–83
*Constitutions of the Society of Jesus and
Their Complementary Norms*, 130,
132–34, 136–55, 157

conversion, xvi, 13, 24, 41, 97, 102,
105, 109, 112, 133, 158, 159, 172,
181, 197; *see also* bishop
Coriden, James, 83
Crowe, Frederick, 38–40
Crowley, Paul G., 32
cultures and histories, xi–xiii, 1, 3,
5–10, 12, 14, 15–19, 22, 24, 25–26,
30, 33, 39, 41–42, 48, 53, 64, 70, 86,
88, 92, 94–96, 114, 131, 162, 167–68,
172–73, 181, 186, 194
Cusack, Barbara Anne, 77–80

Dei Verbum, xii, 3–4, 6
"The Deliberation of the First
Fathers," 134–35
dialogue, dialogical, xiii, xviii, xx, 2;
discernment, 30–41, 71, 73, 142–43,
150, 158, 163–64, 186–87; Society of
Jesus, 138, 141–43, 146, 148–56,
158, 183–84; *The Spiritual Exercises*,
111, 112, 114, 126, 158, 175–76;
structures, diocesan, 73–80, 190–
93, 195–97, 204; *see also* bishop
Dillard, Annie, 1
*Directory on the Pastoral Ministry of
Bishops*, 86
discernment: authentic, limited,
communal, and transformative,
125–27, 165, 184; communal or
ecclesial, 136–37, 139, 143–45, 147,
156, 165, 184–85, 187–96, 198–99;
Ignatius, xix, 38–41, 97, 99, 102,
166; learning, xvii, 3, 70, 90, 92,
123–24, 146–47, 157, 163, 180;
ministry of discernment, xx, 44,
48, 51, 55, 81–83, 86, 89, 92, 130,
163–64, 199, 202–3; mission, 131,
134, 136–37, 144, 156, 165, 183, 185;
person of discernment, xv, xvii,
xix, xx, 55, 69, 82, 86–87, 90, 93,
128, 137, 146, 156–57, 159, 163–65,
176, 178, 181, 196–99, 201, 203;
practices of discernment, xx, 2, 41,

bishop, 130–31; discerning love, discrete charity, 131, 143–44, 147, 157–58; distinctions, 143, 147, 158; God's will, divine will, 140–43, 146–47, 149, 156; mission, shared, 131, 134, 136, 147, 156–58; person and ministry, 148, 154, 155, 159; person of discernment, 146, 156, 159; superior general, 130, 135; superior's will, 139–48; *see also* authority; authentication, process of

teaching. *See* church, bishop
Tillard, J.-M.R., 4, 16, 19, 20, 26–29, 39, 51
Trinity, 4, 22, 53, 56, 65–66, 106, 166
truth, 17, 24, 26, 31, 33, 35, 37, 40, 57, 65–67, 71, 138, 141; *see also* external and internal

Unitatis Redintegratio, xxi
universal church. *See* bishop, local church, reception

Veni, Sancte Spiritus, 203
vocation, xxi, 15, 41, 44–45, 47, 50, 53, 56, 58, 60–61, 65, 68, 70, 74, 101, 125, 126, 127, 133–34, 137, 143, 176, 178, 183, 189, 191–92, 197, 201
vulnerability, 169, 171, 196

Wangsness, Lisa, 170
Wood, Susan K., 44

Zanca, Kenneth J., 10